Enjoy the Journey !
O'Caruso

BORN AGAIN IRISH

O'Caruso

A story of disaster at sea,
the joy of Ireland, and the vortex of fate.

Published by

CGI Books, Inc.
Centennial, Colorado

BORN AGAIN IRISH

FIRST EDITION: March 2007

ISBN 978-0-9785471-0-3 (ISBN 10: 0-9785471-0-1)

Library of Congress Control Number: 2006910648

Visit our websites at www.cgibooks.com
and www.bornagainirish.com

The Cover;
Soldier photo by Alberto Maurer, Jr.
Author photo by Dan Grothe
Scenic photo by Ellen Caruso
Layout and graphic design by
Karen Saunders, McGraphic Services
Design concept by Sandie Ihlenfeldt

The triskele, or tri-spiral, found on each chapter page, is an ancient Irish symbol related to the sun, afterlife and reincarnation. Triskeles are one of the most com-mon elements of Celtic art. The symbol form used in this book comes from the Megalithic passage tomb at Newgrange, built about 3,200 BC in the Boyne Valley north of Dublin. It is drawn in one continuous line, suggesting the movement of time.

Contents

(Continued)

Part III

Part IV

BORN AGAIN IRISH

Part I

Disaster at Sea
and the
Joy of Survival

Chapter 1

An Abrupt Beginning

Even the longest of journeys begins with but a single first step.

My journey to Ireland and Irish citizenship started with an airplane crash. There were no first steps at all.

Ireland wasn't in my travel plans. I didn't want to go anywhere except back home to New York. I was a disheartened and unhappy passenger sitting in a doomed airplane headed for another place entirely.

It happened about midnight, in the raging North Atlantic, some 500 miles west of Ireland's Dingle Peninsula during a cold and brutal windstorm just two days into autumn. The date was September 23, 1962. That is the time of year when temperatures drop steadily and the wind and seas grow increasingly turbulent.

Of the 76 passengers and crew on board, only 48 lived to reach land. Twenty-eight died at sea, three of them in our life raft. Seventeen were airlifted to Ireland by helicopter. I was one of those fortunate few and thus began my journey.

An airplane crash in the middle of an ocean is an abrupt way to begin a new identity, and I do not recommend it. Nevertheless, I am grateful. Without the airplane crash, I'd still be an overly excitable, fast-talking, arm-waving, loud New York Italian, living in a perpetual state of distress. Because of the Flying Tiger incident

3

— that frightening, cold and deadly crash — I'm Irish. I'm a full-fledged Irishman with an Irish passport, an Irish wife, and a home in Ireland to prove it. I'm surely more an Irish "O'Caruso" today than the Italian "Caruso" I was so many years ago.

The aircraft was a four-engine Lockheed Super Constellation, an old turbo prop with a very distinctive arched tail accented by three vertical tail fins, resembling predatory sharks swimming in close formation.

The Super Constellation was known by some insiders to be "the most reliable three-engine aircraft of its day." Even though it had four engines, by the early '60s, the planes were getting so old that flight crews could only count on three engines working properly at any given time. Fortunately, no one passed along that bit of inside information to the passengers.

Our commercial aircraft was on contract with the Army to move troops from the United States to Germany during one of the many international periods of crisis that accompanied the building of the Berlin Wall. Our flight was known as "Flying Tiger Flight 923."

The Flying Tiger Airline was the civilian successor to the original Flying Tiger fighting team of World War II. The Tigers were the first to bomb Tokyo. On this flight, the commercial pilots were taking us to an air base near Frankfurt, Germany.

Of course, no one was expecting the plane to crash. We had a mission to carry out. Unfortunately, soon after reaching the midway point — the point of no return — we knew we were never going to make it to land. We had engine trouble and knew we would be hitting the water at some point. Our emergency landing was supposed to be a controlled and orderly ditching of the aircraft. We all hoped it would be as close to land as possible. There was no alternative.

"Routine" is the word the captain used to describe our impending fate, almost as though ditching at sea was a regular occurrence. He didn't want to create any more panic than already existed. In spite of the good wishes of the captain and crew, the forces of nature caused the end to turn out very badly.

We hit a monstrous, churning and unforgiving mountain of water, belly first, at a speed of more than 120 miles per hour. At the moment of impact, all calm, orderliness and routine — and yours truly — literally went out the window. The plane broke open, a wing sheered off, and by the time it was over, 28 people were dead. Under the circumstances, it's a wonder any of us survived.

Our relative good fortune was due in part to the time of year. Late September is the warmest time for water temperatures in that region of the North Atlantic. This is the result of the warm waters of the Gulf Stream that originate thousands of miles away in the Caribbean.

While the waters are warm (and that is simply relative to how dreadfully cold it eventually gets), it also happens to be one of the stormiest and most volatile times of the year. The Spanish Armada was battered to splinters along the same Irish coast during the same time period 374 years earlier, while escaping from the British. Like me, some of those unfortunate mariners in 1588 were lucky enough to reach the Emerald Isle.

The "we" of the disaster were the 75 others on board and me. Most of us were Army paratroopers, comrades in training for the previous two months, nearly four dozen or so of us, most between the ages of 18 and 22. There were also seven members of the crew, a few active officers and retired military, and a dozen women and children, all related to the military in some way.

Despite the abruptness of the collision, 51 of us made it to a lone 25-man life raft. Only 48 survived the ride. The other three died from the cold or drowned while in the raft. None of the children survived. Only a few of the women made it, along with a small number of the crew.

Five rubber life rafts were stowed on the plane. Two were lost when the right wing broke off on impact. Two others stored in the left wing inflated on impact, but they were quickly blown out of reach for most of us. The few who made it to those errant rafts, all crew members who must have known what to look for, quickly died from exposure. Those who stayed alive on our lone surviving raft had the benefit of body heat generated from the overcrowding. Our raft was the one stored inside the aircraft cabin. It was thrown out the back door after impact.

Land was hopelessly far away. There were no islands, not even an iceberg to cling to. There was only the icy, foaming sea and a raging, gale-force wind.

Life rafts in those days had a very definite top and bottom. The first survivors to pile into the raft got started all wrong. The raft was top-side down, meaning the safety lights were hidden beneath the water. So were the first aid and emergency kits that held the flares and signal devices that might have helped in our rescue.

By the time the mistake was noticed, not a single occupant was willing to jump out of the raft and back into the water in order to turn the raft right-side up. No way. Not one of us was getting out. We would take our chances in the dark. Fortunately, one composed fellow had the presence of mind to snatch a flashlight from inside the cabin.

For six frigid and dizzying hours, we tossed and turned, splashed and twirled in the tiny, overcrowded and upside-down lifeboat designed for less than half as many passengers.

The wild, freezing winds blew us some 22 miles in six hours from the point of impact to the point of rescue. That's a rate of about 3-1/2 miles an hour at open sea in a grossly overloaded craft, swamped with water and without the benefit of a sail.

Our rescue ship was a Swiss freighter named the *Celerina*. The incredible exuberance of being snatched from the sea by the freighter's crew was followed by two turbulent and unsettling days of tossing and pitching at sea aboard the ship.

Once the storm cleared, most of the survivors sailed on to Antwerp, Belgium. For 17 of us, however, there was an exciting, dramatic and glorious helicopter ride over the most beautiful and spectacular green fields in the world. We were evacuated from the ship to Mercy Hospital in Cork City. I was the last of the group to be tapped for Ireland, and my selection was almost an afterthought. For me, however, that unexpected bit of happenstance has been worth far more than winning the national lottery.

The brief event of our medical evacuation by helicopter was my deliverance, my second chance at life, my rebirth. It was a glorious and incredibly beautiful day. It was a spectacularly brilliant rescue. I was saved and back on land, my land, my new land, and I laid claim to it. Ireland!

That incident, that day, that moment, is when I was blessed with the destiny to become Fred O'Caruso, the "Born Again Irishman."

There were no bells or flashing lights. There were no medals or proclamations. I survived. I made it. The Italian boy from the suburbs of New York was welcomed by Ireland herself.

And, thus it was that my journey began, without the legendary single first step.

BORN AGAIN IRISH - *O'Caruso*

Chapter 2

It's Not Easy To Be Irish

You don't just wake up one day and proclaim, "This is my day. I think I'll be Irish."

Whether you fall into it by an airplane crash, or you decide it is something you want to pursue later in life, it is not easy to be Irish, especially if you started out as I did – Italian, New Yorker and nearly Jewish. It is not like changing your clothes or your social identity on St. Patrick's Day. It can be a lot of hard work.

Even with my abrupt and unexpected debut in Cork City, I had a lot of adjusting to do, not only in my way of thinking, but more basically in my way of being. To a great extent, I had to quit being who I was. And, I had an awful lot of quitting to do.

For starters, I had to quit being a cocky, second-generation Italian with a serious New York-New Jersey accent and an even worse case of East Coast attitude.

If you grew up where and when I did, you would know there was no place else outside of the New York metro area. If there were other places, you surely wouldn't want to live there, much less grow up there.

No kids outside my world were tougher, wiser or more worldly. Other kids *begged* to be from New York, while the best they could do was stay where they were and eat their hearts out, forever destined to be less than superior New Yorkers.

We heard rumors of kids living in far off places like Indiana,

Illinois or Ohio and even more far out places like Alabama, Mississippi and Texas. As a New Yorker, it was hard to even imagine being from somewhere like that. We had a family move to our school district from South Carolina. Those poor kids talked and acted so weird they were pitiful. I don't think they ever fit in.

It was one of those simple facts of life. I lived in the center of the universe!

I was first born as Fred Caruso, an Italian and Roman Catholic, in May of 1941, in the suburban community of Nyack, in Rockland County, New York. This small town is 20 miles north of the George Washington Bridge, on the New Jersey side of the Hudson River, only a few miles north of the New Jersey state border.

I grew up surrounded by what seemed to be dozens and dozens of rosary toting, prayer-mumbling aunts, most of whom wore black all of the time and who had apparently come over on the original boat from Italy. Besides the aunts, I had at least a dozen or so uncles and cousins whom I saw less, or at least were less noticeable as I grew up.

My mother was the unlucky eldest of 13 kids, eight girls and five boys. If you could choose your rank, it would be far better to be the last of 13 rather than the first. Number One acquires the lion's share of responsibility in a family of that size. In any case, we all know what bad luck the number 13 carries. Back then, many hotels dropped the 13th floor designation from their rosters. No one wanted to stay on the unlucky 13th floor.

My mother's parents were of southern Italian and Sicilian stock, all Corsos and Yaccopinos. My father was the "Caruso" of the family, with roots in Naples. We were not related in any way to the great opera singer, Enrico Caruso, although I was asked that question over and over again in my early life. Enrico was rich and famous. We were not.

My father was the youngest of eight children, of whom one was a girl, which made him his father's seventh son. That was a bit of family history he told me often and with pride. He was the seventh son, but, he would inform me, he was not the seventh son of

10

a seventh son, which would have been a very lucky thing to be.

So, in the end, my father's lucky position really didn't count for much. He would have to have seven sons himself to make the magic work, and he had no intentions of trying for that legacy. I would have to satisfy myself with knowing I was at the very least the firstborn son of the seventh son, and that should count for something.

I had two younger sisters. In a string of only three numbers, of which I was number one, they didn't have bragging rights, nor did they have anything to concern themselves about.

An opportunity to point out a good or bad omen, or a sign for good luck or bad, or even near-luck, was never missed by any of my relatives. They all had important dreams and premonitions on a regular basis, covering anything from knowing what was going to be on the supper table that night to something as grave as an impending death.

Birds seemed to have special powers. One might say, "I knew something terrible was going to happen. A bird flew into the window and broke its neck. Poor Uncle Antonio died in his sleep last night."

I always wondered if Uncle Antonio died because of that poor dead bird? Or was the bird just sending a warning? If it were sending a warning, why was it telling us? I never really knew, except that another bird was dead and so was another uncle.

From my childhood perspective, all my relatives seemed strange, but of the whole lot, none were more peculiar than my great aunts on my mother's side. Great aunts carried a very important status in the family, compared with, say, just regular old aunts. Hardly anyone paid attention to the great uncles and even less to the ordinary uncles.

My great aunts were the sisters of my grandmother, whom I grew up knowing as "Grandma Proctor." She acquired a non-Italian sounding name when she married a non-Italian, largely out of financial necessity. That occurred soon after my Grandpa Corso met his early demise when he drove his vegetable truck off the roadway and into the rocky Tappan Creek just south of the village of Nyack.

Grandpa Corso left the family destitute and on its own. At age 12, my mother, being the eldest of the brood, was obliged to quit school to take charge of baby-sitting and housekeeping. Her mother, a master embroidery seamstress, went to work at the embroidery mill to earn what little she could at her trade.

My mother never forgave her father for the grief he caused by his periodic disappearances before his death and his permanent disappearance at the time of his fatal accident. Apparently he had difficulty dealing with large crowds at the dinner table and simply took off for weeks at a time when the pressure got to be too much.

From what I could tell, life was really desperate in those days, in the midst of the Great Depression, but evidently not as miserably awful as it must have been in the old country they left behind. In Southern Italy and Sicily, the poor were really, *really* poor.

English was the spoken language at the Corso home and not Italian. That was because my grandmother's side of the family came from the village of Calabria at the toe of Italy. My grandfather came from the village of Reggio, across the waterway in Sicily, where Italy appears to be giving Sicily a big kick. They were raised with different dialects and couldn't reach an agreement on which dialect to pass on to their kids, Sicilian or southern mainland Italian. So my mother and her siblings never learned Italian, except for a few unfriendly-sounding curses.

Evidently conflict over such things as what dialect to use at home was very common. The poor immigrants seemed to be unfamiliar with notions such as compromise. Everyone was always fighting with someone over something of very little consequence. Hard feelings were apparently far better than having no feelings at all.

Italians have a reputation for drama, and it seemed as if some of my relatives were competing for the Academy Award.

My great aunts who lived in the city all wore traditional black dresses, black sweaters and black coats to show reverence for the dead. I never knew who it was that died and I wouldn't dare ask. I had to guess what event might have motivated them. They went nowhere without their rosary beads in hand, mumbling continuously a combination of prayers, profanities and ill wishes on the people in their lives. It seemed like everyone qualified for ill wishes.

This mindless and continuous chatter – prayers mixed with profanities with no consistent reason, just babble – seems to have been the main source of entertainment before television. The babblers didn't even require a listener. God was always listening, I suppose. He must have been listening to the prayer part of the chatter and not paying any attention to the profanity part.

It appeared that everyone had an overwhelming need to let it out – to vent whatever was pent up inside – whenever and wherever they happened to be at any given moment. It was a very common New York-Italian thing, but especially among the women who claimed any kind of relationship to me.

Oh, yes. In order to play the role properly, don't forget this part. When you go about ranting, you must be very dramatic, get excited, speak loudly as if everyone in the world is stone deaf, shed a tear or two, and wave your hands a lot. There seems to be an art to the whole process of being really, *really* Italian and really, *really* a New Yorker. Whatever that art, it is contagious for those growing up in its midst.

The most fearsome of my relatives was my Great Aunt Elizabeth, who was a bona fide, genuine witch of the Cult of Maluk. The name came from a translation of the Italian word "mallocchio," meaning "evil eye." Believers in the power of the curse had their children wear a tiny horn on a neck chain to fight off evil spirits. Witches wore the horn amulet, hidden at all times, to ensure that it would never be seen by a passing Catholic priest. That kind of superstition and the practice of witchcraft were forbidden by the church.

Not everyone had an aunt who was a real witch and could cast and break spells for good and evil. I was very proud of that. I thought that some day I might have to call on her to do me a favor.

Maybe she could put a curse on someone for me when I needed to get even. In any case, I always wanted to stay on her good side. She and that "evil-eye thing" terrified me.

Most of my great aunt's work, I was told, was curing people who had been cursed by spells cast by others under the evil spirit of envy. We could never compliment someone or something without following up with, "God bless you!" or "God bless it!" If you forgot the magic words, you might cast the curse of the evil eye by accident. This could call forward any number of serious consequences such as sickness or misfortune, whether it was intended or not. Often the curse was simply an oversight or a slip of the tongue.

I remember one day my grandmother made a surprise visit to our house in the suburbs. One of my kinder, not-so-colorful uncles had driven her out on the day after my folks had purchased a brand new car, a fact they kept to themselves for fear of showing off. After seeing and enjoying the garden and the flowers my mother had planted, all of which were anointed with an appropriate "God bless," Grandma Proctor came upon the new car. She apparently didn't want to acknowledge that we had avoided mentioning it.

I remember her stroking the right front fender, commenting how beautiful it was, but failing to utter the magic words of "God bless" in appropriate follow-up. There was a lot of discomfort around the house that night after she left, and sure enough, — absolute truth — the right front tire was flat the next day. My mother was not herself for weeks, knowing with certainty that it was the work of the evil eye.

My Great Aunt Elizabeth could cure a sick child by tacking the child's undershirt to the wall, saying the right prayers, and slashing it with a knife to drive the dark-side spirits away. In most cases, the sickness wasn't caused by disease at all. Someone had looked at the child with a bit of envy, and they might not have even known they were doing it. They called it "the overlook."

The Catholic Church, Italian style, was a dominant factor in the midst of all of this superstition, gossip and spell-casting. In those days, the church rituals were recited in Latin, so no one could understand them anyway. The priest performed his magic with his back to the congregation so you couldn't see what he was doing. You had to listen to the bells, kneel, stand up and sit down when everyone else did. You also had to go to church on Sunday, have a big church wedding, make your sacraments such as baptism, confession, communion, and confirmation, and that was about it.

Evidently you were also supposed to say thousands and thousands of rosaries and novenas before you died if you had any hope of making it to heaven. That was especially so if you happened to have the misfortune of being female.

Novenas were strings of prayers with a certain theme. Each had to be said in a specific sequence, depending upon the patron saint being called upon, and in a special number of repetitions to achieve full benefit. Each saint had his or her own requirements. Some saints were less demanding than others. I tended to lean toward the less demanding ones. That was how I knew I wasn't intended for the priesthood.

By the time I was a teenager, the practice of saying novenas to get the things you wanted was losing favor to other forms of enterprise and entertainment, except in the case of my mother and my great aunts, all of whom ignored the trend. They said more and more of them.

My mother used rosaries and novenas as a way of telling my father that he was driving her to the edge of insanity. She must have been close to the edge for a very long time because she said at least a million of them. I grew up knowing that all men were put on this earth to bring mental anguish and misery to women through the highly-prized sacrament of marriage. Regardless of the misery that marriage caused, there was no end to couples willing to line up at the alter. With as many aunts and uncles as I had, we went to a lot of family weddings.

While the Italian version of Catholicism was being passed on to me by my relatives, piece by excruciating piece, I was actually surrounded by and being influenced by the far larger Jewish community. I went to the public schools where more than half of my classmates were Jewish, a few were Catholic and even fewer were Protestant. Nearly all of our neighbors were Jewish.

My growing-up years were spent in the communities of Monsey and Spring Valley, both of which were populated mostly by highly Orthodox Jews, who wore long black coats, long pigtails or straggly locks of hair for sideburns, and yarmulkes, the Jewish skull cap, which they wore at all times, including under their black hats when outside.

Fortunately for me, most of my Italian relatives lived some 25 miles south in Jersey City and West New York, New Jersey, just across the Hudson River from Manhattan. In the New York metro area, 25 miles is a very long way off indeed, not even comparable to 75 or 100 miles in other places.

During World War II, after my father was drafted into the Army, my mother moved us to Guttenberg, New Jersey, at the northern border of West New York, to be close to her family. After the war ended, we moved back to Rockland County, closer to my father's family, to the village of Spring Valley, just six or seven miles from where I was born in Nyack.

Even though we went to visit relatives almost every weekend, or they came to visit us, the distance gave me a margin of possibility when it came to sorting things out about the world on my own. I observed at a relatively early age that my uncles who lived the farthest away had achieved the highest level of economic and social success, quite in proportion to the distance. The farther, the better, it seemed.

A short two to three decades before my youth, Spring Valley was about a 90-minute trip from New York City by bus, train or motorcar, making it an ideal escape to the country. During the early part of the century, a number of resort hotels catering to the Jewish community sprung up in an area known as "Jew Hill," which is what my father and all of his friends called it, including all of his Jewish friends.

By the time I was a teenager in the late 1950s, many of the Spring Valley resorts had slipped into a shabby state of disrepair.

The Catskill Mountain resorts to the north were stealing the show. New highways and transportation systems brought the Catskills to within an acceptable travel time from the city center. Spring Valley had lost much of its appeal and parts of the village were becoming slums.

My father worked for Widman's Bakery in Spring Valley, proud home of Widman's "Splendid" bread as was proclaimed by a giant billboard on the New Jersey side of the George Washington Bridge. My father operated the bread-wrapping machine that packaged those splendid loaves, but he didn't earn a whole heck of a lot of money doing it. The best part of his job, as far as I was concerned, was that he always came home with an abundant supply of free pastries and coffee crumb cake, my favorite.

My father worked nights all of my early life. He liked it, he said, because he could earn an extra ten cents or so an hour doing exactly the same thing people did in the daytime, and he didn't have to put up with as many bosses as during the day shift. His mother thought night work was good for her seven boys because it kept them out of the bars at night and out of trouble. No one seemed to worry about the trade-offs, such as a lack of family life. If a person had to work, he might as well work at night and make a little more money. An extra $4 a week was, indeed, an extra $4 a week.

My folks became very close friends with Molly and Frank Nordhauser, a Jewish couple who were neighbors across the street from where we lived in a very low-cost tenement building on West Street in Spring Valley known as "The Block House." This project was built, as it sounds, out of cheap cinder and concrete block.

The Nordhausers must have been better off than we were, at least by a little bit. They had a *real* house, however small it might have been, complete with a *real* backyard and a porch to sit on, and they owned it, or at least we assumed they did.

Molly Nordhauser walked with a cane and braces, a victim of polio during the epidemic of the early '50s. Even so, she was one of the most delightful, enthusiastic and endearing women I have ever known. Frank was an avid Boy Scout leader, always taking a troop somewhere, and always in his Boy Scout Leader's uniform. Maybe it was his way of not having to wear the dress uniform of Orthodox Jews. No matter, he and his son, Frankie, who was a couple years younger than I, were never seen without their yarmulkes, even if they were covered over by a Boy Scout cap

Molly's nephew, "Moey" Sharf, was our family dentist. I hated the smell of his office, the sound of his archaic drills and, worse, the vibrations they would send through my head. My father loved him, so we all went for regular checkups. Dad was so proud of his accomplishments as a dentist, you would have thought that Moey was *his* nephew instead of Frank and Molly's.

There is no doubt in my mind that the Nordhausers provided the support and encouragement my parents needed to get up the courage to leave the Block House on West Street to buy their own home in the nearby and slightly more upscale and rural community of Nanuet. They did it with $200 down and mortgage payments of $79 a month, a scheme that all of my Italian aunts and uncles were certain would break them financially as well as morally.

Our friendship with the Nordhausers and our time at the Block House opened my eyes to an appreciation for Jewish people. Jews could be educated and wealthy, but they could also be very poor and they could love. They were family-oriented and supportive of their kids and their cousins, nieces and nephews, and were eager to help the youth progress up the economic ladder. They were also respectful of those who came before them and even to the little ones who came later.

Unfortunately, the good qualities I saw in our Jewish friends were not as evident on the Italian side.

Jews had a tendency to overindulge their kids, while my Italian relatives believed in the axiom that "children should be seen and not heard," and they never let us forget it.

It was a matter of principle and honor that children should help their parents financially, and not the other way around. It didn't matter if the help was only marginally needed or not needed at all, or if the help felt like pain and sacrifice. "Helping out" was a requirement if the older folks were to maintain their dignity. It didn't matter if that help generated bitterness and resentment. Everyone had to do it.

Jews, on the other hand, didn't concern themselves with such notions of dignity. Sometimes entire families, including aunts and uncles, pooled their money to help a promising scholar make it through college or to help a couple get a start in home ownership.

The Jews we knew were a fairly cheerful lot. That was not necessarily the case among the older Italians we knew. Bitterness and resentment seemed to be the emotions of choice and I learned a lot about those attitudes, and how to show them with appropriate dramatic emphasis. It seemed to be a part of wearing the time-honored badge of martyrdom. It may have been a poor man's way of somehow affirming faith.

I also learned at an early age about "venting." It seemed that everyone did so to anyone within listening range, about whatever minor frustration came about and whenever it came to mind. The practice was so common among my relatives and their friends that I never gave it a thought until years later when I saw the nasty habit in myself.

There must have been a brighter side of life, but I wasn't sure there was one, based on all of the complaining I heard. Everyone did a very good job of keeping all things good a secret. That "evil eye" thing was always lurking in the background, creating a fear that kept good words and kindness to a minimum.

Maybe life was a lot worse than I thought. It didn't seem so bad to me, but as a child, I saw anger, bitterness and frustration as the emotions most often expressed by those around me. I suspect that people didn't necessarily feel the way they acted. They simply played out mini-dramas. As I learned later in life, the actors and actresses in my family were the ones listening most intently to themselves. Others had already learned how to ignore them.

The Nordhausers were very modern and upbeat Orthodox Jews. Some said Molly took a special liking to me because I looked like a little Jewish boy myself. I had a dark complexion and was woefully chubby, at least until I turned 13. All I needed was my own yarmulke and I might have been treated to a Bar Mitzvah. I had to settle for a relatively lackluster Catholic Confirmation.

Godparents held a special place in our family and in our social circle. My parents used to tease me about Molly being my godmother when, in fact, my real godmother was my mother's younger sister. I rarely saw my Aunt Angelina so I was very happy to have Molly Nordhauser as a godmother. She was much closer to home.

My godfather, on the other hand, was a very genuine Italian by the name of Dominick Fasano, owner of the Venice Restaurant, a fine establishment, nightclub, pizza palace and dance hall on Route 9-W in Nyack. He seemed to be very successful and was a welcome contrast to the poorer side of the family.

"Gumbadi" Dominick, as I was taught to refer to him, was all of 4 feet 8 inches tall. He kept two giant Great Dane dogs at his living quarters in the basement of the restaurant at all times. Those dogs stood at eye level with my Gumbadi and would scare off any potential thieves. The dogs had full run of the restaurant from the moment the place was closed.

Dominick had no direct blood connection with our family. He was from the tiny village of Casamassima near the eastern city of Bari, on the Adriatic Sea. He had come to America during the glory days of silent movies to play the violin in the orchestras that accompanied them. His wife stayed behind to raise their family and to continue in her career as the village midwife. She never joined him and, in fact, she never visited the States to see what she might have missed.

My father's mother, Ethel Caruso, became friends with Dominick very early on. It is possible they got to know each other through my grandfather Alexander Caruso, who was a barber in Nyack, where both my father and I went to high school. Alexander died when my father was only 11 years old, long before I had a chance to know him.

As long as I can remember, Grandma Caruso was always working at the restaurant, washing dishes. She was Dominick's loyal friend and probably the restaurant's most dedicated worker, even late into her 70s.

My Gumbadi wore a tailored suit and tie at all times, projecting authority and looking far taller than his height. He was constantly walking around the restaurant, greeting guests, checking on service and ordering my family our favorite treats and never charging us for what we ordered. Besides that, he always had a little gift of a dollar or two for me, his godson. He was rich and successful, at least in my young mind, and I was very proud of that.

So there I was — Italian, New Yorker, strongly influenced by my Jewish surroundings, and darned close to being poor. Of course, I didn't know about all of these challenges at the time. My world was very close to the center of the universe. A lot can be overlooked when you are at the top of the mountain.

BORN AGAIN IRISH - *O'Caruso*

Chapter 3

Why Me?

It was looking dark and forbidding on the horizon as our plane droned eastward toward Germany, away from the setting sun. Another Cold War military crisis was bubbling over, and my jump school class had been drawn right into it.

The ocean far below looked like a frigid caldron of churning black sea water, a witch's brew spotted with low-lying, swirling dark vapors. It looked alien, other world-like, hostile and intimidating, yet I couldn't take my eyes away from the window. I was fading in and out of thoughts, wondering what I had done to deserve this exile from America. I was leaving the center of the universe to protect some unknown, hostile corner of the world. It was anybody's guess, in my mind, as to what we were defending, or why, or against whom.

Storm clouds were building. Soon there would be nothing to see at all except for the wing and the prop with blue exhaust shooting out from behind the cowling, just a few feet away, nearly touching my right shoulder. I was off to Germany, exactly where I did not want to go.

What did I do wrong? How did I get here? How could I be going where I did not want to go? I was indifferent to Germany itself. The thought of being assigned anywhere farther than a day's travel from New York had not even entered into my plans.

I knew where I went wrong and I had to admit it. I did it to myself. I had only me to blame. I joined the paratroopers as a volunteer. I didn't want to go overseas and, while staying stateside was never promised to us by the Army recruiters, it was pretty safe to assume that a stateside assignment went along with the parachute wings. As far as we knew, airborne troops were all stationed with the 101st Airborne at Fort Campbell, Kentucky, or with the 82nd Airborne at Fort Bragg, North Carolina, and that was it.

At least that was the way it was until about three weeks earlier. An international crisis was occurring, and that changed everything. It was another Berlin crisis, this time in September of 1962. U.S. paratroopers were being sent over to reinforce a small detachment already in place and to deliver a message: We were on standby to kick butts with bullets if the Commies tried to stop traffic passing through the narrow Berlin Corridor. The East Germans, dominated by the Soviet Union, started reinforcing the Berlin Wall and began building a barricade along the entire border between East and West Germany.

I had never even heard of Mainz, Germany, and would have been just as happy if I never did.

Adding insult to the injury of our sudden change of plans — talk about bad luck — the Berlin crisis disrupted all jump school assignments, and that dumped all time-honored and sacred jump school tradition. The kitchen staff on base was left short of help. New recruits were put into the fast track, skipping the first week of pre-training down time. Jump school dropouts were suddenly reassigned. There was no one around for the dirty work except for the new graduates.

My class became the first graduating class of paratroopers in the history of jump school ever to have to pull kitchen patrol. What a dirty, low blow! We had to kill four or five days after graduation waiting for orders, some of that time in total humiliation on KP duty.

This was an emergency. There was no time for an overnight pass. "Hurry up and wait" is the Army motto.

Finally, we were off from Fort Benning, Georgia, to Fort Dix,

New Jersey, where I had begun my basic training. We loaded up at Maguire Air Force Base, adjacent to Fort Dix, and were sitting in an old Flying Tiger Super Constellation four-engine propeller plane, off to the Old World somewhere to the east.

My heart sank lower with every foot of altitude we gained. Darkness was closing in. We were on the last and longest leg of our flight, having just refueled at one of the most desolate and God forsaken places I have ever seen, Gander, Newfoundland. The flight was to take another 18 hours. The old prop planes were slow and a bit noisy, but very reliable, we were told.

"Yeah, reliable," I thought, "Reliable as long as everyone along the way remembered to say God bless it!"

My mind wandered again as I gazed ahead into the darkness. What am I doing here? Why me?"

I wanted to go home. My thoughts were gaining momentum. "Poor me." They raced. "Poor miserable me. I shouldn't have to be here. Why me? Why nice guy, me? What in the hell am I doing here?"

It was that airborne madness! A running chant was haunting me, playing over and over through my mind as I sat there in my misery, "Howdy, howdy, howdy ho. We are airborne, off we go!"

We repeated those songs so many times in infantry and airborne training that they never really cleared out of your head. Run 1,000 miles in formation. And then do five million push-ups, ten million pull-ups and twenty million jumping jacks. Nothing to it. And the continual repetition of mock jumps, "Get ready. Stand in the door. Go!"

How did I get here? What a damned mess this was.

Who in their right mind would want to jump out of a perfectly good airplane anyway? Well, that was the kind of question any non-airborne "leg" soldier might ask. For paratroopers the answer came naturally.

"We do! We are airborne! We jump out of perfectly good airplanes to kill the enemy! We jump to protect your freedom! We

25

jump into the heat of enemy fire, and we love it!"

I even told myself all of that stuff in my sleep.

I hated all that airborne chicken-shit stuff — all of that contemptible, petty and insignificant nonsense meant to add to the training torment — but at the same time, I loved it. I liked being around other paratroopers. We were different. We were fit. We were tough as nails and half crazy, all of which suited me just fine. And besides, I wanted to be a paratrooper so I could stay in the States. Yeah, right!

Oh, well, you win a few and lose a few. I wasn't staying stateside. I was headed to Germany.

The Mark of a Man was the title of the Army brochure that drew me in.

By time I saw the brochure, I had graduated from a two-year community college and was a junior at a four-year college. It was my third change of schools and my third change of career paths, and I was only 20 years old. When anyone said I lacked direction, I would always say, "Don't worry. I'm heading in the direction of finding my direction."

I was at Albany State Teacher's College at the time, in upstate New York, studying to be a physics and chemistry teacher. Unfortunately, I was totally unmotivated from the day I set foot on the campus. I loved science, especially physics, but I had developed a capacity for resenting things that were not the way I wanted them. And I had learned how to make a really big deal out of it. You name it and I had a reason for not liking it, whatever it was.

What kind of reasoning is this, coming from a high-strung, macho Italian youth from New York?

There were more women than men at Albany State Teacher's College, at least 60 percent to 40. And besides having more women than men, most of the guys were wimps from "Nowhere, U.S.A.," little bitty towns upstate from the city. They were no competition at all. Girls — really cute ones — were everywhere.

This was prime picking grounds for a guy from the center of the universe, but I wasn't that interested in the girls on campus. I just wanted to study in order to move on. I had a sweetheart at home at the time, and home was less than two hours away.

I was simply an unhappy camper. I found all kinds of reasons to dislike my teachers and to dislike my new career path, and I made very little time for study.

The Introduction to Education professor taught his class over a TV monitor, not even face-to-face. I remember complaining to nearly anyone who would listen, "Why, of all things! Who wants to teach when you don't even make contact with the kids? Why be a teacher?"

My mind kept after me with a continuous bombardment of questions and statements aimed at proving I was in the wrong place. I needed a drastic change of scene. I had to do something different. That Army brochure, *The Mark of a Man*, the one I found at the Army Recruitment Center, caught my attention.

"Only an action guy can qualify to wear the insignia of combat arms," it said. It even offered a quiz to help a young man find the answers to life's deepest and most searching questions:

How do you stack up as an ACTION GUY? If you can truly answer yes to these questions, chances are you can qualify as a combat soldier.
... Am I man enough to take a new direction and give up the old routine?
... Will I really enjoy the chance for adventure?
... Am I in tough physical condition?
... Am I able to think for myself in a tight spot?
... Am I better than average in character and responsibility?

Well, I couldn't say no to any of those questions. I was sure I had been born to be an "action man," someone who could cut down the enemy and simply could not be killed himself.

That was how I felt *before* I had gone through training. Now I was unstoppable.

But there was more.

Under combat arms came the choices of infantry, armor and

artillery – none of which really fit me except for a category listed a little farther down on the page under the section entitled,

SPECIAL JOBS FOR SPECIAL MEN! PARATROOPERS —
They don't come any tougher than these Professional Fight-
ers.

Wow, that was me. And those professional fighters get to kill people too! (You only got to kill the enemy, of course, but the Lord knows we had plenty of enemies.) What more could a young man ask for?

I have no idea why becoming a trained killer was so high on my wish list, but I wanted to be one. Really! I wanted to be an unstoppable, Rambo killing machine before there even was one. I was bulletproof and looking for a chance to prove it. A dozen en-emy machine guns couldn't stop me.

The brochure kept on with teasers. Some of them dressed up as warnings:

Your training for these rugged outfits requires absolute sharp-
ness of both mind and body ... So before you consider sign-
ing up, you had better understand just what it's all about.

I was already sold, but it kept sounding better, warnings or not. I wanted to do something different, and this sounded more like the ticket the farther I read:

These career combat soldiers thrive on danger. They take
great pride in being on their own... taking chances ... push-
ing their minds and muscles to the limit. Unless you thrive
on excitement — rugged living and bullet-fast competition
— better back out right now, because, buddy, this just isn't
for you.

No, no, this is for me! I kept going, looking for more. Another little flyer pulled me in a little further. There they were, the air-borne action guys on the front fold, all floating to ground in their silken "chutes," their planes flying off into the distance. The brochure title consisted of only one word, aimed at grabbing the reader, "Airborne."

> *AIRBORNE is a word. A shout. A way of life . . . The train-*
> *ing — the toughest. The tradition — the strongest. The men*
> *— the proudest. Airborne — the best! Here there is no sec-*
> *ond place. No maybe. No letting up. Airborne means confi-*
> *dence. In yourself. In your fellow soldiers. In the cause*
> *you're all fighting for.*

Wow! That was it! I wanted to be airborne. Airborne all the way! I had to enlist in the United States Army.

So there I was on Flight 923, staring off into the darkness, miles above a hostile-looking ocean, asking myself, "How did I get myself into a mess like this?" I always had the capacity for forgetting what really got me into things.

In this case, I volunteered to do what I wanted to do. I wanted to be airborne and I got it. But I wanted to stay in the States.

Once you complete training and start jumping out of airplanes and impressing your friends with your accomplishment, the thrill begins to fade fast. Reality sets in.

My reality of the moment was that I was sitting in an old, out-of-date, propeller-driven Lockheed Super Constellation (not even a jet), flown by an airline I had never even heard of (the Flying Tiger Line), and headed to a place I didn't want to go. I'd be away for 30 months, nearly 1,000 days. Put another way, I would be gone for some 24,000 very long hours. I might as well have been going to prison.

We left Maguire Air Force Base in New Jersey fairly early in the day and headed for Gander, Newfoundland.

I learned in later years that Gander, Newfoundland, and Shannon, Ireland, both pretty much owed their existence to trans-Atlantic propeller aircraft flights. Planes had to refuel for the last time leaving North America at Gander and for the last time leaving Europe at Shannon.

Our stop in Gander was totally uneventful. You couldn't find a more remote place. There was nothing at Gander except for a few aircraft runways surrounded by endless forests and one small terminal building with a coffee shop and cafeteria. The food on the plane was far better than at the local cafe. We were glad to get going again.

While boarding, I somehow got separated from the rest of the guys. I wasn't paying attention to anyone else anyway. It was open seating, first come first served, and I wanted a seat by a window, so I lined up as soon as I could. I found a perfect window seat immediately behind the right wing.

Without my noticing, a major sat down next to me in the center of the row with his wife on the aisle. I didn't have anything against officers, but you just didn't chat with them beyond the courtesies. Besides that, he was a "leg" officer, just a plain old foot soldier, not even airborne. How could we relate? I never did ask him his name and I doubt that he asked me mine. We all wore name tags, but I didn't pay attention.

We weren't very far out of Gander when the pilot announced that we had encountered turbulent weather and that he was going to try to get above the storm. By then he didn't really have to tell us about the turbulence. We were bouncing around rather wildly and the hostesses were having a hard time getting us a Coke. The captain announced he was going into overdrive to bring us up to 21,000 feet, which in those days for that type of aircraft was a pretty big deal. We would hear some changes in engine noise, but not to worry. Everything was routine . . . so he said.

Chapter 4

Fire in Engine Three!

*F*our miles above the water, I could see the white caps on the waves below from my seat against the window.

The ocean looked so cold and desolate and was getting darker by the minute as we flew away from the setting sun. The view gave me a horrid chill, but I couldn't take my eyes away from it. I waited and watched, seeing nothing at all but the engine and the raging sea. We were flying toward the unseen, that foreign land called Europe.

The engine's blue exhaust grew more distinct as the skies blackened. It cast a hypnotic spell against the eerie backdrop of darkness. I wondered how hot that exhaust gas was.

Then, in a flicker of sparks, my spell was broken. Against the black of night, first came orange sparks mixed among the blue glow of the exhaust. Then yellow and red sparks. Then the engine burst into flames. I could nearly touch it.

No more sparks now, just fire rushing out of the engine. Fire, real fire! The kind of fire that burns. Oh, my God, I can't stand the thought of it. I hate fire.

That little episode ruined what little was left of my already perfectly miserable day. What do you say at a time like that? "Help?"

I was speechless — in shock — and so was everyone else who was aware of what was happening. No need to shout "fire." There was only the dreadful silence of fear — the horror of knowing something really terrible was happening and not knowing what to do or say about it.

The fire went out quickly. The engine was dead. A few minutes later I noticed that an engine on the left wing was also silent. I assumed that it had been turned off to balance the plane, but that wasn't the case at all. In a hasty attempt to extinguish the fire in the engine on the right, the flight engineer had mistakenly shut off the oil supply to an engine on the left. We didn't know what had happened at the time. We only knew that we were running on two engines instead of four, and we still had a very long way to go.

The stewardesses told us not to worry.

"Not to worry?" I thought. "Who are they kidding?"

They assured us that two engines were all that were needed to get us to our alternate destination, Shannon, Ireland. "As a precaution," however, we were to prepare for a routine ditching operation.

"It's just a drill," the stewardesses told us, but I knew we were goners. We had had it. It was over. You don't just look into a burning engine and think everything is fine and dandy. While I was no expert on airplane engines and how they should sound when they are running correctly, our airplane hadn't sounded all that great to me when it was going on four engines. Now we had only two engines to carry all that weight. We were a flock of dead ducks, just looking for a place to cash it in.

"It's just a drill," we were told again.

Suddenly, I became very calm. I began writing a letter home to say "Thank you, Mom and Dad, and farewell," as if the letter would ever get there.

I was scared. Yes, bullet-proof me, scared to death, but resigned to wait for the outcome. We were getting ready for a routine ditching operation. Step by step, we went through the procedure, not all at once. First at one level, then on to the next, all just part of the "drill."

As our drill proceeded further and further, it appeared to me and most of the others that our situation was becoming hopeless. I found time to finish my letter. The passengers were starting to loosen up a bit.

I was proud of my letter, which I carefully tucked into the inside breast pocket of my uniform. It told my folks how much I appreciated what they had done for me and acknowledged how far they had come, meaning their progress from the children of very poor Italian immigrants to where they were now, owning their own house. How do you say it all on the occasion of your unexpected and premature departure from this life?

I was very proud of them, and just a little disappointed I wouldn't be able to tell them in person. I figured there would be some kind of exercise to gather up bodies, when someone would find the letter and mail it for me.

"Just a drill." Shit! We were all dead troopers. The guys who didn't know it were the guys who weren't looking into the engine the way I was when it caught on fire. It was burned out dead! That was no drill.

I could see the water raging right out of my window. How could that be? We were so far up, yet I could see it churning and foaming and rising into enormous swells. I could see the water clearly in the darkness as if it had a light of its own. I felt I could touch it with my bare hands if I could open the window.

We were assured again it was just a drill. We could get all of the way to Shannon on just two engines, we were told.

"Yeah, yeah we can," my mind shouted, "provided, that is, every saint and angel each one of us in the plane knew personally was out there giving us a lift." I found very little comfort in that thought. I couldn't think of even one saint or angel I could call on, and I doubted any of the other troopers on our plane could either.

"Excuse me! Anyone!" My mind was racing, "Anyone who might be listening!"

I was calling desperately inside my head.

"Shit! Oh, shit!" At a time like this, what else could come to mind besides, "Oh, shit!"

I tried praying. I knew the "Hail Mary" and the "Our Father," but at that point in time, Mother Mary and our Holy Father seemed very far away. With my luck, they were vacationing in Florida or somewhere safe. Certainly they would not be here within eyesight of a freezing ocean. Why would they want to be here? "Oh, shit!"

Under those circumstances, praying seemed to serve so little purpose.

Nothing more happened for what seemed like a very long while. We limped along, actually for several hours, with me looking down at the churning, foaming and frothing sea.

My road to this disaster had been a rough one.

I signed up for jump school and was promised it as long as I continued to qualify and provided I could bear the pain. The Army managed to gloss over the long months of agonizing prerequisites. It was nothing less than torture.

Everyone had to do basic training, of course. I joined up with a buddy, Donald Godwin from Monsey, who was a cousin to my girlfriend at the time. Her brother, whom I had known since fourth grade, had joined the paratroopers about six months before I did and became a parachute rigger, one of those guys who pack the chutes for all of the others after a jump. No doubt his assignment inspired me further toward the airborne madness.

Donald and I went together for our physical exam and formal induction at the Whitehall Center in lower Manhattan, a week or so before we had to show up for duty. That dilapidated, archaic, and musty old building in lower downtown Manhattan and the cold, impersonal and bureaucratic pre-induction process were enough to get me thinking about running off to Canada. Whitehall Street was about enough trauma for me, but it was too late by then. There was no turning back. We were going in, like it or not.

Our first day on the Army payroll was punctuated by one of the briefest and most unexpected surprises of the next three years. It came without the benefit of even the tiniest of Italian premonitions.

As a final act of leaving civilian life, we had to discard our street clothes and stand in line in our underwear to get our brand new Army issue. Handing out the olive green fatigues we would wear throughout our training was my Great Aunt Elizabeth's son, who was fresh into his first weeks of training himself. He was pulling extra work duty, certainly a few steps up from KP.

Was that an omen? My cousin was there to hand me my first Army uniform. No time for chitchat. Just a brief hello between cousins and a "Good luck to you. It's good to see you!"

Donald and I were to be in basic together, under the buddy plan guaranteed by the U.S. Army. There would be no separation during training, except that I fell out with pneumonia two weeks into basic. We started boot camp in March, which is not the greatest time of the year for training outside, rain or shine, at Fort Dix. My pneumonia ended the buddy plan contract for both of us.

Donald went on after basic to administrative training and became a payroll clerk. He was married before he got out of the Army and was stationed at Fort Mammoth, New Jersey, barely 50 miles from home.

I didn't smoke when I entered the hospital at Fort Dix, but I was hooked by time I left, pneumonia or not. The Red Cross nurses at the time passed out free cigarettes to the troops, even those on the pulmonary ward. Nothing could really make my cough worse than it already was, and besides, the codeine syrup kept the cough pretty well under control. Then there was one week at home for rest and recovery. It was a rough start for me in the Army, but actually not all that bad. I had three weeks on duty and one week back in Nanuet with a starting pay of $90 a month.

I lived through the rest of basic training and actually took a liking to it.

My next assignment was advanced infantry training at Fort Gordon, Georgia, somewhere near Augusta. I've never had a desire to go back to either place — Fort Gordon or Augusta — and I've never even taken the time to look them up on a map.

Advanced infantry training, or AIT, taught a man a lot of useful skills; however, very few were of any value outside of the Army. We were going to get into some very serious fighting techniques and even more serious physical training.

The Fort Gordon experience was a shocking giant step into the past. I found myself in "deep south" Georgia.

I rode an overnight bus to the closest town to camp and stepped out into a backward, old southern country village that seemed to be more like an abandoned movie set than a place where people lived.

It was about 9 o'clock in the morning. The first thought that came to mind was, "Do people really live here?" But I wasn't waiting around for an answer. I was just a soldier passing through and wouldn't be there long. I wanted to find a beer and then be on my way to post.

The first and only place I could find for an early morning drink was an eerie old country bar. It was not a Western bar like I had seen so often in the movies. Old men were hanging around at that early hour, catching up on gossip. The back door was wide open to let in a little air, and a chicken was standing there at the threshold, clucking away. It must have been an invisible chicken as the old men paid it no mind at all. I was getting sick of the South already.

I had my beer, found out where to catch the bus for Fort Gordon and left. The few minutes I spent gathering my thoughts while waiting for the bus to arrive was just enough time to melt the shine off my military shoes. It was early May. We still wore our woolen dress greens up north. It was almost summer time in Georgia. I had to get out of that heavy outfit.

I got to post at about noon. Check in time was 6 p.m. and most recruits waited until the last minute to arrive, and for good reason. Instead of an opportunity for quiet time, I was reminded that I was in the Army and was handed a paint can and told to help the other early birds get the barracks ready for the late ones. They were opening up a section of old buildings that had not been used for many years.

What a dismal, hot and desolate dump. My training mates were all new faces, none that I recognized from basic, and I saw none that I would want to hang in my photo gallery. There were a lot of black guys there, a lot more than we had in basic.

It didn't take long for me to realize that advanced infantry training was not my cup of tea.

It wasn't that advanced infantry was so physically impossible or mentally demanding. It was just that hell itself could not have been hotter than Fort Gordon, Georgia, in June and July. No way! No air conditioning. No shade. Just miserable, God-awful, blistering, humidity-drenched, breath-sucking heat.

Prickly heat — that is what I remember most. It was the red, bumpy, prickly kind of rash that babies used to get around the edge of old cloth diapers, especially during the hot, humid days of summer. Prickly heat was my curse and my scourge.

I may have been the only soldier in the camp to get it. I didn't ask around to see who else had it. All I know is that I had it really bad. I was covered with prickly heat from the tops of my boots to the top of my shirt collar. It was from the sweat, dirt, humidity and moisture from those unpredictable, lukewarm Georgia rainstorms, all rubbed into the skin by the coarse fibers of Army fatigues. Since most of the training consisted of push ups, squats, running and other sweat-generating Army exercises, there was always plenty of motion to be had for rubbing the crud deep into the skin.

Maybe I was allergic to Georgia. In any case, I was certain I would die from prickly heat before it was over. With my luck, I thought, I would be the world's first and only fatal case of body-wide diaper rash!

On one especially hot and stifling day I decided I had taken as much punishment as a human being could tolerate. My skin was swollen and sore from my neckline to my boot line, with every rub point in between blistering with infection. I could barely take another step. I was convinced that if the heat, the stress and the humidity were this bad in advanced infantry training, no one at all – and especially me – could possibly live through airborne training at a still hotter place in Georgia during the even hotter month of August. I couldn't get out of advanced infantry, but I could get out of another four weeks of hell that the Army called jump school. I was told that jump school made advanced infantry training look like kid's stuff. I wanted to drop out before I died.

37

I begged for it and got permission to go to Army administration to sign my waiver with the recruitment sergeant. He had to handle the paperwork because I enlisted specifically for airborne duty. The Army had to let me stay in airborne training, according to my enlistment contract, as long as I kept qualifying. Quitting, however, was my option.

The old sergeant was very calm and pleasant, a stark contrast to the barely sane fanatics at the training camp.

He questioned why I wanted out. "Airborne is surely the best of the best," he said.

I rolled up my shirt sleeve and pulled open my neck collar and showed him.

Prickly heat! My God, I was a mess. It didn't itch any more. After so much soreness, it hardly hurt, or at least you couldn't tell what part of the skin was hurting. He looked as if he had seen it before.

He smiled reassuringly and said, "You'll live through it, Soldier. Don't worry. Most people do."

"Yeah," I thought, "except for those who don't." I was trying to be pleasant and appreciative, but I had to know more.

"How do they do it?" I insisted, "How can anyone do airborne training and live through the heat?"

"Simple," he said. "They run you through cold showers every hour during the ten-minute break."

"Cold showers every hour? You're kidding! How do they do it? Do you have a locker room? What do they do? How do they get from the field to the cold shower?" I had to know.

"No, no, they don't go to a locker room. They have outdoor showers right out there in the training field. Every hour you get a ten-minute break and can stand in the cold shower as long as you want," he assured me.

"Do you get undressed? How do you do it?" I insisted. I had to know. I was dying to be airborne, but I didn't want to die first from prickly heat.

"No, no, no. You go through the shower with your clothes on. It doesn't hurt because you're wet from sweat anyway. You wash the sweat and dirt off. You cool down and you're ready to go again for another hour."

"You're kidding." I insisted.

"No, no. You can make it, Soldier. You'll get through it. I promise you."

He was telling the truth. I was sure of it, as unbelievable as it sounded. I went back to the sweaty hell hole and toughed it out for another three weeks of running, pushups, pullups, squats, and playing soldier in the woods night and day. I was going to be airborne if I didn't die from prickly heat first.

Airborne here I come!

Our ditching drill kept interrupting my thoughts.

The stewardesses were giving us instructions. First, we took off all of our medals, anything that might be sharp and poke a hole in our life vests. That was just about anything we had of value, including our parachute wings on our dress uniforms. Then we put on our life vests and secured them properly, making sure everything was in order, just part of the drill.

It was becoming more realistic and more urgent as time went on. How far were we into it? Two hours? Three hours? Four hours? Where the hell were we?

Next, to make our "drill" more realistic, some time after everyone was in their life jackets, the stewardesses told us we had to take off our shoes, our beloved, spit-shined paratrooper boots. Stocking feet only. The stewardesses would be coming around to collect our footwear. My God, this was going too far.

We paratroopers hated to part with our jump boots, but we were too scared to complain. The stewardesses locked our boots in the tiny toilet up front to keep them from flying around. Just in case we had to ditch that is. We were still only in drill mode.

A latrine full of paratrooper boots. Who can use a latrine full of paratrooper boots?

What a waste of good stuff. Spit-shined paratrooper boots.

Can anyone use a whole airplane latrine full of spit-shined paratrooper boots?

What a crock of shit! A drill, just a drill. What bullshit. Months of it all — bullshit, chicken shit, and just plain shit.

No point looking back to the beginning again; we were getting right up there to the end for keeps, paratrooper boots or not. We were like cowboys being robbed by bandits in our final moments. It just wasn't right or fair to let a trooper die without wearing his boots. My God, every one knows a cowboy wants to die with his boots on. So do paratroopers!

Oh, well, what the hell. When you're dead, you're dead. But at that moment in time, I felt I'd rather be dead wearing my boots. Once again, I wasn't going to have my way.

Everyone was thinking the same thing: "This is it. This is the end of the line."

We were flying so close to the water that I could almost feel the spray on my face, and they were calling it just a drill. We had to drop down — way, way down — to below 1,000 feet. In fact, much of the time we were at 200 feet to allow us to keep going on just two engines.

Just a drill? Excuse me, but this seems pretty much like the real thing to me. My thoughts were running wild. "Shit." That was about all I could muster.

I felt as if I was watching a movie and I was one of the actors. It couldn't be real, but who are we fooling here? It was real. No reason to panic. This is it. Relax. We are dead already, Fred. You might as well get used to it.

"Keep a stiff upper lip," I said to myself, as I had heard others say before. Who said that? I don't know. I must have seen it in a movie.

"What a revolting development this is." That was a line my father used to say a lot. It was from his favorite radio show, "The Great Gildersleeve." Goddamn! How those ridiculous thoughts jump into your mind. What a revolting development indeed!

I said something mindless to the major beside me. He was kind and consoling. He was whispering to his wife.

There we sat, in our life vests, in stocking feet, waiting for what might come next. I pulled the letter out of my inside jacket pocket, looked it over once more, then wrote on the envelope, "If recovered, please deliver to my parents at ...". I carefully wrote out my address in Nanuet. I was ready now. I made sure the letter was properly folded and ready to be found and delivered.

Another long wait. In fact, it seemed like an incredibly long wait. Silence.

Invincible paratroopers! Jump school! Blood and guts! What a crock of you know what!

From less than 200 feet above the water, I could see the foam splashing off the waves. The water was vicious. Won't be long now. You might get to see some real blood and guts. Your own.

It got very quiet in the cabin. Praying seemed like a very good idea. Swearing and profanities were not going to get us anywhere.

The captain turned off the cabin lights so our eyes would adjust to the darkness. We eased into the ditching position — legs bent loosely before us, head forward almost touching knees, then with both arms reaching down.

Try to relax. Yes. Relax.

We would hit the water with a thump, thump and another thump, just bouncing along on the surface. Our ditching position would give us the angle and flexibility to handle the water landing, they said. And we wished it to be the case.

We waited, and waited . . . and waited. Silence.

Chapter 5

The Crash
of the Flying Tiger

*T*he stewardesses knew the children didn't stand a chance on their own. They needed volunteers to hold the little ones on their laps. No one was expected to swim. Everyone was to walk out onto the wing in an orderly manner and then climb into one of the five life rafts. That was the game plan. Should the volunteers need to swim, which was unlikely, it would be for just a short distance to bring the child to safety.

Obviously those optimistic, would-be heroes couldn't see what was going on outside. The waves were in a fury, waiting to grab every last one of us.

When the stewardesses matched the last child with a naive, optimistic soldier about two rows ahead of me. I thanked God for that bit of kindness. I wouldn't have been able to say yes if they had asked me to take one — I was worried sick over the prospects of saving myself — but at the same time, just like the others, I would have had a hard time saying no. How could an airborne trooper say no?

Everything was quiet. Our boots were gone, stowed in the latrine. Our pins and medals were taken hours ago. We were in our yet-to-be-inflated safety vests. The plane was nearly clipping the foam off the crests of the waves.

Five long hours after the first two engines went out, a third sputtered and died away from the strain. Only one engine remained. Captain Murray calmly announced, "Well, folks, it looks like we're going to have to ditch."

We didn't have any altitude to lose. We were sitting on the waves already.

Everyone was in the brace position, with hands behind the legs and head resting on the lap. Only a very dim light remained. Everyone was waiting for impact.

Silently we sat, hunched over in the ditching position, waiting, waiting, and waiting some more. Now, now, waiting, silently. When would the waiting end?

The water below our wings was a raging, chaotic, moving landscape of jagged, mini-mountains with steep slopes and yawning valleys between. The pilot was looking for a relatively flat stretch of water between the peaks where he could level off as best he could and slide his craft into safety. Having only one engine made the maneuver all the trickier. He was waiting for that stretch of open field, waiting, waiting. We were coasting in.

Now, now ...

not yet ...

now, now — COW-WHAM!!!

It was a gigantic, heart-stopping, teeth-jolting belly whopper landing. Everything broke loose! It was as close to a dead stop as you could get, with an ear-shattering cow-wham! Someone flew over my head. My seat held fast. The people in the row in front of me were gone. Vanished.

Freezing water rushed in and soaked my feet up to the ankles before I made a single move. The icy cold on my feet filled me with horror. I popped open my safety belt and jumped out of my seat, reaching in the same motion for the emergency window in front of me. No one was there to slow me down, no one.

In a single jerk, I pulled the emergency window right off the wall. I was out! One of the first, I thought, "Thank God! Thank God! I'm out!"

44

The water was so frigid cold that it knocked the breath right out of me. I gasped for air. The waves were choppy, splashing and frothing, swirling violently, throwing water everywhere, especially into my face and mouth. I could not catch a breath. I was gasping.

"Head up! Head up!" I was screaming to myself, "Keep that head up! Out of the water!"

But where was up? Where was out of the water?

I was spinning and tossing, and the waves were throwing buckets of water at me. Gasping for air, I could not find those goddamned inflate strings. Panic. No strings. Where are my inflate strings?

I was screaming and thinking no words at all, just inhuman panic.

You have heard it before when you take a flight over water. "Grasp firmly on the draw strings and pull down to cause your vest to inflate," they say. No way! No goddamn way! My draw strings weren't there.

The life vest strings flew up beyond my neck the instant I hit the water. I had to find them. They were not at my waist where they were supposed to be.

I was gagging and gasping, trying to keep my head out of the pitch-black, icy water. It was dark, the water so choppy and wild. I found the draw strings at last. In a final fit of panic, I yanked hard on them, and in a blessed, grateful hiss, I was floating in my life jacket. Sort of floating. I was drowning while wearing my life vest.

Just an hour earlier, we were told that the plane would probably float for 20 minutes. We were to step out of the emergency window and onto the wing in an orderly manner. The life rafts would inflate automatically. There would be two near each wing and one inside the cabin.

There was no wing. At least I couldn't find one. If it was there, it was too deep under water to reach. We wouldn't be floating any 20 minutes. We wouldn't be floating at all. We were on our own. The plane was sinking fast.

I was desperate, in a total panic and alone. "My God, where is everyone? My God! Help me! Please help me!"

For those first few seconds after inflating my life vest, I floundered among the waves, gasping for air and praying for help. I couldn't breathe. The cold water stole my wind. Buckets of water were being flung in my face no matter which way I turned.

This wasn't working the way they said it would!

I couldn't see anyone. Where was everyone? I was alone in the dark, left to die! I couldn't stay afloat, even with the life vest. The freezing sea was pulling me down. Down! Down!

I couldn't think. I couldn't breathe. I could only scream my lungs out for help, but there was no one there to help me. There was no one to even hear me.

For a fleeting instant I thought I saw a raft and heard shouts in the darkness a little off in the distance. It was dark, but the water let off a tiny phosphorescent glow. I was certain it was a life raft. It looked like there might be some people getting in. I started swimming out toward the vision, but lost it in the crests and trenches of the swirling waves.

The wet fury was joined by mighty arms and icy fingers reaching out to drown me. I was locked in a desperate death struggle to keep them back, to gasp a breath. I pushed away from the vision of the distant, lonely raft. I started swimming back toward the sinking airplane.

"My God! Is there no one here but me? My God! Help me God! Please God, help me!"

Baggage was swirling all around me. Gasoline covered the water. I gulped a mouthful of salty petrol while gasping for air, then vomited. I latched onto a floating duffle bag and drifted toward the sinking fuselage and toward the tail. The water was less violent right against the side of the plane. The mighty Flying Tiger Super Constellation looked like a giant, dying shark with an evil tail intent on smashing me in its final throes.

The tail! That evil-looking, three-finned, Super Connie tail! Its silhouette loomed in the darkness like a blood-crazed demon. It was flapping up and down in the water, waiting for me to slip under it.

It was a wicked illusion. The tail wasn't flapping at all. The water was thrashing up and down to meet it. The water was trying to beat the plane to death, just as it was trying to beat me to death. Horror raced down my spine and grabbed me by the gut. That evil looking tail was after me. It was trying to kill me!

I slid along the hull to gain my bearings and lunged for the tail fin as if I was going to fight with it. I grasped it with both hands to hold it back and screamed at the top of my lungs, "God! Help me! Someone! Please help me!"

And then, in an instant, I snapped to awareness. The panic vanished and I could think again. I pushed away from the tail, that giant shark, and the remains of the aircraft sank from view. For a few seconds, at least, I was back in control.

My God, it was so dark and desolate.

I could hear cries for help, but I could see no one. How could I be so alone?

No matter how hard I tried, I was going nowhere. I was drowning. I was freezing and I was dying.

"Help me!" But there was no one to lend a hand. No more airborne bravado or cursing, just begging, begging! "My God! Please God! Help me! Please help me!

Then, a flash of light. Now that the plane had sunk beneath the waves, I could see some motion and what must have been a raft. I started swimming toward it with the strongest breast stroke I had ever mustered in my life. That let me see where I was going and kept my chin up far enough to keep from drowning as I swam.

My God! The waves were gigantic. The water was spraying and frothing from every direction. The raft kept disappearing from view. The wind and water kept fighting to keep me off course. Was that a vision, or was it a life raft for real? Is it there? I saw people and heard shouting and screaming, cries for help. Keep on going!

The water kept breaking in my face. One after another, the waves threw buckets and buckets of ice cold sea water in my path. "Don't slow down! Keep on going!" I was coaching myself. "Keep on going! Catch your breath! Keep on going! Don't quit now!"

It seemed like miles from the sunken Tiger to that life raft. What-ever the distance, it was enough to kill off most latecomers. Lucky for me, I was a strong swimmer. I could keep my head up, swim fast and hold out for quite some distance. And thank God I was airborne! The training gave me the stamina I never dreamed I had.

"Got to keep going!" I kept shouting to myself, as I continued screaming for help. "Keep on going!"

A horrifying scene was playing out before me. The closer I got to the raft, the farther away it seemed to be. My arms and legs were stiffening from the cold. I was begging God, praying in wild screams for help. "Keep going," I kept on coaching. "Keep on going! Faster! Harder! Harder!"

It was so cold, so dark and so turbulent! The raft kept on mov-ing away. I was going to die! I knew it. I would drown before I got there!

"Help me, help me," I was screaming in what seemed like one long and continuous scream. Can't someone help me? "Help me, please help me!"

At last, the raft! Just a few more feet. I could see people. Some were in, some were climbing in, and some were falling away, sink-ing under.

I caught hold of that slippery raft. The waves kept fighting to drag me back into the darkness. The raft was slimy and slick, no handles to hang onto. The top edge I was trying to grasp was actu-ally the bottom, but I didn't know that. No matter, slippery or not, I had to get over the top.

The raft was crowded. I could see that much. It was packed with people, but not with me! I could barely hold on. So slick and cold. I couldn't climb in. My clothes were too heavy with water and gasoline and my muscles were getting stiff. The waves were pulling me back and dragging my legs downward and into the center of the underside of the raft. I kept slipping back and fight-ing forward. It was impossible. I couldn't get over the side. I was losing control and began screaming like a raging madman. "My God! Help me get in!"

Others were hanging on, screaming too. The wet rubber was

impossible to hold. Slippery and slimy. It was a desperate sensation. My life was hanging on a thread. "Slippery," I hate the feeling. Rather it would be an arm full of nettles than a slippery rubber raft pushing me down and under.

The people inside the raft just sat there, staring at those of us who were desperately clinging to the rim. The frantic, freezing waves kept tearing and tugging from behind, yanking us away from life, away from safety and back to the pitch-black depths of the ocean. Most of those on the inside were troopers, just staring ahead with no expression on their faces. Weren't they going to pull us in?

Then a panicked scream came from inside the life raft. Some one shouted in total desperation, but with heart-stopping authority, "The raft's too crowded!"

Too crowded! The raft's too crowded? My God, no!

I couldn't believe it. My life was done, finished. The raft's too crowded! I was being left to die. The shock! The horror!

My God, no! The raft's not too crowded!

Wait! Wait for me! Help me!"

I was in a panic all over again. The thought of it! No, no! Don't tell me the raft's too crowded! Don't tell me that. I don't want to die! No! No! Don't let me die!

I screamed at the top of my lungs, *"Help me! God! Please help me!"*

After what seemed like hours of hanging onto the slippery, slimy rubber, fighting the waves for my life and screaming at the top of my lungs, begging and praying for help, someone from inside the craft finally grabbed my jacket and helped me slide over the top.

BORN AGAIN IRISH - *O'Caruso*

Chapter 6

The Raft and the Rescue

*E*veryone was sitting on someone else's legs, 51 of us in a raft made to hold just 25. Once in position, a person couldn't budge, even if they wanted to.

Someone piled on top of me, more like fell over me, ending up in my lap. I don't know how he got there, but there he was, bleeding from his forehead, squeezing in as best he could. You couldn't see his eyes for the blood. He made it over the side and landed in my lap.

Once inside the raft, as crowded as it was, there was some hope of survival. Outside there was no hope at all, that was for certain.

It was icy cold and dark. The waves around us were so high that you couldn't see more than a few feet out. By this point, you were either dead or in the raft starting the process of dying. We were all praying for God to help us, at least those of us who were not so far into shock as to be silent. We were desperate, in dire need of help, and right away.

The raft was filled with water. The giant, ferocious, icy waves were splashing in, spraying us with phosphorescent sea life. The light was an eerie green, the water so cold, it took your breath away again and again. In a few minutes we were all submerged from the chest down. Some had to struggle to keep their head up just to keep from drowning in the raft.

The sea was tossing us around without mercy. Up to the top of a wave we would go, only to drop back down to the bottom, then spin around, up and down, never slowing, always moving, round and round, up and down. Splashing over the sides, the waves interrupted screams as they cast that phosphorescent glow. Everyone was sick.

As our mass of humanity stabilized, each person wedged into position, the planes came, seemingly out of nowhere. They were flying low, with night lighting and occasionally dropping flares.

There they were. First one, then two, then three of them, beautiful, beautiful planes. They knew where we were even though they couldn't see the raft's safety lights hidden under water. They saw our beacon light, that one lone flashlight, and dropped flares to reassure us.

So pretty they were, so beautiful! The planes were watching out for us even though they couldn't reach down to help us.

Our captain and the flight navigator were on the raft. Captain Murray, it turned out, was the burly fellow on my lap. His head was cut from hitting the control panel on impact. His life vest was slimy with blood and gasoline, and it kept rubbing against my face every time he moved. But no complaints from me! He had saved us. Thank God, he was safe. He even gave me some protection from the freezing surf.

The navigator said that a ship was coming. He had contacted it by radio before we ditched. I prayed to God to make it hurry.

But it didn't come. Was he just trying to make us feel good? Our raft just drifted on and on, blowing in the violent wind. The skies had cleared. There was no moon. The stars spun around and around above us. I am sure there were millions of individual stars, but the constant swirling of the raft made them seem like one big blur. Occasionally, someone would start a song.

Someone suggested we call out our names to see who made it. We were packed so tightly in the raft that you couldn't see anyone. Many simply didn't answer. Some were too scared. Some were in a serious state of shock. Others just listened. Some were dead.

After nearly four hours in darkness, except for an occasional flare from one of the planes above, we caught a glimpse of light on the horizon. Sometimes we would lose sight of it for ten minutes or more. It took almost an hour to make certain it was a ship and not just drifting flares or the rising moon. Then we were certain. Frantically, we signaled the planes. They kept dropping flares to mark our position.

After what felt like many long and agonizing hours later, the ship was in full view. It was a freighter. You could tell by the cranes on deck. Its spotlights were on us. The planes had guided it to us. It stopped about two hundred yards away.

I couldn't see much. The captain was still sitting on my legs and my head was too low. We sat there, wondering what was happening. They were waiting for us to drift in. It took so long, so terribly long. It was so freezing cold.

Finally, we made contact. The ropes, the beautiful ropes! They were thrown over the side to secure us to the ship. Then, ladders came over the deck railing. I prayed for God to help us the rest of the way.

The sea was furious. The ship was pitching violently. One second the deck was five feet above us. The next instant it was 20 feet up. One by one, we climbed on to the rope ladders. Only a few were strong enough to make the climb. Most held on to the ladders, and the ship's crew hoisted them up over the railing.

In the ship's floodlights, you could see how full our raft was with water, now dark with blood. People were thrashing around in that bloody water, waiting their turn to reach the ladder.

My legs were tangled in the ropes that had been thrown down from the ship and into the life raft. It was hard to get free. The raft was pitching violently up and down and to every side.

My God, don't let me fall back into the water again. I had to struggle to keep from being tossed out of the raft during those final frantic moments.

Then Captain Murray got on the ladder. I was right behind

him. The ship pitched, and he swung up 10 to 15 feet, but couldn't hold on. He fell back into the water and under the icy waves.

My God. What a horror.

"No! Don't drown now. Please don't drown."

I grabbed him by his shirt and pulled him back into the raft. He caught his breath and tried again. He made it up on his second attempt.

At last, I was able to grab the ladder. The crew pulled me over the side and onto the ship. I couldn't walk in those first few moments, but I was safe. Thank God. I was safe.

The ship was a Swiss freighter, the *Celerina*, headed for Antwerp, Belgium. It would take two nights and nearly three long days to reach Ireland due to the violence of the storms. Three people had died on the raft from the cold. Others were not doing well due to chemical burns. The gasoline mixed with salt water, combined with the rubbing of woolen uniforms, took the skin off of exposed areas. Some had more rubbing than others. My right leg had a bad case of abrasion, from the back of my knee down the back of my calf, and I had a little patch of burn on my left calf. No problem for me. Certainly my injuries were minor compared to what might have been.

The crew gave everyone towels and dry clothes, and somehow they found warm bunks for everyone in the safety of the hull. The water outside was fierce and splashing over the deck. Planes were still flying overhead to make sure we were picked up.

One poor soul was stretched out in a hallway in the ship, laying there in his skivvies, totally blue in the face, with several of the crew making motions over him. I saw him and nearly gasped in horror. That could have been me. Having been a lifeguard, I ran forward to give mouth-to-mouth resuscitation.

"Clear the air passages, clear the tongue, grasp the nose, mouth-over-mouth, blow in, let it out, blow in, let it out, blow in, let it out, blow in, keep on going."

I kept at it for ten minutes, then 20 minutes. Nothing was happening. I kept on going.

A crewman signaled, "forget it." No, I wasn't going to forget it. "Blow in, let out, blow in, let out. Keep on going."

Finally, after more than a half hour of trying, I gave in. They were right. He was dead. I was horrified, broken. The crew members who watched me try to revive the poor fellow led me away to a bunk, where I apparently slipped into a deep and badly needed sleep.

The ship rocked and pitched and rocked and pitched. There was no special order, no special time to get up, no special time to eat, but when we awoke, everything was waiting for us: coffee, warm food and juice.

Since the ship was small, only about 150 feet in length, it felt as if it struggled up each swell, hesitated at the top, tipped, and careen down the opposite side, ending with a crash at the bottom, only to start the process over again. The crew must have been accustomed to the sounds and strange sensations. This didn't seem to bother them. We thought the boat might break in half. Heck, we were airborne. "We'll stick to the air, thank you." The sailors could have their ships.

Settling down on the rolling and pitching *Celerina* meant licking wounds for most of us, or at least checking to see if we had any. A few of the survivors had pretty serious injuries at the onset. Others developed them slowly. Puss began oozing out of the abrasions on the skin. Depending on how deep the abrasions were, the repercussions came right away or a few days later, as was the case with me.

The seas were still far too furious for any kind of rescue mission, but the British Royal Air Force was able to land a medical team on our ship late in the day following the crash, amidst all of the tossing and turning. The team was able to administer emergency treatment for those most in need.

Unfortunately, that turned out to be a big mistake for several of the survivors. Bandages and ointment felt good at first, but they quickly fused with secretions from the open skin abrasions just like glue. That was not good at all. I didn't ask for any treatment, so I didn't get any. My leg wounds simply ran a sticky liquid and started to turn red.

We all had fairly private quarters, at the most two to four in a room. There was no dining area on the ship large enough to accommodate us for a group meal, so our schedules were staggered. As a result, we didn't see much of each other, which was fine with me. I enjoyed a few hours by myself.

One of the crewmen found me a few pages of graph paper and a ball-point pen. I was glad for the gridlines on the paper, because my handwriting, which is bad at best, was dreadfully uneven with all of the pitching and rolling of the ship. I started writing about the plane crash. It was a stream-of-consciousness type of writing in the form of a letter to my parents. I named my story, "Oh, Thank God!" It wasn't a very creative title, but that was about all that was on my mind from the moment I got into the raft until I got on board the *Celerina*.

I wrote to my parents and my sisters, to tell them how horrible the crash was and how I lived, thanks to the good will of God! I wrote in a style we learned in Henry Larom's creative writing class at Rockland Community College, just a long rambling description of the horror of it all.

I wrote and I wrote, for the best part of a full day. I don't remember if I ate or slept. What a hideous affair! I wanted to get the story out while it was still fresh in mind. The saga wasn't over yet, but I felt as if it was. "Thank God!"

I had a hard time getting over the mouth-to-mouth resuscitation that amounted to swapping spit with a dead man. I had no idea who it was and didn't want to know either. How sad it was! What if he were me?

Sad. That's an understatement. When it is someone else who dies, maybe it is just sad. When it's you, well, that is the end of the line. That is it, end of story. It is a lot more than sad! It wasn't me who died, so I guess the word "sad" fit the situation. I was ready to move on to what might come next.

Chapter 7

Born Again in Ireland

*I*t didn't hurt very much, but it was a burn for sure – a burn without the fire. All I had to do to get relief was roll up my pant leg to keep the ooze from sticking. Others had more severe burns, and their skin was sticking to their sheets and the bandages the medics had put on them the day before. Some with the worst burns started to moan.

The sound of people moaning in pain is absolutely horrible, but it may have been the moaning that caused the ship to call in a chopper to take the injured to the nearest hospital. The seas were calm enough by the third day, and we were not too far from land.

A rescue helicopter came in for its first pickup. Very, very exciting! I had a front-row seat, so to speak, to a real live helicopter rescue.

The sun was brilliant and the seas were blue. The British chopper hovered about 30 feet overhead, lowering a stretcher and a medic. One by one they went up, the ones moaning and groaning in pain. Then the chopper flew off, coming back an hour or so later. Each time the weather showed improvement.

I had no idea that I would be one of the evacuees. I doubt I was on any kind of an injured list. I may have been an afterthought — simply a person standing in a handy spot at the right time. In any case, there was room at the last moment for one more survivor.

"Yes, I have burns," I heard myself shouting.

The calf of my right leg was getting infected. Not terrible, mind you, but infected and running.

"Do you want to go?" the airman shouted back.

"Yes, I want to go!" I shouted and he nodded. "Go where? What did you say?" I couldn't hear above the roar of the helicopter hovering above.

"Ireland?" I shouted. "You say Ireland?"

I could hardly make out a word, so I shouted again. "To where? Cork City?" I shouted. He nodded.

"Where's that?" I shouted.

(What a stupid question to be asking under the circumstances. Who really cared where Ireland was when salvation and rescue were the issues of the moment.)

"To a hospital in Cork City, Ireland," the RAF man shouted. "Get on now!" He shouted in a very patient but commanding way.

The chopper maneuvered overhead for a final swing. With nothing to pack – all I had were my Army dog tags and my Rockland Community College graduation ring, both of which I was already wearing — I was ready to go. I was ready for the rescue.

I was strapped into a harness, hooked to a rope and up we went. Everyone was standing on deck, watching and waving.

Up, up we went as the cable brought us to the copter. Then a forward dip and off we went . . . To where was it?

"Cork City?" It must have been my New York instincts. We had to question everything, even as our life hung on the end of a rope. I got no answer of course. I could hardly hear myself in the roar of the helicopter.

It was a day like no other I have seen. How beautiful was that day!

By the time we left the ship, the mist had cleared, the winds had died down and the sun was brilliant, not a cloud in the sky. The helicopter flew at just a few hundred feet. I could see every detail of the sea and shoreline. From that low altitude, I could almost see the look on people's faces.

The countryside ahead was a magnificent and majestic green! Oh, yes, Ireland, the Emerald Island, I had heard about it before. A place where everything was green.

Even the ocean turned green as we approached land, for at least a half a mile or so. A green finger of shallow sea seemed to be reaching out to welcome us. A brilliant emerald green against the otherwise deep blue sea. The sun was shining brilliantly.

That green finger of water must have been an Irish welcoming carpet. What a beautiful sight to behold.

The Royal Air Force rescue helicopter, like all military choppers, had a noisy way of announcing its approach. It is an awesome, deep and throaty "whoop, whoop, whoop" of the propeller blades and a horrifically loud groan of the engine. The Germans call helicopters "Whoop Sloffers," or something sounding like that, which is pretty appropriate to the sound they make. Anyone in the area who hadn't heard about us and the Flying Tiger incident was surely aware that something was going on by now.

"Whoop! Whoop! Whoop! Whoop!" There was no way to keep our arrival a secret.

An Irish farm woman stepped out of a tiny cottage to see the source of all of the noise. She held a broom in her right hand and cupped her left hand over her eyes. I could see her so clearly I can remember the color of her dress. I am certain she had red hair.

As she watched us approach, a small flock of sheep in the field behind the cottage, hidden from her view, began to panic and race to safety, moving at a frantic pace, first running one way and then the next.

When we were directly overhead, one of the wildly frightened sheep found the open back door and ran right into the cottage. The entire flock took pursuit after their reckless leader. The woman dropped her gaze from the sky and began to chase after the sheep, but she couldn't stop them until the last one made its way in the back door and out the front. There was the "Missus" in hot pursuit after them with her broom outstretched.

What a hoot! What a glorious view! What a hilarious, glorious ride! What a show! What a glorious and happy welcome to Ireland! My heart was racing wildly.

An ambulance was waiting for us at the landing pad. I was the last of the injured to be taken aboard and was probably the least injured. I was in no hurry. I was sure I qualified for evacuation simply because there was an empty space. I was standing in the right place at the right moment, and I even had the New York gall to question our destination. In retrospect, it was sort of like winning the lottery and not realizing it.

From the first moment of contact, the people were so friendly, accommodating and welcoming that I found it all hard to believe. The ambulance crew asked if I wanted to see the city, just as if they might have been working for the local visitor's bureau. Of course I wanted to see all that I could, so the driver took the long route to the hospital. We passed a beautiful lake with giant white swans. It was Lough Cork, near the university, between the airport and the hospital.

The sun was brilliant. Every face I saw had a smile on it. I saw hundreds of them — hundreds of smiling faces! They were acting as if they were happy to see me there, alive and in one piece.

My God, the Irish are beautiful people!

As I was getting out of the ambulance to be taken to the hospital, a reporter from the Irish and British *Daily Mail* newspapers stopped me for an interview. I remembered my story, the one I had written on the ship in the form of a letter, and said, "I told all about it in this letter to my folks. I'll give it to you if you promise to get it to them."

He snapped my picture on the steps of the hospital and promised he would deliver the letter, and he did. He said he would ring them on the phone if I gave him their New York phone number, which he did. He gave his thanks, tipped his hat and was off.

I was there at last, at the place of my new birth, so to speak, at Mercy Hospital in Cork City, County Cork, Ireland, a very old, outdated relic of a hospital, but nonetheless a beautiful place to be and crowded so full of absolutely beautiful people.

There I was, little old me, not quite naked, but nearly so. But not to worry! I had my Army dog tags, my Rockland Community College ring and the clothes the *Celerina* crew had given me. I was well.

Oh, those nurses, those beautiful, smiling nurses. They all seemed to be clutching oversized needles and appeared to be totally committed to poking me in the backside as they flashed their beautiful Irish smiles. Were they chasing me with needles for real, or were they chasing me just for fun?

It must have been for fun. It was hilarious. I could hardly stop laughing. Of course, when I was laughing, they were laughing too.

Seventeen of us were taken to Mercy Hospital, but they only had room for ten. Other accommodations had to be made. They did what they could while they waited for a back up, but I couldn't just sit down to wait. I had to keep moving. I was wild with joy. The others needed treatment. I didn't. I was there to meet and greet anyone willing to meet and greet me in return. I didn't even care about the return. I was in a one-man greeting frenzy.

I was in Ireland, and not knowing at the time that I had only five or six hours to test the sod. An Army medical aircraft was coming to fetch those of us who could not stay. We were to go to an American hospital in Swindon, England, an Air Force hospital.

I paid no attention to the news that we had to leave. I was delirious with joy over my reception and my new chance at life. I couldn't be bothered about what was to come, and in fact, I probably didn't even hear it. I was in love and would have been brokenhearted at the prospects of leaving those beautiful nurses behind with hardly even a kiss.

How unfair can you get?

I still had time, but no time to stay in one place and lament. I had to see all that I could of Ireland. Maybe I could meet everyone in the city. There couldn't be that many more to see. After all, most of them had come out to greet me already. There were dozens of them – no, hundreds of them – or maybe even thousands of them for all I knew. There were so many I couldn't begin to count them. My mind was racing. I was getting drunk on adrenaline and getting still drunker by the minute on love.

Some of the nurses were better at catching me and stabbing me with needles than others. Whatever they stabbed me with seemed to get me racing faster and faster. I was going wild. All I needed was a high point and I could take off flying. I was wild with silly jokes and silly tricks. There seemed to be no end to the hospital's halls and wardrooms.

I knew it. Those nurses had never seen a Casanova like me before, an Italian Romeo from New York. What beautiful nurses, red-haired ones and black-haired ones, all chasing me around with those long needles. I gave them a good run, but I didn't mind getting caught. It was just a little poke in the butt, that's all. First one needle poke, and then another one; they kept coming at me. It had to be all part of the game. Poking needles in people's butts is what nurses do, you know.

Undoubtedly, some of those needles were filled with something aimed at taming me down. I was wild for sure, but I didn't need any taming down. I didn't need to sit down, nor did I need to lie down. I had people to see and places to go. I was intent on visiting every ward and every bed in the hospital, just to introduce myself to old men and old ladies, and to young men and young ladies as well, to say hello and to acknowledge the glorious day in Ireland!

If those needles carried sedatives, they were weak or slow acting. I was in a buzz right up to the time they caught me, strapped me to a gurney and rolled me off to the Air Force MediVac plane.

There was no room at the inn. Couldn't stay in Cork City, not at the Mercy Hospital. Only the really hurting patients could stay. Several of them were already in their own private rooms, moaning from the pain of bandages having been stuck to their chemically burned skin.

The one thing I hate about hospitals is all of those sick people. Sickness is depressing. I wasn't sick. I was celebrating, having a party. I felt fantastic and I was wild! I had just been born again.

It was dark by time we took off from Cork. Sleep or the sedatives caught up to me. All of a sudden the lights went out. I don't remember leaving and I don't remember arriving at the hospital in England. I just remember a few seconds of the flight when I looked out of the window to see the lights of the villages passing below.

Ireland was fading into darkness.

BORN AGAIN IRISH - *O'Caruso*

Part II

Trauma
and
Mending

Chapter 8

Postnatal Trauma

*A*fter the electrifying and euphoric episode at Mercy Hospital in Cork City, I awoke to find myself a prisoner in what appeared to be the stage set of a science fiction film. It was obvious to me that I had been drugged into unconsciousness and taken to a foreign planet.

No more Ireland. No more welcoming crowds. No more celebrity status. I awoke very much a nobody in a squeaky- clean, sterile, white and surreal-looking hospital ward. A bevy of faceless American Air Force nurses in impeccably clean uniforms – all with the peculiar nurse's caps of their training schools – were buzzing around me. The odor of pine-scented ammonia filled the air.

In comparison to that great celebration the day before, I felt like I had been unceremoniously reduced to the level of a common, garden-variety accident victim. I was a non-noteworthy hospital patient hidden in the back wing of a totally alien institution.

About a half a dozen of us — survivors of the Flying Tiger ditching — had been evacuated to the 7505th U.S. Air Force Hospital in Swindon, England. It was a sprawling, mostly vacant series of highly polished hospital wings connected by ramps. There were no stairs as the hospital was designed for wheelchair convalescence. It was Wednesday. The crash had occurred on Saturday night into Sunday morning.

I was in a ward with at least five others, none of whom I can remember, even though we spent nearly two weeks together with nothing to do except race wheelchairs up and down the vacant corridors.

I've often wondered why it was that I couldn't remember anyone on the rescue ship, after spending nearly three full days on board, or anyone on the life raft, except for Captain Murray, and that was only because he sat on my lap for six hours. And even given this, I couldn't remember his face and wouldn't have recognized him anywhere.

How can a person not remember important things after an event like that? Before the crash, and certainly since the crash, I have made lifelong friends literally within a fleeting five-minute encounter.

We certainly talked a lot on our hospital wing, sharing our stories of the Flying Tiger, the raft and the *Celerina*. People came to see us several times a day. Some of the visitors were news reporters, some were insurance investigators, and a few were Army or Air Force doctors. I don't remember a single one of them. And, of course, we had lots of nurses and Red Cross volunteers. We had plenty of free cigarettes. I was totally hooked on unfiltered Pall Malls by that time.

If we had a difficult time sleeping — and I believe all of us did at the beginning — we were reminded to let the nurses know and they would give us something to calm us down. I started asking for "calmatives" about an hour after waking up in the morning just in case I found the opportunity for a catnap. It is difficult to sleep while the nurses and orderlies are going about their chores. I liked napping while people worked around me.

I did a lot of assisted sleeping, especially during the daylight hours in order to avoid everyone. That meant I was up a lot at night when there were very few people around. I could cruise the deserted ramps of the vacant wards in a favorite wheelchair, which I found to be especially fast and quiet. I could spend my time visiting with other patients who might be doing the same thing, and I was having a jolly time with the lone night shift nurse on our ward.

She seemed to like the company and apparently had very little to do for the patients.

By Friday night of that first week the euphoria of rescue had faded entirely. Everything was starting to feel very much out of place. I was edgy and unsettled. The rumors I was hearing around the ward and the logic I was crafting in my mind made it clear that the Army was out to kill me. I didn't know about the others, but I was certain someone wanted me dead.

Our plane crashed the weekend before, either on Saturday or Sunday, depending on your time zone. It hardly mattered. Dead is dead, and it seemed as if death was stalking me.

I'd cheated death just last weekend and way too many times before. It couldn't have all been coincidence. Someone had my number and was just waiting for me to slip up. Whoever it was, he would be standing nearby to collect on my soul the minute I faltered.

I made up my mind: those bastards weren't going to get me out of bed on Saturday or Sunday, no matter what. No way.

I stopped talking.

People continued to come around to talk to me even though I had no interest in talking to them. I didn't know who they were, or what they wanted. They were saying words, but I wasn't hearing. They might have been doctors, but they could just as well have been spies or even janitors. It didn't matter. None of them would believe anything I had to say anyway. The Army was tuning me out, shutting me off, and apparently was out to get rid of me for good.

Don't ask me why. I didn't know any secrets worth knowing. And besides that, didn't the Army need all the fighting troops it could get? I made it through training. I was airborne. I was at least as good a soldier as the next one. It hardly made sense. Why were those bastards after me? Little old me?

There were clues, a lot of separate incidents, a number of close calls to support my speculation. Some of those close calls were pretty serious business, even though I brushed them off as bad luck. The more I thought about them, the more there seemed to be, and the bigger each incident became. I was seeing a pattern of evidence indeed. I didn't even count my bouts with pneumonia just two weeks after I began my tour and that miserable struggle with prickly heat.

I tried to forget the seemingly disconnected incidents, but I couldn't. There were too many. Then came the high-priority, rush orders to Germany — no days off to go home, even though we were only 60 miles away — and then along comes the Flying Tiger incident! Could all of that have been coincidence?

There was a lot of misery that simply went with Army training, but the bad luck events seemed to string together with increased rapidity toward the end of jump school. It could have been the evil eye, but I doubted it for the simple reason no one knew me well enough to envy me. Before I finally connected the dots in my imagination, I was certain I was carrying a basket full of bad luck.

There was my first free fall jump only a month before.

What a thrill it was! We got hoisted up with the parachute partially open above us, 250 feet high. Then, when we hit the uppermost point, we were left to fall with nothing between us and the ground but our parachute. We all made it without injury and were all very high on the idea of free flight. Yes, us! Paratroopers! Airborne!

Then, lunch time. Our band of 30 or so hungry troopers jumped into a high riding open-bed dump truck that was sent to take us to the mess hall. I was standing on the tailgate facing out so I could be one of the first to get in line. I was learning to like that Army chow.

The drivers shared our elation over a morning of jumping and were really hot on the accelerators. We were kicking up a cloud of dust as we zipped into the unpaved parking lot. Our driver jammed on the brakes. We all swept forward, then we all tumbled back, with me going over the tailgate, head first. By that time I was such an expert at the parachute landing fall that I tumbled right back on to my feet.

"Ho, ho, ho!" I shouted, clutching my head with my right hand, "No damage done! Just my head!" And I went on in with the rest of the troops, nursing one heck of a headache.

"They tried, but they didn't get me that time," I joked. "Ha, ha, ha." (Well, not that funny.)

The next week it was our last, long-awaited "jump week." The first four jumps from the "big iron bird" had gone perfectly, with lots of shouting and stomping, much bravado, and lots of adrenaline. Those jumps were without any fighting equipment.

Our final jump was with all of our combat gear. That required us to be all suited up with everything we would need to face the enemy. My jumping buddy was a big, kindly black fellow named Johnson, one of the few I remember by name. He was the one who helped me chute up. Someone on his other side helped him, and I helped the fellow behind me.

It was a short, smooth flight, hardly more than a few miles, and a brisk, perfect jump, with a technically perfect landing, except that my rifle butt slipped out of its covering and hit me on the back of the head.

Wow! Did I see stars. Some of the black guys said it was "The Hawk." They were a little superstitious. It was the Hawk who waited out there in the wind and gave you a jab in your soft spot when you weren't looking.

"Got to watch out for that Hawk! That Hawk will get you!"

"The Hawk, my ass!" I growled back. "It's the Army. They've been out to get me for some time now." I could still muster up enough mock humor to send out a hearty laugh.

Maybe I was at the center of a comedy. The prickly heat didn't kill me after all. Those other little irritations didn't do me in. Incidents just started adding up. Maybe I was the center of a conspiracy.

By Friday night we had finished training, got our wings and actually had a weekend off, and KP duty wouldn't start until Monday.

KP, kitchen patrol! Can you believe it?

No new airborne school graduate ever had to pull kitchen patrol, ever, we assured each other. That was a job for the new, raw recruits, the ones who weren't into training yet. What an insult! We could go downtown on Saturday if we wanted to, but from what I could tell, going to town wasn't worth the effort, so I planned to spend my weekend in an air-conditioned base library, or just hanging out reading, or simply doing nothing at all.

Somehow, given all that free time, I just barely made it to the mess hall before closing time. They ran out of the main course, but came up with a not-so-good-looking substitute, chicken salad, Southern-style, with lots of creamy mayonnaise. It didn't taste nearly as bad as it looked.

Just another meal, and quite okay for a lazy Saturday night on base — okay, that is, until about four hours later. Most of us late chow hounds had planned just to hang around, as it was finally starting to cool down on post and the barracks were a tolerable temperature. Our own bunks felt pretty good for hanging out.

Then one trooper got sick, like really, *really* sick, throwing up and choking, retching his guts out. He could hardly stand up.

This was not your normal upset stomach. Someone called the clinic to see if we should be asking for help. Then it hit another, and another, and another.

My head began spinning. My stomach started getting queasy. I made a dash to the latrine, but didn't quite make it, missing the toilet bowl. I puked and puked, got dizzier and dizzier, and then, out I went.

I didn't wake up for the next 48 hours.

When I did come to, I had a horrible taste in my mouth and a swollen, aching, right arm full of needles and tubes, not having a clue about what had happened or where I was. I groaned and the nurse came running.

My right arm was swollen to twice its size. I must have tried to move when I began to wake and the needles and tubes came loose. Saline solution had seeped into the muscles and caused the swelling. It would go away I was assured. All I had to do was get some rest.

By late Monday afternoon, most of us were ready to go back to the barracks. We could walk and actually hold down water. There was no point in our taking up a hospital bed. We were all perfectly fit. Rough, tough paratroopers, and brand new ones at that.

So I survived another Army attempt on my life. But the bad news was that I had to show up for KP duty at 5 the following morning.

"You must be joking! You *are* joking, aren't you?" I thought I was getting sick again.

"But Sarge, I just got out of the hospital. Just two hours ago." I tried reasoning with the message bearer.

"But Sarge, isn't there anyone else who could do it? I can switch a day."

"But Sarge."

"Well, okay Sarge."

"Thank you, Sarge."

"I'll be there, Sarge."

First thing next morning I was in that Army "killing field" they all called the mess hall. It was 5 a.m. and I wasn't exactly feeling my best. My attempts at reason had failed.

The Army mess hall must have gotten its name for a very good reason. Most of the time the food is really good, especially if you are half starving to death as we were in jump school, but sometimes it is bad — really bad — bad enough to kill you.

I dragged my poor pitiful body around all day long in an attempt to be a decent soldier, at least as decent as one could be in my condition pulling KP duty. The supervisors were easy on me.

About two in the afternoon, after the midday meal, an Army investigator came around to interview me. He was talking to everyone affected by the "chicken salad incident." I could take a break. We sat with a cup of coffee at a table against the wall.

The investigator was calm and efficient in his questions, mechanically writing notes on his clipboard. Despite his calmness and military command, he managed to touch my fast-talking, New York-Italian hot button.

I never left the post on Saturday. I got sick as a dog on mess hall food. I was out for nearly two days, then I got dumped out of the hospital and put on KP duty. I was hardly fit for living, much less KP duty, I told him. It simply wasn't fair.

"Aren't I right?" I said as any self-confident New Yorker would say. He just ignored me and worked on his notes.

An inch-long cockroach started walking up the wall between us. I hated those creatures. They were everywhere in the South. We had them in New York, but they were more domesticated, smaller, and there were fewer of them.

I said, "Look at this thing," and pointed to the cockroach moving up the wall. He ignored the roach. I kept on, "They're all over the place. I know we were sick from food poisoning, whether they caused it or not. We all ate together in this mess."

He pretended as if I wasn't there, just writing his notes. I kept on talking and complaining.

The investigator left quietly, but politely. I finished out my day of KP and sulked all the way to my bunk, and down went one more day of Army life. How many more did I have left? Two years and seven months? How many days is that? Some 930 days and a wake up. (Not to worry. It will be over eventually.)

The investigator wrapped up his study. His conclusion: "The subject became violently ill from drinking too much hard liquor in town."

Those dirty bastards! I didn't even go to town! I didn't even have a drink. I stayed right there in my own little bunk! The Army tried to kill me with poisoned chicken salad and wouldn't even own up to it!

Talk about Army chicken shit. This was getting to be a little too much. This was *chicken salad* chicken shit. This was way too much for me. But nobody cared.

From there they sent me north again, back to Ft. Dix, New Jersey, where I did my basic training, with no time at all for leave to see my family or my girlfriend, not even a simple four-hour break, nothing. We were on hold to leave immediately, but we waited until early Saturday to ship out on a low budget aircraft,

Flying Tiger Flight 923.

The Army didn't care in the least whether I lived or died.

BORN AGAIN IRISH - *O'Caruso*

Chapter 9

The Army Cuckoo's Nest

*S*aturday and Sunday were my unlucky days.

I made my decision. I was going to stay in my hospital bed all day, with the drapes pulled around me. I got up only once to use the toilet when I knew no one was around to do me any harm. The rest of the time I used a bedpan. Nurses brought meals to me.

I didn't want to talk to anybody. I didn't even want to tell my story as to why this was such an unlucky weekend.

Maybe I had bad karma. Maybe I was being stalked by the evil eye. Where was my Aunt Elizabeth when I needed her? I was sure she could break the spell, but she was very far away.

It was a year earlier to the day of the airplane crash that I was in a car accident with my good friend Clarence Sweet.

Clarence had a tiny new car. A fuel-efficient, French Renault mini. One of the smallest cars you could get in those days. It was his first day out in his new automobile and he wanted to show it off to me.

We were on a windy back road in Monsey, talking about how he was saving money to go to college, how we both wanted to go somewhere, to be something worthwhile and to do something worth doing, to get married, raise a family and to be just like everyone else. The Army had not yet entered my plans. I was enrolled in Albany State Teachers College and was thinking very seriously about a future with his sister.

We were psyched about what might come. The sky was the limit! We could do it, whatever it might be. Nothing could stop us. And then, wham!

A wild-eyed drunk came roaring around a blind corner and rammed the car from behind. That little Renault looked like a very sad and slightly oversized accordion. It certainly had no value for either driving or music.

We made a phone call to the police from a nearby house. A few minutes later a policeman drove up in a squad car, looking very official and military-like. The bad news was he was a high school friend of the other driver, the drunk one, so he didn't bother to take note of the obvious circumstances.

Clarence must have been driving too slowly. Of course, that was it. He was driving too slowly on a winding road full of blind curves. The poor fellow behind him hardly had a chance to avoid hitting him. It surely wasn't his fault that he ran into that tiny, underpowered vehicle. It could hardly be seen on the roadway. Clarence was lucky he didn't get a traffic ticket.

The Renault was dead and crumpled, and so were the plans.

The good news of sorts was that neither one of us was injured. Clarence, fed up with life in Rockland County, went to an Army recruiter a few days later and signed up for airborne training.

I made it through my unlucky weekend at the hospital in Swindon without catastrophe. I didn't give bad luck a chance. I stayed in bed and everyone left me alone. I enjoyed the peace.

The chemical burn on my right calf seemed to be healing well on its own; nevertheless, the doctors decided I should get some whirlpool therapy to stimulate the healing process just a bit more. I was game for any kind of diversion. The water was nice and warm and alive with swirling bubbles.

I'd never experienced such luxury. I was at ease and feeling regal, until two therapists carried in a very small child, probably not more than four or five months old, and lowered it into the opposite side of the whirlpool. The baby was crying, screaming, and waving its tiny arms and legs in a frenzy of fear or pain. Its backside, cradled in the therapist's hands, seemed perfectly normal, but its frontside was burned and covered with black scabs and water blisters.

I couldn't tell if it was a boy or a girl. Most of the harm was to its stomach and legs, with just a few black spots on its face. The poor little thing. Those kind caregivers were cleaning its wounds. The bubbling warm water must have dulled the baby's pain as it softened the burned tissue.

I tried not to look, but how could I not? I wasn't sick. I didn't need treatment. Could you call that sore on my leg a burn? My burns were hardly worth mentioning. I wanted to get out of there.

I had been terrified by the thoughts of fire, burns and disfigurement ever since I was a child old enough to remember. A family in Spring Valley suffered a fire tragedy, with five kids nearly perishing. All lived, but were horribly disfigured. There was frequent talk of fundraisers to help pay for their surgery and of the agony they had to go through to bring back a normal face.

The kids never hid from the public. Two wore ski masks to cover their scars.

It seemed like I found myself looking at those burned kids every time I went somewhere with my mother and sister, although, in reality, I only remember seeing them twice. But that was twice too many sightings for my weak stomach.

The first time I saw them was during the heat of summer when they were wearing very skimpy clothing. Most of their burns were exposed. My mother was taking us on a bus from Spring Valley to Lake Monsey, about three miles away. And there they were, on the same bus, the whole gang of them.

My sister and I sat paralyzed in our seats, staring as they played around like any other kids, except for the fact that they looked perfectly hideous. Two of them were wearing skimpy, warm weather masks. Their eyes stared out of those large cloth holes, and what you could see was terrible. Their hands and forearms sticking out of their short-sleeved shirts were wrinkled and scarred.

I hardly knew at age 8 or 9 how to have pity. I simply cringed in horror and shrunk inside my mind.

We were relieved when they didn't get out of the bus when we did. Swimming that day helped distract us, but the memory of their burns lingered on.

Then, when we were a little older, old enough to go to the afternoon movie by ourselves, they were there, all of them, cavorting around, looking horribly disfigured and scarred. No eyelids for the most part, no eyebrows, just scars of varying degrees of red and white. Burned kids were just too much for me.

That was it — no more hospital whirlpool treatments for me. I was fine. My burn was curing up just fine. I could hardly see it. I couldn't even call it a burn.

After that incident, I stuck close to my fellow crash mates, none of whom I remember by name or by face. We smoked as many free cigarettes as the nurses and aides could bring to us, raced wheelchairs along the vacant ramps on deserted hospital wings, never declaring a champion that I can recall. We had a good time doing things and telling stories about which I have absolutely no recollection.

It was all one big blank, no names and no faces, except for one visitor from London who was the sister of our family doctor in Nanuet. She was a nurse. She came with several newspaper clippings about the crash, including my front-page photo and the story I wrote and gave to the *Daily Mail* reporter in Ireland. She also brought a cake and well wishes from the family. It was a very nice visit and was written up in our local Rockland County newspaper some time later.

As the end of two weeks approached, I was getting out and around a lot more and we all began inquiring about our chances of going back home for some kind of leave. Army investigators were selecting some of the passengers for an inquiry to be held in New York about the crash.

Wow! A free trip to New York and a few days' leave, just to go to court and testify about what I remembered about the airplane crash. What a fabulous opportunity. Of course I wouldn't be one of them. I knew too much. The Army was trying to kill me. I caught on to the game, and they didn't like it. They were sending me to Germany, but not directly to my post. I was going to a *special* hospital in Frankfurt. I didn't know exactly where, only that it was special and where I didn't want to be. I wanted to go back to New York.

The words of a song began running through my head: "Oh, no, please no, I don't want to go. Oh, oh no, I don't want to go! Not to Germany, no way, please!"

It was just like a little song I remember hearing as a kid. It was a song about the cavalry soldiers headed to the battle of the Little Big Horn. One line went like this: "Please Mr. Custer, I don't want to go!"

I was big on cowboys and Indians and knew all about Custer's Last Stand. All General Custer had to worry about were the Indians, and they did him in out there in the wild hills of Montana.

His battle was nothing. He knew who his enemy was — the renegade tribes of Crow and Cheyenne Indians.

I had to worry about the whole damned U.S. Army. The Army was going to blind side me right there on the Cold War Eastern front. I thought that the East Germany Commies and the Russian Commies were our enemy. We just finished fighting a World War there in '45. Why are they after me? Why now?

Whatever it took — tranquilizers, restraints, a stretcher, walking, I simply don't know — they got me to the hospital in Frankfurt. I didn't remember the trip. I didn't care. It seemed to be all one big blur. But like it or not, I was somehow there.

I was slipping. I was having very bad dreams and vivid flashbacks about the crash and those hours in the water and the raft.

In the middle of the night, freezing water would lap up on the sides of my hospital bed. I was all right as long as I stayed in the middle of the bed, but if I fell out, the waves would get me. Icy fingers would claw at me, trying to drag me under. Thousands of them. They were cold fingers, pulling me, dragging me, tearing at me, down, down, under the waves. I couldn't breathe. I couldn't keep my head out of the water. Someone was splashing water in my face, buckets full of water, faster and faster. I couldn't get away long enough to catch a gasp of air.

Icy cold fingers. Down! Down!

No air! I couldn't breathe! I couldn't get my head out of the water!

Drowning! Buckets of water hitting my face, one after another! I was trying to get my head as high out of the water as I could, but I still was drowning, right there. I was giving it my strongest stroke, my absolute best, my absolute limit. I couldn't breathe, desperately alone, no air, no one to help me!

Help me! Please! I am desperate! Please, someone, help me! Anyone!

I woke up covered from head to toe with a rash. It wasn't prickly heat. It was like patches of strawberry, everywhere. Some would call it the hives. The doctors in Frankfurt couldn't figure out what it was. An allergic reaction? The water? As far as they were concerned, I was going to live and the strange rash would go away in a few days. And it did.

So, there I was, in Germany, isolated and surrounded by strange people who shared my ward as patients.

One poor sailor nearly lost his leg when a launch cable on an aircraft carrier snapped. The shock threw him off the deck. If he was lucky, he would keep his leg, although it wouldn't work as well as before. No one seemed to be too sure yet. They were watching him and his leg very closely.

Another fellow killed someone with an ax. How he got into my ward was beyond me. He didn't seem injured or sick at all. He sounded fairly normal. He looked healthy.

Nearly everyone had some kind of bizarre story or some kind of traumatic and shocking injury or crime, mostly murder. I soon quit asking the others about their condition and they quit telling. The same U.S. Army couldn't possibly be after all of us and especially any of *them*. Most of those guys were nuts.

I must have known something I shouldn't have known. I wasn't like the others. I must have had the top-secret clue to who-knows-what. Maybe I saw "the secret" when I was staring out into the blue flame of the exhaust as we were flying over the ocean. I was staring right out at it when the orange sparks started flying. Then the flames, and that long delay before somebody hit the fire extinguishers, and then, the engine went dead on the other side.

Was it something I had seen? Where did those people in the seat in front of me go? Did their seats snap off? Did they fly into the ceiling and drop down onto the passengers in front of them? Were those seats and seat belts built by the lowest bidder? That's it. I bet they snapped right off. Those poor devils were killed by the lowest bidder.

Maybe that was good luck for me. Not a single person stood between me and the emergency exit in the row ahead of me. All I had to do was jump up, pull the window off the emergency door, and I was out of the sinking aircraft!

Could I have been the only one smart enough, sharp enough and strong enough to get out of that emergency exit?

I was alone. Why wouldn't anybody help me? Were they already dead?

The water was so cold, smashing so hard against my face that I couldn't breathe. Thank God, I had been a lifeguard and had spent so much time at Lake Nanuet. I could swim. You name the swimming stroke, and I could do it. I could float for a month. Well no, not in that cold. A person couldn't float for even a few minutes. Forget about a month. And besides, I hated cold water long before the crash.

While I can't remember a single person from the hospital at Swindon, I found fewer people I could relate to at the Frankfurt hospital. I don't think anyone from the Flying Tiger had been shipped there with me. To this day, everyone is a totally blank face, including that sailor who just about lost his leg, and that odd-ball, nut-case who killed someone with an ax. You know, he wasn't such a bad guy. Some have done a lot worse than that.

I circled the wagons and withdrew to my hospital bed. What

was next? I was ready to move on, but the Flying Tiger incident wasn't going anywhere without me.

I thought maybe I'd have people coming by every day to talk to me or to interrogate me about the crash, maybe do a little Army debriefing. Nothing! At least I don't remember any questioning. In fact, I don't remember much of anything. I had a lot of needles poked in me, but I didn't know why. I wasn't opposed to the idea of lying around sleeping all day, but I thought I should be talking to someone about my condition. There wasn't much else to talk about other than the Flying Tiger wreck. Was there?

What happened there? Where did everyone go? Why was I all alone until I got to the raft? Why wouldn't anyone help me?

The raft. Yes, the raft, that damned, overcrowded, freezing, flooded, slippery, slimy, God-awful savior of an upside-down life raft.

What was I supposed to do? The raft was too crowded. Was I supposed to say, "Okay, no bother. I'll catch the next one. Have a nice day."

I screamed my lungs out. That is what I did and that is what anyone would have done.

Maybe I should have just slipped under the water and died. And I might have except that the water was too cold. I had to get out of the cold and into that raft. I had to. What was I *supposed* to do?

Chapter 10

Lee Barracks

A man without a country. That's how I felt. At the peak of my joy with my new life in my new homeland, after being rescued from that dreadful sea, I was shanghaied off from Ireland to cold, gray England, denied any possibility of going home to New York, then snatched away again to some nut house in Germany. It was all part of a big cover-up, no doubt about it.

What was left now? I was about 210 days into my enlistment. That meant I had only about 884 days and a "wake-up" to go until discharge. That's just 21,216 hours, just 21,216 long and dreary hours.

Somewhere toward the end of my week at the cuckoo's nest hospital in Frankfurt, the Army higher-ups must have decided I had used up their goodwill and my share of recuperation time. I wasn't much of a threat to national security, and I didn't fit the profile of my neighbors on the psycho ward. I wasn't an ax murderer and had no catastrophic physical traumas to worry about, so I had to vacate my bed for a more worthy patient. The Army said I was okay for duty. My vacation was over. They were kicking me out of the hospital.

"What the heck, anyway," I thought. I hadn't made any friends there. I was just passing time.

The staff at the hospital gave me the necessary paperwork,

and I was free to go. No one even showed me the way out. Just follow the signs to the hospital exit.

I was met on the street by a smartly dressed paratrooper driving an open Army jeep. We drove some 35 miles west toward Mainz-Gonsenheim and the Army base known as Lee Barracks, home of the majority of airborne troopers in Europe. That must have been a well-kept secret. I had never heard of Lee Barracks before we got our assignment orders.

The hour's drive gave me my first look at the German countryside. The sky was slate gray, the horizon blurred with haze, the trees were barren, and the roads were mostly cobblestone and bumpy. The buildings, made of concrete and generally unpainted, all looked very cold, institutional and hardly welcoming. It was mid to late October by then. I had completely lost track of time, and it hardly even mattered.

The post was nearly deserted. All the troops from both battle groups were on maneuvers for 30 days with the 10th Special Forces in Bad Tolz south of Munich. I was assigned to C Company of the 505th, but I would be on my own for about a week until the troops returned. I just had to pick a bunk in the common area on the third floor and hang out. I could take my time, get acquainted and avoid anything that resembled a work detail.

Just about everything was shut down except for the post office, the coffee shop, a small portion of one of the battle group mess halls, and a few administrative offices.

Once situated, I began exploring the base.

I came upon the post office and was curious about how it worked within the Army. During my first year at college I worked as a Christmas season deliveryman for the Nanuet Post Office, and I really liked it. I thought I might have a little in common with anyone who might be working there.

The base post office was a small, two-room area on the second floor of the headquarters building, out of the way, but close to the center of activity. It was run by two GIs, a low-ranking sergeant and an even lower-ranking helper. Both were happy-go-lucky fellows. One look inside their workspace was all it took to see why they had such an upbeat attitude.

What a cream puff job, I thought.

The mail clerks were airborne qualified. I supposed that was just in case they had to jump into a battle zone with the mail. That meant they got the extra parachute pay, provided they jumped every now and again. They otherwise pulled no duty other than putting in their quiet eight-hour days. Sgt. Mailman was an Army lifer in his early thirties who seemed to have some formal education, but not much ambition or drive. His helper just hummed away in the background, sorting the mail as we talked.

Sgt. Mailman was genuinely interested in my Flying Tiger story. He knew I was about to arrive and was watching for me. He filled me in on everything I might need to know about the base and which jobs were the good ones and which jobs were the bad ones. You had to watch for a good one and snatch it up.

As a green trooper right out of training, I had no idea a GI could actually go looking for a job. I thought you just took what the Army gave you. The sergeant was interviewing me as we spoke — that became quite obvious — so I let him know all of my good points, my very best assets.

I could type fast and accurately, I was a good writer, and I had a two-year Associate in Arts degree from Rockland Community College. It was a brand new college at the time, but certainly well-known by now, I assured him. I was in the first class of only 44 graduates. I was a hard worker and always loyal to my employers.

He took it all in and asked more questions. Finally, he told me that his friend, Sgt. Perry, at the base re-enlistment office, just lost his typing clerk due to rotation back to the States. He was trying to find a replacement clerk of his choosing, as opposed to waiting for another "Army issue." In those cases, all the candidate needed was the ability to type a few characters and enough breath in his lungs to fog up a mirror, and he was on. The sergeant would have to take the assigned body, like it or not. The recruitment sergeant had enough bad experience to make him want to avoid the assignment process.

Armed with my top-secret, inside information, generously provided by Sgt. Mailman, I wasted no time in going down to the re-
enlistment office to introduce myself to Sgt. Perry. He was easy to
find since his was a cozy two-room office just down the hall from
the mail room and he was the only one there.

Sgt. Perry was not your typical Army lifer. He was upbeat,
enthusiastic, curious and intelligent. He wasn't any taller than me,
only about five feet, six inches. He looked Greek, with big dark
eyes, black hair and bushy black eyebrows accented against his
ashen white skin. He wore a smartly tailored, heavily starched set
of Army fatigues and a trim, neatly cropped airborne haircut. No
doubt about it, he was airborne and he was sharp.

Sgt. Perry — his dark-brown eyes always wide open — was a
constant motion and talking machine. His specialty was making
anyone laugh, at any time, even if they didn't want to laugh. If he
wasn't telling jokes, he was describing some mundane real life
drama in hilarious, sidesplitting detail. Once you knew him, just
catching a glimpse of him brought on a smile.

We took an immediate liking to each other. I matched his qualifications, demonstrated my typing skills, which were nearly twice
the norm in speed and accuracy, and I was hired on the spot. I
hadn't even met my own outfit or my company commander, but
not to worry, Sgt. Perry assured me. He would take care of the
paperwork and dealing with the officers in charge. The Army
needed the re-enlistment office. He was the re-enlistment sergeant
in charge. He needed a typing clerk. That was it.

So there I was. In one afternoon I was transformed from being
a well-trained combat killer, slightly shaken up by an airplane crash
and fresh out of the cuckoo's nest, to being an office jockey, known
with a degree of jealousy by the regular troopers as a "Remington
Raider." Remington typewriters were the standard Army equipment of the day. I had a brand new one. And I was still airborne,
with silver wings and jump pay to boot!

Mail from home was catching up to me. My mother was heavily
into saying rosary novenas on my behalf. She was convinced I

was saved from the clutches of the Flying Tiger for some special purpose, whatever that would be. Maybe my new job as an office clerk was a promising start.

It didn't take long to learn the ropes of Army re-enlistment. We just filled out a few forms when a fellow wanted to re-up. The information had to be perfect, with at least five layers of old-time carbon copies to be distributed here and there. The new re-enlistee took his papers to the payroll department, and they issued the appropriate cash bonus, depending upon his rank, years in service and how long he was willing to commit. Some soldiers were using their money to buy cars, or to pay off debts to loan sharks, or just to go back home to the States for a short visit.

No one ever seemed to have a worthwhile use for the bonus, according to my reckoning, but that was not my business. I just had to get them processed.

After having the whole base to myself, my peace and quiet was broken when the troops arrived in the middle of the night. Hundreds of paratroopers came in dozens of trucks with tons of field gear, clanging and banging and shouting and yelling, all strung out, drawn out, tired, dirty and ready to hit the bunk — with one exception that is — the bunk where I was sleeping.

I learned later that I came closer to death that night than I did the night of the Flying Tiger. There were no waves, no wind, no engine fires, no icy cold water, no news-making drama. There was just me and one dead-tired, half-crazed, Spanish-speaking parachute infantryman. He was a Peruvian national who had been hoodwinked into the Army and decided to make the best of it by going airborne. He was Alberto Maurer, who, I learned, wanted very badly to be the cause of my immediate and bloody demise.

How was I to know that one bunk out of 100 identical bunks could hold such value to a person who had been dreaming of its comfort for so many days on bivouac? I had stolen his little patch of heaven.

I had no idea that there were so many Spanish swear words. I didn't have to know what the swear words meant to know that they were really bad ones. When he ran short on Spanish profanities, he switched to English.

He was really mad, nearly in a rage, but the mix-up wasn't my fault and I wasn't going to move. I had squatter's rights.

Word was out that I might have a loose bolt or two rattling in my head and had some kind of special status. The sergeants in charge stepped in. Somehow they calmed him down and a murder was averted.

A few days after the dust settled around the bunk bed episode, the company commander called me in for an interview, along with several others who had just arrived. We were there for an official welcome and orientation. He called me up last.

"Welcome, Private Caruso. You are being reassigned to special duty with Headquarters Company. You will be the new clerk at the re-enlistment office. You will be staying here in Company C, but you are being assigned quarters with the headquarters platoon. Congratulations on the new assignment and good luck to you. But next time, Private," he warned, "you had better remember to go through the Army chain of command."

He issued a supportive smile.

"Thank you, Sir," I said with a snappy salute.

I didn't say anymore, but I could hardly suppress the urge to grin from ear to ear.

"Well, I'll be darned," my thoughts were telling me. "I knew I was forgetting something when I went looking for a job. Next time for sure, Sir. Yes. I will. The Army chain of command. Sir!" No doubt he could read my mind.

I had already put in a few days of work at the new office before the troops came home, but my brief welcome and exit interview served as my official Army blessing and, at the same time, my official military reprimand. I quickly rounded up my gear and moved in with the headquarters staff in the same building on the first floor.

I was starting to feel better already. "Not doing too badly for having just gotten out of the hospital as a borderline nut case," I bragged to myself. Although there were others on base who were in the Flying Tiger crash, I seemed to have notoriety, partly because of the length of time I spent in the hospital, but mainly because of the story I gave to the reporter in Ireland. My story and photo had been all over the front pages of the British and Irish versions of the *Daily Mail* and probably in other papers too. The main officers on base and all up and down the line seemed to know quite a bit about me before I arrived.

Shortly after settling into my new job as a typing clerk in the re-enlistment office, I was called in for an interview with the base commander, Colonel White. He asked me how I was doing and how I felt about the Army.

Being the fast-talking New Yorker that I still was at the time, I didn't do a very good job of holding back.

"I like what I am doing, Sir," I told him. "But I feel I could do a lot more."

I told him I had been the editor of the Rockland Community College literary magazine. While that was a relatively small achievement, it was significant. I told him I had a two-year Associate in Arts degree and had done a lot of writing and taken a number of a writing courses.

He said he would keep it all in mind, and he did. Within two months of my interview with Col. White, the sergeant who was writing the press releases for my battalion took sick and had to be replaced. I was asked if I was interested in filling his spot on a temporary, part-time basis, on my own time if necessary, just so I could see how I liked it and others could see how I did. I could fit the writing in between my tasks for Sgt. Perry.

I was soon producing more and better work than the base had seen in years. I was happy, the commanders seemed happy, and Sgt. Perry was happy too.

My two jobs — right-hand helper to Sgt. Perry and the new press-release writer for the battalion — helped build a distance between my Army and the other real life Army. It was that "other" Army that was trying to kill me off, and I wasn't about to forget it.

I couldn't let my guard down. Agents of that other Army were stalking me and I knew it. One slip up and I might get it right between the eyes. Staying busy helped get my mind off the need for watching my back.

If a person had a tendency toward feeling blue, Rhineland Germany was *not* the place to be in November and December. The skies were gray all day and the air was soupy with fog and pollution. I avoided going outside unless I had to, except when I went to town on weekends with some of the guys from Headquarters Company.

Lee Barracks was a self-contained base with its own post exchange (PX), a large cafeteria and coffee shop, a very big Enlisted Men's Club, equipped with slot machines and several bars, a bank, travel agency, barber shop and just about anything you might need. The officers had their own Officer's Club and the sergeants and up had their NCO club.

The winds blew the skies clear one day in mid-December, and much to my delight I could see we were surrounded by beautiful countryside, a ring of mini-mountains and high hills, and that the skies over Germany could be blue. There actually was a sun above the clouds.

Christmas was coming, and I was a long way from home, but so was everyone else. I was avoiding Christmas activity as much as possible. With Sgt. Perry around, however, it was hard to avoid the subject. Christmas was the perfect time in his world for joy and humor and storytelling. He had his family with him in Germany, and Christmas was a big event at the Perry home.

One of Sgt. Perry's favorite story topics was Christmas shopping for his wife, who obviously shared his sense of humor. She could not have survived his silly pranks and stories otherwise. He had a tendency toward wild exaggeration and hilarious dramatics.

Our office was on the second floor of the central post building just above the main entry way that went through the building. We overlooked a very big cobblestone village square, which would have been a major parade field for the old village of Mainz-Gonsenheim.

I often stared out at that cobblestone square thinking about how many World War II Nazi parades must have been held out there, with German SS troopers clicking their heels against the stones, shouting, "Sieg Heil! Sieg Heil!" Old town Mainz still held plenty of scars from the destruction of the big war, which ended nearly two decades earlier. Bombed out buildings and vacant lots still dotted the city.

The holidays were just a few weeks off. Sgt. Perry was getting desperate as to what to get for his wife — really, *really* desperate. He couldn't think of a thing.

He finally gave into the buying fad of the season, which was a camel saddle. It was an odd little thing, a footstool with Arabic styling, that looked like, well, a camel saddle. Everyone was getting them. It was the thing to do that year.

Sgt. Perry was beside himself knowing he had given into one of the dumbest Christmas gift gimmicks of all time. He had bought his wife a camel saddle. Now that he had it, he wondered what in the world was she going to do with it?

"You can't sit on it," he shouted. "You can't balance a cup on it."

There seemed to be no practical use at all for such a stupid gift. He was on a roll.

His right hand held his full cup of coffee. His left hand waved circles over his head. He was looking sharp that day, in his perfectly tailored and starched Army fatigues. He was wound up and ready to spring as he told about his wife and the gift he had just purchased.

"A camel saddle! Maybe she can ride it!" he shouted, his voice purposely raised a few octaves. "A goddamned camel saddle! Maybe she can lasso a cow from on top of her camel saddle. That's what she can do!" he was hooting and shouting. "She can lasso a cow."

He was twirling an imaginary lasso over his head and began shouting, "Yippee-ki-yah-ki-ooh!" He was laughing at his own silliness as he kept twirling his hand above his head.

Sgt. Perry wasn't giving up easily that morning. He was going strong as he worked his way past my desk. He kept on shouting, "What the hell are we going to do with a dumb thing like a camel saddle?"

Maintaining his balancing act — a coffee cup in one hand and the imaginary twirling lasso in the other — he made his way to the window.

He was nearly shouting as he called out to anyone within listening range, "I'll bet there's not a single 'f 'ing' camel within a thousand miles of this place!"

"What a joke!" By then he was really shouting. "A goddamned, stupid camel saddle. And I just bought one of them for my wife!"

It just happened that at that very moment a circus was moving into town to set up a special Christmas show, right there in the dead of winter and right there in Gonsenheim. Two men were making their way across the Gonsenheim cobblestone square at that very moment, walking right toward us, leading a very large single-humped camel.

Yes! There it was, an honest-to-God, real live camel walking across the square right outside the gates of Lee Barracks, right in front of our window.

Sgt. Perry caught sight of the spectacle and went into orbit. His eyes were twice the size of Oreo cookies and he was splashing coffee all over the office. Both of his hands were waving.

I saw the camel at the same moment he did, and I couldn't help joining him. "A camel!" I shouted.

"There's a goddamned camel right here in the center of Gonsenheim. Where the hell is that saddle you were talking about? Go get it Sarge! That camel needs a saddle!"

We were both howling by that point and everyone on base must have heard us at the same time. People all around the plaza swung open their windows to see the camel.

Perry had his volume up to full. Everyone knew his camel saddle story, and now everyone knew that there was a camel walking across the cobblestone square. His wife's Christmas present wasn't a complete sham after all.

"That goddamned Sgt. Perry. What a character! It's a wonder

the Army lets him stay." More than one officer and NCO of higher rank held that thought, I am sure.

Work was actually enjoyable. The more assignments I had, the better I liked it. I felt I was doing pretty well as long as I didn't see too much of the regular troops or get drawn into their routine.

I was still officially in Charlie Company, an airborne infantry unit, and roomed with the headquarters staff, along with Alberto Maurer, even though I worked at Base Headquarters. On occasion I had to do what the rest of the troops did, especially during base alert exercises and when we had an opportunity to jump. Otherwise, I managed to avoid contact.

Unfortunately, weekends were my bad times. The mindless, pointless chicken-shit trivia that persisted around me and occasionally drew me in, started to get to me. Worst of all were the Saturday morning inspections and the preparation for those inspections the night before.

BORN AGAIN IRISH - *O'Caruso*

Chapter 11

Taunted by the Devil

*T*he Air Force and Navy had only a five-day workweek. Those guys could get out of town on Friday and not show up again until Monday morning. Not so for us Army grunts. For reasons no one seemed to know, the Army had an official five-and-a-half-day workweek. We had to hang around until Saturday noon, which meant you had to be somewhat cautious on Friday night. Whatever you might be doing during those wasted Saturday morning work hours — no matter how trifling a task — felt like hell if you happened to be nursing a beer and cognac hangover from the night before.

What did we do on Saturday mornings when all of those Air Force and Navy guys were sleeping until 10 or 11 a.m., or goofing off? Well, the Army filled our time with chicken shit, like inspections, or clean up, or some silly 10 minute activity that had to be painfully stretched over three or four hours, until the main sergeant gave the green light for us to leave. Part of the routine was to see if the Army could find something to justify keeping us on base just a little longer, to remind us who was boss.

I could almost tolerate the trivia until I found a real live girlfriend. She worked in the serving line at the base coffee-shop cafeteria. Her name was Hella and she didn't speak a word of English.

I have no idea what she served or if she performed any function at all at the cafeteria. All I knew was she seemed to smile more at me than the others, and that was enough to make me want to go through the line a dozen times a day, for a coffee one time or a coke a little later.

Hella's grandmother also worked on the serving line and she watched over her granddaughter with the greatest of care. I am certain now that grandmother was a lot more enthusiastic about me than Hella was. Whatever was the case, I hardly stood a chance. I was smitten by Hella's smile.

I finally got up the nerve to get someone to write a note for me in German asking her for a date. She wrote a note back, suggesting a walk through the Gonsenheim forest on Saturday afternoon.

Wow! I had a date. However, this assumed our Friday night, pre-Saturday morning inspection was acceptable to Master Sgt. Williams. He was the sergeant in charge. He would have the final say over my Saturday afternoon. That all depended upon our not flunking inspection for some trumped up, chicken-shit reason. The real purpose of the inspection was to cause us to flunk.

I fell into a colossal twit over the prospects that my quest for a few short moments of romantic joy might end up in my complete and total social destruction, all because of Sgt. Williams.

It was my first date in Germany, with a girl who didn't speak English, and if I had a problem with being there on time, I didn't know how to contact her.

It was not the normal inspection. In addition to personal gear, it was to be a weapons inspection. Our rifles had to be taken apart and laid out on the foot of the bed along with our bayonets. Every piece had to be perfectly clean. On command, should you be selected, you had to assemble all of the pieces with appropriate speed and snap smartly to attention.

Sgt. Williams, the "God" of my Saturday afternoon destiny, was one of those guys who I knew was out to get me. There was no doubt about that. He was never satisfied with anyone or anything.

Pre-inspections were used to show how poorly prepared we were for the much bigger non-event scheduled for the following

98

morning. Since Sgt. Williams was always predisposed to dissatis-faction, we could expect a hassle. Our pre-inspection was already putting a three-hour dent in our Friday evening plans.

I was worried sick that he would pick at something of total unimportance, some tiny, insignificant bit of nothing, and use that as the grounds for ruining my life.

I have no memory of what it was that caused the flap, but it had to be something trivial. I was prepared for the worse. It was probably just a trumped up "pre-threat." Whatever, the intent was to cause me to cancel my Saturday afternoon date. With no way to commu-nicate, I would be forced to leave my new girlfriend standing there, upset and alone, wondering why I didn't show up. My God, I went off the deep end!

"Why me?" My inner self whined. "Why me of all people? Why me, the nicest guy in the U.S. Army! Why do I have to be dumped on by the Army hierarchy?"

Scant milliseconds passed as my thoughts flashed into blind-ing lights.

I'd escaped the jaws of death in spite of those Army bastards, time-after-time, and still that son-of-a-bitch, Williams, was trying to figure out some chicken-shit reason to put a stop to my life at this very moment. That rotten son-of-a-bitch!

My heart was racing. My mind was going blank. My eyes glazed over, head spinning.

I was drowning again.

I was up to my knees in an instant, and then to my neck in freezing sea water. I was surrounded by blackness, water frothing and splashing in my face. I couldn't breathe. Those icy fingers were dragging me down, deep into the frigid salt water. Waves were covering me over, smothering me. I was blind, gasping for air. That bastard was trying to kill me!

Sgt. Williams was oblivious to the fact that my brain was explod-ing. I was losing control, trying to hold on, mind raging black, furious and evil, full of the roar of an uncontrollable, screaming sound, a maniacal, shouting whisper, a shout with clenched teeth and sealed lips.

"I'yz xyzxyz betxyr xyn xyan yzx, you basxyzx son yz a xyzxyz! I've xyzxed yzttyz myz anz I'yz xyzx agxy!"

That frantic, shouting whisper that I couldn't hear but couldn't escape played over and over again, fueling my madness.

I grabbed my bayonet from the foot of my bunk and jumped the bastard. He wasn't going to get me, not me, that son-of-a-bitch.

"I'yz xyzxyz betxyr xyn xyan yzx, you basxyzx son yz a xyzxyz! I've xyzxed yzttyz myz anz I'yz xyzx agxy!"

"I mean it, you bastard!" I was a wild man. I was screaming like a banshee, an out-of-control demon.

He must have been forewarned. He ducked me and got the hell out of there. I was raging, pounding on the walls and the lockers with my fists, ready to kill anything in sight. I was full of unfocused rumbling and roar. My roommates kept their distance.

Word was passed in that I was to cool down and get the hell out of there. Go! Get out. I couldn't have cared less. I was going anyway. To hell with those bastards!

I calmed down, slowly, changed into civies and went out to the enlisted men's club, feeling that all was good again, but knowing in my heart that it wasn't. I had a problem. I didn't know what it was, but to hell with it. I was to meet Hella on Saturday afternoon and no one was going to get in my way. She didn't speak English. I didn't speak German. We would get along fine holding hands, exchanging smiles, and being close.

I had gone berserk at the threat of my enemy! It was just like the Vikings and the Celts used to do. It was believed that they could actually change their body shape in a moment of "berserker," and they were unstoppable. I was becoming a "Doctor Jeckle and Mr. Hyde," unable to control myself. I could have killed that son-of-a-bitch. I wanted to.

I shrugged it off as best I could with, "To hell with it. Just get out of my way." But what was that voice? What was I screaming that I couldn't hear?

It was no louder than a whisper, just out of range of awareness, and no quieter than a jet engine, a thought I couldn't even get my conscious mind to think, much less say out loud. It was a thought that blinded me. I could not read it or see it. The thought deafened me. My head knew something, but it wasn't about to let me in on the secret.

That episode was not the only one. Most were mini-rages, triggered by trifles, mainly centered around the slightest inkling that someone was trying to keep me from my objective. My change of mood was typically so dramatic that my "enemy" fell into retreat at the mere look in my eyes. As soon as I cooled down, my thoughts always went blank. My mind was keeping secrets.

"Shit! If you can't trust your own mind, who can you trust?" I remember swearing to myself one day. I knew the Army was after me and Sgt. Williams was enemy agent number one. Now it looked as if my own mind was out to get me too. All I wanted was a little peace.

Thank goodness for the shrink!

A month or so before the bayonet incident, I started going to a one-hour psychiatric session every other week at the Division Headquarters, about 30 miles away in Bad Kreuznach. That was a darn lucky thing for me. Otherwise, my rage over Sgt. Williams would have landed me in jail.

I was learning from the head shrinker. I was indeed experiencing an abnormal reaction to people getting in the way of my objectives. Some of it was the way I have always been, determined and persistent since early childhood.

But there was something else going on.

What is that screaming whisper you can't quite hear? Could it have anything to do with the Flying Tiger crash?

In addition to seeing the base psychiatrist, my re-enlistment office boss, Sgt. Perry, lined me up for sessions with the base chaplain, an airborne-qualified Catholic priest.

Father Kennedy was a tall, soft-spoken, red-haired Army captain of Irish descent and an absolute prince of a man, who always spoke with a bit of a smile, a very sincere and kindly smile. His assistant, Pvt. Bill Wissell, also airborne-qualified, was in our headquarters platoon and roomed with us.

It didn't take long for Father Kennedy to sense that some of my negative attitude was a carry over from my pre-Army years, long before the Flying Tiger crash. He detected a habit of bitterness and resentment and challenged me to work on it.

"Just remember this, Fred," he told me in his quiet way, "being bitter won't make you better."

He wanted me to work at breaking the habit of acting as if I were bitter and resentful even when I was not. I apparently picked up acting like most of the people I knew as a child had acted. I didn't like it at all and I hardly ever really felt that way. Acting the part seemed to go well with the internal quest for sympathy and self-pity. I was getting very good at it.

Father Kennedy's assistant, Bill, was a lot less compassionate and not nearly as patient with the chaplain's clients as the chaplain was himself. Half joking, but in no uncertain terms, he laid it out to me the first time I came to visit.

I was ranting mindlessly about the unfairness of life, thinking for a few moments I was back home. I was just doing that New York "venting" thing. Bill was the only one in hearing distance, trying to type a letter. I was disturbing his peace and wasting his time. He decided to cut me off.

"Fred," he said, "Why don't you save your energy? Why don't you tell someone who cares?"

He said it so calmly and clearly, but so emphatically, that I was stunned speechless! I stared at him, and he responded without my having said a word. "Yes," he said, "Tell someone who cares."

Once I regained my composure, he went on to tell me he wasn't being paid to listen to my problems or anyone else's. That was Father Kennedy's job and, besides, he had enough of his own problems. What gave me the idea that anyone should care anyway?

Wow! Did those two ever get my attention!

"Being bitter won't make you better," and "Tell someone who

102

cares." I had just gotten two heavy-duty pieces of advice, when all I came for was a little sympathy. I promised to work on my attitude, and I repeated the advice in my head for years, but at the time I really could have used a little sympathy too. Oh, well. You can't have everything.

Father Kennedy was right about my attitude being a carry-over from pre-Army years. However, I learned later that there were other issues driving the drama. They would be sorted out in time, but for the moment I had to start the process of mental transformation.

Despite my progress, I could see my attitude changing for the worse. Bitterness and self-pity are bad enough. Uncontrollable rage makes the mix all the worse, especially for a well-trained Army killing machine!

What was my problem? I had a great job. I was young, physically fit, reasonably at ease with the girls, and I was invincible. Unfortunately, I was also totally depressed.

My mother kept on praying and writing to assure me that I was saved for a purpose. Surely, God had plans for me. Those words of encouragement provided me with very little consolation.

Thanks largely to Sgt. Perry's humor, Father Kennedy's kindness and advice, and the patient ear of the shrink, I made it through the first holiday season, just three months after the Flying Tiger affair. I was hoping for improvement in the coming year, but I wasn't willing to make any bets. Things could get worse.

In the meantime, my relationship with Hella didn't last long, which is probably just as well for me. We both seemed star-struck right up to the end. All of a sudden one day there was only Grandma on the serving line. No more Hella. Her estranged husband, who I learned later was an elderly, alcoholic and abusive man, decided he wanted his sweet little child bride back again. He was taking a job in the north German city of Hamburg and was going to try to make it right. They were still legally married, and it was his right to take her.

I buried myself in my two jobs, cranking out news releases and typing up re-enlistment papers. End of story!

BORN AGAIN IRISH - *O'Caruso*

Chapter 12

Secrets of the Sinking Tiger

Alberto Maurer — the raging, wild-eyed Peruvian, who was willing to take my life in exchange for his prized bunk bed — had a German-sounding surname because his father, the senior Alberto, was one of two brothers who emigrated from Germany prior to World War II. One settled in North America, in San Francisco, and became an architect. The other, Alberto's dad, settled in South America, Lima, Peru, and became an enterprising adventurer. At the time, he was owner and manager of a jungle lodge in a remote corner of the upper reaches of the Amazon River.

Alberto became my older brother who kept an eye on me when I needed a monitor, which was fairly often. He became my younger brother when he needed help, but that was very seldom. On occasion we would find ourselves trapped in a drinking contest with the locals. The Gonsenheim firemen had regular festivals, and central to their endless games and contests was drinking beer from a large, silver champagne ice bucket. It was impossible to win, but Alberto was not an easy quitter. He was a lot heavier "under tow" than he looked while walking upright, I can assure you of that.

A year earlier, he was going to school in San Francisco, but dropped out and hung around campus in violation of his student visa. He was discovered by the authorities and confronted with a choice. He could go home immediately, or "volunteer" for the U.S. Army. At the end of his three-year tour of duty, he would become

105

eligible for U.S. citizenship. He decided to go airborne for the adventure. He still had a few wild oats to sow. His friends and family in Peru would understand, so there he was.

When Alberto got ready to go out on a Saturday night, he dressed like a European, donned a silk neck scarf, a fine shirt and slacks, and cologne, but no hat, and would be off to someplace like the Wiesbaden Scotch Club. Everyone else headed off to the Mainz red-light district or, just as bad and generally more expensive, to the B-girl dance halls, where the barmaids cajoled the troops into buying watered down, expensive drinks. The suave Latin actor of TV's "Fantasy Island," Ricardo Montalban, could claim to be an Alberto Maurer lookalike, although he may never have been as physically fit.

While my first meeting with Alberto was anything but sociable, we unexpectedly became roommates soon after I became a typing clerk at the re-enlistment office. He had become a base photographer and joined the staff of the prized Public Information Office, the PIO.

I was already a stringer for the PIO, writing stories about our battalion while working for Sgt. Perry, but I was not a part of the PIO staff. While Alberto covered the whole base as a PIO staffer, he maintained his bunk and official position in the organization charts in our company within the 505th. (The Army had a lot of people assigned to one place and working in another.)

Alberto was exceptionally good at his work and eager to teach me what he knew.

He taught me the art of black and white film processing, photo cropping and enlargement, and the basics of composition and artistic setting. Lee Barracks had a photo lab for the use of the GIs for a very nominal hourly fee, and it was open just about any time a person had a few hours to put into it. We were both regulars.

I was making progress of sorts. My writing improved and nearly everything I wrote was published. I even started getting an occasional photo published along with my stories.

But in spite of the attempts by so many good people trying to serve as mentors to me, and regardless of all the good advice I was getting, "they" were still out to get me. There was no doubt in my mind. The bad guys were out in full force, hiding in the shadows, out to dash my plans to the floor, to do me in, to utterly destroy me for no good reason at all. I hated that feeling.

"They" were waiting for the perfect moment. I didn't know their motives. Why me?

Maybe they just got pleasure out of hurting people. Maybe they were simply devious. All I knew for sure was I couldn't trust anyone, Alberto and Sgt. Perry among the excepted few. Anyone might end up being one of "them."

The reality was I had tons of goodwill and opportunity being tossed in my path by dozens of people who had no need at all to do so. In fact, some were going way far out of their way to help me. They were stacking cards in my favor, yet I seemed to be totally unaware. That is the nature of reality for many people who have undergone similar traumatic situations — not ungrateful for help and opportunity, just preoccupied with mental turmoil to the point of being unaware of the good fortune right in front of their doubting eyes.

Sgt. Perry was my number one supporter. Somehow he tolerated my erratic behavior that included far too many unsociable and losing drinking bouts with orange-flavored vodka. It seemed just like drinking orange juice to me. I knew orange juice was very good for you so, I reasoned, the more the better. Sgt. Perry always had a good supply on hand.

Another one of the good guys was Jack Odgaard, who later was my boss at the PIO. Jack got into a heck of a nasty fist-fight in my defense over, of all stupid things, my having played the hit song "Soldier Boy" ten times in a row on the jukebox in our company club.

I thought everyone was in love with that song. The first time I heard it was the morning of my first full day in the Army, and I seemed to go into a trance the moment it played. I couldn't understand why the guy objected. I played it at least a dozen times the night before, and no one complained.

The truth was beginning to show itself.

I was on a roller coaster of highs and lows, weighing far more heavily toward the lows. Up and down, and down and up. Those rotten SOBs. No matter what I or anyone else did, I was outnumbered. The bad guys were one hell of a strong force and were getting stronger by the day.

"To hell with them all!" I might flare out, just thinking to myself, for no particular reason, no matter where I was, be it typing a form, writing a story or sitting in the latrine. I might burst out, muttering mindlessly, "To hell with them all! What do they know? Shit! That's what I think of it all." Then I'd go back to doing what I was doing as if nothing had happened.

The German beer and cheap Army booze didn't do much to douse those flashes of rage, and we surely had plenty of opportunity for dousing. There were few restrictions on keeping alcohol. In any case, we had virtually no supervision by anyone who might tell us otherwise. We had our private beer supply stashed in our office file cabinet.

We also had a mini-club in our building, just a few doors down the hall from our office. It opened at the end of the workday and stayed open until the last man left. If you wanted slot machines or more company with fellows from other units, it was a short walk to the enlisted men's club beneath the mess hall, barely 100 yards away.

I might be calm all day, or for two or three days in a row. The periods of calm were always when I found myself working like a madman, writing news stories, typing re-enlistment papers, working in the photo lab, socializing and writing lengthy letters home.

Abruptly, the wild flash of thought would come out of nowhere. Even in the middle of a sunny day, those icy fingers would reach out at me and grab me by the throat.

My God! Wet, cold, freezing fingers were reaching out, trying to pull me down below the surface. Buckets of cold splashing water cut off my air.

Wind! Blowing water! Buckets of water! Splashing! Splashing faster than I could possibly gasp a breath.

My God! Get a grip on the nearest anything! Get a grip! Don't slip under!

By that time I was going to the Division psychiatrist at least once every two weeks. For all of those hour-long visits, I don't remember him in the least. He was like a shadow, hardly ever saying a word. He could have been a mannequin with a hidden recorder for all I knew. Our sessions were my time to talk and my time to whine without someone telling me I should save my talk for someone who cared. I don't know if he cared, but he at least pretended.

It wasn't too long after the bayonet incident that I got into telling the shrink how that bastard Sgt. Williams was trying to do me in and how he set me up over a silly, stupid thing I couldn't even remember.

What was it that was screaming and whispering in my head? I couldn't remember.

What was it?

I couldn't hear it.

Say it again. What was it?

It was either too loud to be understood, or too quiet to be heard. What the hell was it?

"I'yz kyzlyz betxyz xyn txyz yyz, yyz xyn xf z xyzch, ayz I'yz xyzl axyzn!"

What? What was that?

Okay, so I can't say it. But what is it I can't say?

"Try to re-create the situation. Close your eyes and think about it."

Out of the dark. Out of the cold. Out of the wet, icy cold! Those goddamned icy fingers would grab for me!

"What are those icy fingers wanting to do to you?"

"They are trying to kill me, damn it! That's what! Those goddamned icy fingers are trying to kill me! Why kill me? Damn it all. Why me? Help me!"

Sometimes I would get dizzy and have to sit quiet for a while, nearly sick from the seawater and gasoline I swallowed, out of breath from trying to catch a breath between the blowing waves.

What is drowning me? What the hell is it that is drowning me? And, why me?

That was the big question. Why me? But the answer wasn't coming. Maybe the answer will come next time and so I would end another session with the shrink. Not much happened, as far as I was concerned, beyond bringing up bad memories.

Alberto started driving me to my doctor's appointments in Bad Kreuznach in his beaten up and overused, secondhand Volkswagen. Besides the battle scars of age, the old car had acquired a number of new dents and dings from Alberto himself during his many girl-hunting expeditions and drinking patrols.

He looked for any excuse to get off base, and going to "Bad K" was a particularly good reason. He could drop by the *Arrow* newspaper headquarters and lay some airborne PR work on the Division staff. He was already the most widely published photographer, and he was intent on keeping that status.

It was on one of those trips that he raced a train and nearly lost with me sitting in the passenger seat beside him.

We saw the train cruising alongside the highway a few minutes earlier. A road crossing was coming up, and we seemed at that point to be pretty far ahead. The warning bells at the crossing started ringing and lights began flashing, but that was not about to stop or even slow Alberto down. He pushed the gas pedal to the floorboard, downshifted gears and braced for a race.

The train was gaining on us to our right. Warning lights flashing, bells screaming in our direction, the massive iron and concrete crossing bars were swinging downward.

But clear the way! Alberto was coming through.

Faster and faster he drove, and faster and faster the bars dropped down, like a mad pair of scissors out to clip us in half. Not to bother my Peruvian driver! He pushed faster!

The crossing bar to my right was perfectly positioned to cut the little Volkswagen and me in half, just about at hood level a little more than waist high. It would have been a clean cut at the speed we were going, right across the rib cage, even though the crossing bar was thick, round and blunt.

I saw myself right there, half of me on one side of the track and the other half on the opposite side, sliced right through at the waist. That was the end of invincible me.

And Alberto? He had gone insane, or as he would say later, had gone into a state of total mental control.

Faster and faster drove the Volkswagen, and faster and faster raced the train. And faster and faster dropped the crossing barrier!

Wheeeyooowee!

We made it by a nanosecond.

One more coat of paint and the roof of the car would have scraped right off. I was speechless. As a matter of fact, Alberto was speechless too for quite some time, until he gathered up enough resolve to point out that he had lots of time and I was simply overreacting.

Well, I wouldn't be missing my appointment with the shrink after all and Sgt. Williams would get at least one more chance at doing me in. What a lucky day for Sgt. Williams!

The train incident must have softened my mood because the shrink got me right into the Flying Tiger episode, icy water and all. Was he getting tired of my whining and hoping I would get to the point? (Maybe those guys who were out to get me were pressuring him to wrap up our sessions so they could get at me without restraint.)

In any event, I settled down and got right into my story.

The darkness was closing in on me. The wind was howling. It was wet, soaking wet. The black, icy water was breaking in my face, the cold was taking my breath away. My God, it was dark and I was alone! The waves were coming alive, splashing froth in the direction of the wind. Won't anyone help me? Please help me. Help me! Am I alone? Someone, please help me!

I was between the waves, surrounded by floating baggage and debris, covered with foaming seawater and aircraft fuel, and other thrashing passengers, screaming for help, some hidden by the waves, some above on the side of a crest, some below in a trough. We were gasping, fighting to find the inflate cords for our life vests. We were all trying to find a raft. Some couldn't swim.

Desperation!

But wait. I was alone.

Alone, yes? Alone, no?

Was I alone or not alone?

And then the truth: *I couldn't remember anyone after impact because I didn't want to remember anyone.*

Yes, I was screaming my lungs out. I was screaming, "Please help me! God! Please! Please help me!"

Help me? GI Fred?

Yes, help me! Yes! Me!

The whole story was more like: "Yes! I'm Fred, the great swimmer! Please help me. I'm drowning! I'm Fred, the great lifeguard of Lake Nanuet! Help me, please! I'm Fred, the great airborne paratrooper, the invincible one, the indestructible one! I can't breathe!"

Yes, I was screaming my lungs out.

"I beg you God! Help me, please! I'm Fred, the incredible Army fighting machine! I'm dying!"

Yes. And was there more?

"Yes, I'm Fred, Mr. Nice Guy! I'll kill anyone who gets in my way! Yes, me! Mr. Nice Guy! Don't get in my way! Don't let me die!"

Who was doing all of that screaming? It was Fred screaming. Yes. Fred, the great swimmer, the great lifeguard, the great airborne superman. It was Fred, that selfish, killing son-of-a-bitch!

I couldn't remember anyone after impact because I didn't want to remember anyone. I didn't want anyone to remember me.

The truth was out. Some poor devil came to me from out of the darkness and raging sea, screaming, horrified and drowning. His eyes wide open and not seeing a single thing! Panic and desperation. His grasping, icy, gasoline-soaked fingers were reaching for me and got me by the neck.

He was pulling at me and begging for help. He was begging for help from me, "Fred the Great," and I did the only thing I could think of.

I pushed his face down and under the water. I drowned him right there, in an instant, to save myself, then I proceeded to put him and anyone else who might have been a witness right out of my mind.

That was why I was alone on that dark side of the airplane in the middle of a storm amidst all of the floating debris. My mind wouldn't allow anyone else to be there to witness my response to someone begging me for help. It was better for me to be alone, drowning in the icy, splashing, pitch-black windswept sea, than to have someone be there to see what I had done.

There was not a single witness to the event, not even me!

What was that?

Who said that?

Why did I say that?

Who was that son-of-a-bitch?

You can't trust anybody. I told you that, you stupid son-of-a-bitch!

I was wild, banging my fists against the psychiatrist's file cabinets. For a tiny instant I was able to hear that muffled scream — that blasting, deafening, silent, inaudible scream that drove me in my fit of anger. I finally understood.

"I've killed better men than you, you son-of-a-bitch, and I'll kill again

I didn't want to drown anyone. I would have helped him, but I couldn't. He was a good trooper. A better man than most, I am sure. There are so many rotten people alive. I had my chance to save a good one, but I didn't. I couldn't. I wanted to live, and no one was going to stop me.

There it was, at least the part of truth I could squeeze out of myself. My own mind was keeping secrets from me. Damn it all! My own goddamned mind!

My mind was racing and raging, "If you can't trust yourself, who the hell can you trust?"

It was "me" who was not leveling with me. It was "myself" who wasn't telling me the whole story. Who was I trying to deceive? Me, obviously. I was the last person who really wanted to know. I was fighting to keep it a secret from myself.

Stupid! Very goddamned stupid!

Just think about it. If your own mind will stop you from remembering something that really did happen, how do you know that what you do remember actually happened at all? Memories can be wonderful gifts, but one's memory is sometimes quite unreliable.

The whole drama haunted me intermittently over the years, but for the time being, the excess pressure had been let out of the overinflated tire in my head. I at least knew what it was that I didn't want to remember and I proceeded again to forget as thoroughly as possible.

I don't remember much more, except that I experienced one heck of a comedown. I left the shrink's office as a very quiet and subdued trooper, intent on remembering as little of my unhappy revelation as I possibly could. I decided there was no point in my trying to rehash the past. Anyone would have done the same as I did under those circumstances, I assured myself.

When I closed the door to the office, I closed that chapter for a long time. In fact, I couldn't remember what it was I had decided to forget for nearly 25 years.

The ride back to Lee Barracks was uneventful. There were no more races with trains and little conversation. I didn't even mention my episode with the headshrinker. Alberto's mind was on other pursuits, undoubtedly of the female kind. I just wanted to get back to work.

Chapter 13

"Hey, PIO! Take My Picture!"

*I*n a world of lucky breaks, it could hardly get any better than this. An opening popped up at the base Public Information Office — the PIO — and I jumped at it.

Sgt. Perry wasn't eager for me to leave, but he gave me his unqualified support. It was a great opportunity. The PIO covered news for all of Lee Barracks as well as all airborne activities in Europe.

Getting the job was not an automatic shoe-in, even though I was already writing a big portion of the press releases as a second job. I had to pass a live photography test and darkroom exercise. Alberto was there to monitor and judge results, since he had already worked his way into a senior photographer position.

My test required that I shoot a whole roll of film of anything on base that caught my eye, then process the film to demonstrate my potential as a photojournalist, as well as my skill as a lab technician. Thanks to Alberto's tutoring, I was confident I could do it.

The position opened when Specialist 4th Class Dick Smiley, a low-ranking lifer, was being rotated back to the States. I knew him long before the opening occurred and did my best to avoid him. He was a total jerk. Now I had no choice. I had to deal with him.

Smiley had a warped sense of humor, as far as I was concerned, and he just couldn't resist one last opportunity to abuse the blind enthusiasm of a dumb private like me. Smiley gave me my assignment. He handed me an Army-issue camera and an Army-issue roll of film.

"Just go out there and do your best work, Caruso," he said. "Come back, process the film, then show me a contact sheet. I'll let you know if you passed."

I did my best work ever that morning, knowing my entire future was on the line.

I got back to the lab on schedule to develop the film. Breathlessly, inside the pitch-dark chamber, I fingered the newly exposed roll of film, winding it on to the developing reel. Then I added the carefully prepared chemical solution to the canister.

I set my timer and waited for the results. I was "on a roll!"

The bell rang at the prescribed time and I prepared to open my prize, an award-winning set of negatives.

"Voila!" I sighed with confidence as I started stretching the film off the metal reel. Here it is. Alberto was watching quietly from the sidelines.

But, wait. What? I was sinking fast. I was shocked, horrified and dumbfounded! Shattered!

"What is this?" Nothing at all! All I had was a blank roll of negatives. The whole roll of film was ruined, totally exposed.

What did I do wrong? What a wreck. I did it to myself. What a jerk. I was devastated, ruined. Then I realized what had been done.

"Who was the son-of-a-bitch?" I demanded.

Alberto was smiling by then, attempting to suppress one of the world's most uproarious laughs. It was as if he was going to burst apart from holding it in. That bastard Alberto. It wasn't him. You could tell. On the other hand, it was obvious he wasn't totally innocent. He was on the inside track of what I thought was a very sick joke.

It was Smiley. He had exposed the film and rolled it back into its container before sending me out on my assignment.

"You passed the test!" Smiley broadcasted, as he burst into the photo lab, laughing like a delirious hyena. "You're on, Caruso! Welcome to the PIO!"

I got the job, so what the hell. Let him have his fun.

116

We had deadlines, long hours, and had to get up with the rest of the troops to fall out for roll call every morning, but that was about it. We didn't have to pull kitchen patrol, or guard duty or any other bothersome detail. We worked with virtually no supervision. We got to be creative and see our work in print. We got to know just about everyone on base and became known by everyone, including the highest-ranking officers.

We were even allowed to have our own cars, which I eventually did. In those days, an enlisted man in Germany had to be in the Army for at least four years and have the rank of E-4 or above to have a car on base. I was only a private first class, PFC grade E-3, with less than two years of service, yet I could own one if I could scrape together the money. There was nothing in writing to support this privilege. The fact was we pretty much set our own rules and came and went as we pleased. We typed our own press passes and were always very liberal with ourselves.

There were five of us: Maurer, Jack Odgaard, Jim Edwards, Ivan the Hungarian refugee, with a last name as long as the alphabet but pronounced simply as "St. George," and me. There was no officer or sergeant in charge as near as I could tell, and it was that way for a very long time.

We loved our work, all of us, and it was a continual contest to see who could have the most fun doing the most of what he liked best, whether it be writing stories, taking photos, or both. We never kept track of time, but if time were tallied, we certainly all clocked far more than our share, and we loved it.

Maurer was a great photographer and dark room lab technician. He used the photo lab as his own personal public relations headquarters, taking pictures of all of the right people in all of the right places, and delivering copies to them very quickly. His specialty was dramatic "Stand in the door" airborne action shots aimed to please even the highest ranking generals.

Alberto was a great teacher and taught me everything. Edwards and Ivan were strictly photographers, keeping a lower profile.

Odgaard and I did all of the writing, but we shot photos as

well, mainly to support our stories. No one cared about being up-staged by another. We made it a game to see how much we could get published, and it was fun, every bit of it.

The only catch to the notoriety, a minor one, was that everyone on base thought our job was to take their picture, to make them famous somehow.

We all heard it thousands of times, "Hey, PIO, take my picture! PIO! Hey! Take my picture!"

The GIs were always looking to have a little fun, and it seems like everyone likes to have their picture taken, even if they never see it.

When someone shouted the magic words, "Take my picture!" we usually stopped right there and took their picture. What the heck. More often than not, the incident was forgotten, but when we could, we made prints of the photos for them to send home. Just hearing the words made us feel important. We felt good, and so did they.

To make sure we didn't end up with thousands of pictures of others and none of ourselves, we got into the habit of taking pictures of each other. We each made our own "Me Book," a personal photo album that would serve as proof of our Army days.

I was changing since my confrontation with what I refused to re-member during the Flying Tiger disaster, and Alberto was becom-ing a major player in my transition. My unruly subconscious mind was no longer screaming for attention, and I was able to put the truth in its own box somewhere in my mental archive. From a semi-nut case suffering from post traumatic stress, which was not recognized at the time, I was evolving into a professional man of the world, and I was ready.

Soon after joining the PIO and after signing off with the Division psychiatrist, I was asked to apply for a higher security clearance. If I was going to write about military action, I might have to ex-pose myself to sensitive material.

For starters, we had top secret nuclear weapons assigned to

our outfits. They were just little things, jeep mounted missiles with nuclear warheads, but nonetheless sensitive. We couldn't write about them and couldn't take pictures of them. We couldn't even shoot pictures in their direction. No one ever checked on us, but it wasn't necessary. We were all "straight arrow" soldiers writing and shooting film for the weekly 8th Infantry Division *Arrow* News.

We could live with our top secret restrictions, but the civilian media wouldn't stand for it. *Time* magazine featured a cover photo and inside story about one of our most common nuke launchers, the Davy Crockett jeep-mounted launcher, while we were obliged to look the other way and pretend they weren't there. The magazine article filled in a lot of blanks for us. It was interesting reading material, but really, it didn't matter to us.

Once I got my secret clearance I could get deeper into the workings of the U.S. Army. But becoming so important meant I had to deal with one odd little trade-off.

Due to the nature of my clearance and the information to which I would have access, I would not be allowed to travel to Berlin, which was then an island on the other side of the Iron Curtain. I couldn't go within five kilometers of the East German border, either. I might be kidnapped and tortured for my secrets. I tried to ignore the possibility of kidnap and torture and reveled in knowing I might have some information of value, even though I didn't know what it was.

I ended up in the Flying Tiger mess as a result of one of several Berlin crises. The wall was already built, at least in its earliest stage. The rest of the East-West German border was open, with the exception of guards and gates at all road crossings, and a flimsy border fence that looked the same as it did at the end of World War II, nearly 20 years earlier.

The crisis that turned our jump school class and my life upside down was when the East Germans began partitioning off the entire border. The new barrier was complete with barbed wire fences on both sides of an open no man's land. Machine gun towers were built all along the way, and the strip between fences was seeded with land mines.

The relatively loose borders prior to the crisis resulted in an occasional GI being lured into espionage. Some met local females who were really enemy spies from the other side. Some soldiers were actually kidnapped. Others managed to find themselves on the other side of the border and in serious trouble without even knowing it.

By the time I was settled in as a reporter, the wall was very solid and the fence from north to south was nearly complete with its contingent of armed guards and other obstructions to keep their people in and our people out. Mainz and Lee Barracks were some three or four hours west of the forbidden zone, so I didn't feel deprived. I could live with my special rules. There would be no visits to Berlin and I would avoid the border. There was plenty of free Europe left for me to see.

The past was growing smaller and the future was expanding. The Flying Tiger was fading into history, at least as much as was possible at that point in my life. I was working at developing a new world vision, which began to include South America.

Alberto's Peru was a mind-opener for me. It was as different a world from the one I knew as a person might find. When he showed me a new set of rules or a different way of being, it wasn't a contradiction. It was just another way entirely. I liked a lot of his ways. I had a lot to learn.

He must have gotten a kick out of teaching me etiquette, because he devoted a lot of time to doing it. I was far behind the curve, so to speak, and had a lot of catching up to do. I accepted everything he taught me, like opening the door for a lady, offering to light a cigarette by striking the light before even being asked, or calling and paying for a taxi when needed.

He was a social success in my eyes and especially when it came to the area that counts the most for soldiers — girls and romance. It seemed as if he could charm any woman, anywhere, at any time into almost anything. Charm was his sport, no matter what the outcome. Lucky for me, talking me through the rituals of romance was about as much fun for him as doing it himself.

"You see that girl at the table over there?" he would ask. "Near the window, sitting with the other girl?"

"Where?" was my typical response. I was very slow to catch on.

He would say patiently, "Over there by the window. Turn in her direction. She's looking right at you."

Then he would prod me, "Buy her a drink. Buy a drink for both of them."

Before I knew it, he would be calling the waiter over, asking him to bring a drink to the lady and her friend and to tell them it came from me.

From that point he would talk me though the toast, *prost* in German, using the proper gesture with the glass, and like magic, we'd have a new set of friends.

He must have been the hunter and I his decoy. I didn't care. It worked for Alberto and it worked for me. And I learned a lot by watching him.

Within a year of my getting to Lee Barracks, the base did some serious consolidation. We became the 1st and 2nd Battalions of the 8th Infantry Division and we were airborne/mechanized. Soon every company had armored troop carriers with metal tracks meant for serious terrain. We could hit the enemy by air or land or both.

Best of all, the PIO living quarters were moved out of the fighting units into battalion headquarters. That gave us more status and even less supervision.

We had a big office on the second floor of the three-story central headquarters building, sharing our space with the one-person base communications center where orders were reproduced and important messages were distributed. Mike Farmer, who roomed with us, took care of that function. Our sleeping quarters were just down the hall.

Our photo lab was one of the largest in the entire 10th Corps, which covered nearly all of Europe, taking up several pitch-dark rooms in the basement of our building. We each bought our own cameras (that is one thing we didn't want to leave to Army issue), but other than that, everything was provided, including an endless supply of film, provided free in huge quantities by the U.S. Air Force. It was the same film they used in their aircraft, mounted along side their guns to record encounters with the enemy.

Since we had status as official reporters and photographers, we had the opportunity to meet some of the world's best civilian media people, including those who covered stories for *Life, Time,* the *Los Angeles Tribune,* and *National Geographic.* The pros all shared with us the same important piece of advice: "Take an endless number of pictures, but only keep the best."

We took their advice and shot hundreds and hundreds of pictures, always printing the best. We dominated the pages of the military newspapers.

Most evenings were spent in the dark room, making prints for PR purposes, experimenting with new techniques, and getting better at our skills. Our free time on weekends was spent mixing with the civilians off base and taking pictures. We kept up with our jump status and competed to get the best action shots during maneuvers and in midair during parachute jumps.

Army war games were fun for us.

Chapter 14

The Stars and Stripes

*O*ur self-prescribed objective as base PIO was to fill the Division newspaper with as much news and photography of paratroopers as possible. And we did.

Jack Odgaard, a trooper from Columbus, Nebraska, was the most prolific writer I have ever known. He was a total news hog. His greatest moment every week was when he could grab a copy of the Division paper literally right off the press. As soon as the papers arrived at Lee Barracks, he would snatch a handful, run to our office in a dead heat, and then, one at a time, circle all of the stories and photos by any of us with a bright red crayon. (We didn't have highlighters in those days.) He would go around the base and place a marked-up copy on the desk of all of the top brass. He made sure we all shared in the glory of the week.

The longest stories in the 8th Infantry *Arrow* usually had his byline, "Story by Jack Odgaard." I wasn't into length. My stories were shorter, "tight, terse and telegraphic" as they say in the world of print media. He specialized in human interest, and I specialized in facts. The Army needed both.

While the Division paper responded well to the human-interest approach, the *Stars and Stripes* was another venue entirely. It was a daily paper of the highest prestige. Stories had to be to the point, or they didn't get in. Very few photos of military action were used. With the *Stripes*, we were competing for space with at

123

least a quarter million American troops stationed in Europe at that time. These soldiers were part of hundreds of battle groups and thousands of companies. Each one had his own little publicity effort.

The *Stripes* was printed in Darmstadt, 45 miles southeast of Mainz. The paper was Army controlled, but thought of as a "civilian" publication. It was distributed free and had no advertising.

Somehow, Odgaard got word that the *Stripes* was offering something of a scholarship to writers and photographers to come to headquarters and intern for a week on the military desk. The *Stripes* provided housing and a meal allowance and offered an incredible opportunity for one-on-one training with the best news writers in Europe. Odgaard went first, then several fellows from Division. Finally it was my turn.

This was a real newspaper that demanded real journalism. Work there was total journalistic immersion. Living there was just like being on an intellectual, but relaxed, college campus. Most of the staff were civilian. The few Army and Air Force guys assigned to the *Stripes* got to live in what was very much like a fraternity house, nothing at all like the Army barracks.

The closest we saw to military brass was in the form of an old sergeant, who took great pride in calling himself the local "Forest Meister," the man officially in charge of the grounds, trees and wildlife. Indoors, he stayed as far out of view as he could, but was prepared to regale anyone in range with stories and jokes for as long as they were willing to listen. Hunting in the traditional German style was his specialty. He organized rabbit and fox hunts, dressing in a typical German green felt hat and Bavarian lederhosen to add color as he entertained his guests.

I got to know the civilian editors and became familiar with their expectations and journalistic style. I grew especially sensitive to the limitations of the "news hole." If a two-inch space needed to be filled, I could think of something to fill it in my own tight style. Even I would marvel at times at how much could be said in two short inches.

The campus experience led to my getting to know the German printers in charge of the commercial print shop located in the basement of the main building. They sold services as well as printing the newspaper. It reminded me of when I was editor of the college literary magazine at Rockland Community College, developing relationships with the printers as well as developing the content.

That got my creative wheels turning.

It was soon to be the one-year anniversary of the rotation of our colors (the old 505th and 506th was moved back to the states and our outfit was renamed First and Second Battalions of the 8th Infantry Division and became airborne/mechanized). Rotating colors meant all markings of the famous Screaming Eagles of World War II would move stateside. All emblems, shoulder patches and signage had to change. The history of the unit and its flags and banners were packed up and moved, while we, the troops and equipment, stayed behind under a different name.

Within days, the idea of a special anniversary yearbook for our "new" outfit, with new colors and new commitments, emerged.

Of course we needed a commemorative yearbook. Who couldn't see that? We were the *Airborne*! Were we not the original and most famous liberators of World War II? In spirit at least, we were still the same Screaming Eagles. In fact, we were a supercharged version of the same thing.

Why not have a yearbook to commemorate our transition?

We were writers and photographers and now we were trained as editors. We even knew a commercial press that could print it at a special rate for us. We could do it, Odgaard, Maurer, Edwards and me. And we did.

We got every company, every platoon and every squad to participate. Within a month or so we got photos of them all, got our photos identified, and assembled them into our own anniversary magazine. It even featured a welcome by the base commander and the *Uber-Bergermeister* of Mainz, the mayor of the city and its suburbs.

Our yearbook was produced in magazine format on slick paper, but was only 32 pages, which kept the price down and made it handy to distribute. It was a tremendous success and the talk of the entire Division. We did it entirely on our own, with no official military supervision or financial assistance.

Only one thing slipped through the cracks.

We decided early on that there would be no advertising or sponsorship. It was our yearbook and ours alone (we being the Airborne). We charged the troops $1 for each copy and thought we would at least break even. We weren't out to make a killing. We just wanted to commemorate the troops. We figured most of the guys would want more than one copy. They would keep a copy for themselves and send one home to their families in the States.

Our costs were exactly as planned. Unfortunately, we came up short in the end by about $600 and were left holding a small stash of unsold anniversary yearbooks. The debt was more than a month's base pay for all of us put together. By our reasoning, one little old U.S. dollar each for our fantastic, stupendous anniversary yearbook was cheap at twice the price. But, alas, in spite of our success and generous accolades, we ended up in debt.

I talked the German printers into an installment plan, paying all I could from what we collected from the troops. This would stall them for at least another month. But, as the publication ringleader, I was the one who had to come up with a solution.

By that time I knew all of the base officers. One of them put me in contact with the Army recruitment office in New York City. He set up a telephone call with an important contact. I spoke in my best New York accent and with fingers tightly crossed. The recruitment office in New York decided it would be a very good idea to buy all remaining copies of our yearbook for promotional purposes. They had a little extra money in their budget for promotion.

Done! That wiped out our debt. One phone call was all it took. No profit? We hadn't planned on a profit anyway, so no problem. No more debt. Unbelievable.

Good luck strikes again! Zap. Zap. Zap.

Shortly before our foray into the yearbook publication, another bit of good fortune occurred. It was during one of those "talk-Fred-through-the-motions" scouting expeditions with my guide and social advisor, Alberto Maurer.

It was at the Gonsenheimer Gasthaus, in our own little village, a short walk from Lee Barracks. It was late summer, soon after I had gotten back from my first and only leave to the States. I finally got the whole New York homesick business out of my system, re-establishing relationships with the family, old friends and my former girlfriend.

She was getting letters regularly from the "stressed out" side of myself, while the other side of me was really having one heck of a good time. I don't remember the words being said directly, but the understanding was clear. Whatever happens, will happen. I suggested it at about the same time she was about to approach the subject. She agreed and that was that.

Back at the "new" home front — which by then was Mainz, Germany and not Nanuet — Alberto provided me with his best "on the job" social training and never missed an opportunity with women. He always got me involved.

There were two girls at the next table, real cute ones, right there at the Gonsenheimer Gasthaus. They were obviously taking an interest in our conversation and straining to listen in. Alberto broke the ice by getting me to buy them a drink. Elke and her friend were more than eager to get acquainted and joined us at our table without our even asking.

Elke soon became my personal "interpreter," although by that time I was studying German on my own and getting pretty good at it. She was a medical technology student at the University of Mainz, where her father was a professor. My being a journalist, even if I was in the Army, gave me enough status to allow her to feel she could bring me home for an introduction.

Unfortunately, it was dislike at first sight between Elke's father and me. Our relationship never warmed up. My feelings were a lot more congenial toward him. I was naïvely oblivious to how poorly I fit into his plans for his daughter's future. I reasoned, after all, that I was a journalist and not just a common, run-of-the-mill GI. Besides that, I was airborne. It became quite obvious that he would have been a lot happier if I just went away.

At one point I did a special assignment for the *Stripes* on a subject I was certain would please him, as he taught meteorology.

The story was about a new international weather-link that electronically networked all airports in Europe and several on the other side of the Iron Curtain for up-to-the-minute weather information. It was a great story and of special interest to aviators and meteorologists. It was of joint civilian and military interest and got a lot of highly-prized front-page space. I was eager to show him the story and he was impressed, but not for long.

Although he appeared to tolerate me, Elke worked hard at keeping me out of his sight. I rarely saw him, except in my dreams.

It started one evening when Elke showed me the family photo album. Her father was in the German Army during World War II, just as my father was in the American Army. I couldn't determine his rank, and it hardly mattered. All I needed to see was the German uniform to have his image as a sinister force burned into my brain. I felt an immediate and constant need to keep watch over my shoulder to make sure he wasn't following me.

If those bad guys were still out there trying to get me, as I had so vividly imagined in the past, Elke's father would have been one of the first to close ranks behind me. Of that I was certain.

My nightmare always began with an especially sunny and cheerful morning as I stood on Elke's doorstep. Elke opens the door and greets me with her sweeping gesture and cheerful welcomes. I step inside to find she is not alone. Standing there in the entryway, just out of sight and to my rear, as the door closed behind me, is her father in his German Army uniform. My imagination elevated him to the status of the dreaded SS. He holds a Nazi sub-machine gun.

Without comment or explanation or the tiniest ounce of mercy in his eyes — just that cold, steel-blue Aryan German glare with a touch of defiant arrogance — he pulls the trigger, not uttering a word. The gun is open to full automatic. Ratta-tatta-tat! Ratta-tatta-tat!

The bullets rip through my invincible airborne body, hurting like hell as they drill through my flesh. I double over in agony, falling into a pile of twisting, bleeding muscle and bones, right there on the entryway floor. Elke is still smiling as I writhe in a growing pool of airborne blood. She was part of the trap.

Damn! Did that dream ruin my day. I could never forgive him for ambushing me like that, literally shooting me in the back. I was always able to forgive Elke, of course, knowing her father forced her into it.

I have no idea how many times he gunned me down. Maybe he did it in his own imagination a lot more than I did in mine. I'll never know.

From that point on, Elke didn't have to work hard at keeping me out of sight. I found my own ways of avoiding her father without ever giving up the chase.

Elke played a big part in our anniversary yearbook project. Simply serving as a cheerleader, she kept us moving at an even more feverish pace than normal. At our prodding, she orchestrated the interview with the Mayor of Mainz.

Elke's father was impressed with her photos with the mayor. Of course, we didn't tell him until after it was done. He didn't have to know ahead of time. He didn't have to know about all the other time she was spending at the base, giving us moral support, taking unauthorized rides in M-60 tanks, watching us shoot mock battles. Some things are best kept from Dad.

I had my own car by this time, a brand new, shiny gray Volkswagen Beetle, for which I paid $94 as a down payment and committed to $94 a month for the next three years. I was in seventh heaven.

Having a car gave me a chance to make more frequent trips to the offices of the *Stars and Stripes*. In fact, I started going there nearly every Tuesday and Thursday afternoon. I would stop to see if they needed any help or had any holes in those two tight military news pages that needed filling before deadline.

"You need three inches? I have the perfect story for you." And I could fill it on the spot. Of course, I always saved my best photos for the *Stripes*, which they began using with ever-greater frequency.

For that incredible year or so, the Flying Tiger incident barely came to mind and never became an issue. I had a fantastic job, all kinds of freedom, and I even drew extra pay when I stayed at the *Stars and Stripes*. That was to cover meals, since the *Stripes* had no military mess facilities. I still earned airborne jump pay for making my required number of jumps each quarter. And I always expanded those into a photo news event.

I never claimed automobile mileage. That would have required a trip to Bad Kreuznach and a lot of paperwork each time I wanted reimbursement. I was able to get more gasoline coupons than I needed, and besides, fuel on any military base was only 15 cents a gallon. In the field, no one ever objected to my filling up from an Army tanker truck. (One time my little VW was seen waiting in the gasoline line between an M-60 tank and an even larger tank retriever.) My personal expenses were very low. Work was fun and life was good.

At our PIO offices, Odgaard kept on producing volumes and volumes of special interest stories for the Division *Arrow*. Maurer produced rolls and rolls of photos for whatever publication would take them, but mostly for scrap books and memory walls of the airborne leadership.

I got more serious into covering combat maneuvers and staging action photography. As long as I was there to record it, I would go to any length to make a common bivouac seem like the greatest adventure in military history.

Chapter 15

It's Good-bye, Army!

*M*y soldier days were running out. I was getting down to just a hundred or so. I had less than 15 weeks to fit in all the things I still wanted to do, only 2,400 short hours to go.

The thought of getting back to civilian life excited me, but the thoughts of leaving the *Stars and Stripes* and Germany — well, I simply put those thoughts out of my mind. I was having too much fun.

Owning my own car opened up entire new worlds for me. I could explore new territory, when and where I wanted. I was no longer dependent upon hitching a ride with someone, which gave me great flexibility in covering operations. If I had the coordinates and a map, I could find any place — almost. I got fooled a few times. Sometimes the command post was relocated to an undisclosed point for security reasons, and I didn't get the word.

A Volkswagen bug could get through nearly any amount of mud, snow, ice and ruts and, if it couldn't get through, a paratrooper could lift it over the obstacles with a little help from his friends. The latter became a necessity on numerous occasions.

It was my last autumn in Germany, and the time of my most interesting military maneuver. By that time I had logged quite a few mock battles, more or less as a free-lance reporter. I typically stayed close to the command post and avoided anything that looked like military regimentation. I was now my own assignment editor and was supported by a staff of photographers and writers. I was free to jump into the action when and where I determined.

"Panther II" was to begin on Saturday morning, a week before the actual war games began. The opening exercise was to be in of all unlikely places, Rudesheim, the festive wine center and home of the famous Father Rhine monument overlooking the Rhine River, about 30 miles west of Mainz. It was a joint venture with the German Army, combining their train transportation system with our need to move tanks and other heavy armor, along with our savvy in potential nuclear confrontations. Rudesheim had an appropriate rail head for loading tanks.

I was invited as a reporter to the opening ceremonies, which would conclude with a German-American fellowship luncheon at a restaurant in the village. Of course, my girlfriend, Elke, known to the outside world as "my interpreter," was more than welcome to join the affair.

So there we were, among dozens of German and American soldiers and scores of armored vehicles, early on a cold, winter Saturday morning. I was in my standard "uniform" by then — my civies — and Elke was on hand to do my translating, which in that group, of course, was totally unnecessary. She was looking very important and official nonetheless.

Between the events of the day I snapped a photo of Elke. She was sporting an Army jacket and wearing a soft, woolly-eared cap, sitting in a jeep and acting as if she might be giving orders to the troops. It was a great photo, and the *Stripes* used it later in a feature entitled, "Wo ist Elke?" or "Where is Elke?" The story gave her credit for volunteering to help with our PR efforts and livening up the environment with her smiles.

We sat at lunch that day with the military muckety-mucks of both armies. Elke, all of 21 at the time, turned on her charm. She was in her element, and I was politely accommodating.

An American full-bird colonel from Division Command, seated right next to us, turned to me at one point and said, "You are a very lucky man, Caruso, to be out here on such an interesting assignment, in civilian clothes, with such a pretty girl. You are very lucky indeed!"

I responded as professionally and graciously as a hyperactive, New-York-born-and-raised, son of Italian immigrants, who was more Jewish than most, could possibly do.

"Why, thank you, Sir." I said. "I'm very proud of my assignments. I love the work and I enjoy reporting on Army events. I am very proud of my interpreter, Elke. And, frankly, I wouldn't be wearing civilian clothes except for the fact that I am just a little embarrassed to let people know I am still just an E-3, a Private First Class."

He looked surprised.

Elke was armed and ready to wade in, as if I had issued a well-rehearsed theatrical cue. She had seen what we had been doing, having gone through the anniversary yearbook exercise and dozens of other adventures. She got right to him, while he still held a look of surprise on his face.

"Yes, Sir, that is amazing to me," she said. "I see a lot of other people on the base getting promoted, and they hardly seem to do anything. Fred works so hard, but I don't think anyone has ever talked about promotion. I hardly think it's fair."

She was on a roll, but I didn't want her to go too far with it. I was actually feeling a bit embarrassed. I was too busy to bother about promotions and, besides that, I was on the company's shit-list and would never get off as long as the likes of Sgt. Williams were around. Elke slowed her pace, and we quietly moved on to other subjects.

The following Tuesday, however, orders were slipped under the door of my office at Lee Barracks. I was promoted to Specialist 4th Class (E-4). That was progress of sorts, but I was still at least a dozen ranks short of being an Army officer. No bother. I didn't need the rank. And besides, I wouldn't be around much longer. I was to be discharged within the next three months. No way I was going to stay in.

Along with my unceremonious promotion, I was notified in the same envelope that I would be assigned to the *Stars and Stripes* in Darmstadt for the remainder of my tour of duty and was "welcome" to move my belongings out of Lee Barracks as soon as possible. Official orders would follow.

What a heartbreaker. Kicked out *and* promoted. I was leaving Lee Barracks for an adventure as a full-time staffer at the *Stars and Stripes*. I would be sharing a legacy with legends the likes of Ernie Pyle, Lowell Thomas, Andy Rooney and other journalistic greats.

My popularity at home base had been dropping steadily. My company commander seemed to resent my special assignments, even though I didn't even work within the Company. Someone from Division or higher up the chain of command might call to order an "administrative leave" for me to go to some rather fun place, sometimes with just few days' notice. I would be provided free transportation and a small amount of cash for spending money and living accommodations. Administrative leaves were a quick way to get around Army paperwork.

One trip called for reporting on an all-European NATO boxing match in Oslo, Norway, where our troops, mostly from our paratrooper units, struck a stunning victory. Seven days in Norway over the Thanksgiving holiday and seven rolls of film in one night of boxing was payoff in itself, but the sugar frosting came when I earned a front page photo in the *Stars and Stripes*. It was my best photo out of more than 200 shots. Quite a prize.

My understanding of my assignment to the *Stripes* was I would be on temporary duty status, still assigned to my airborne unit at Lee Barracks. I would keep getting jump pay, plus a generous temporary duty allowance. Only now I would spend most days in Darmstadt practicing real journalism under the tutelage of real pros.

Everything seemed to be on fast-forward from that point on. I was free to go to Darmstadt, but I had to finish the Panther II story. The maneuver was to go on for another week.

I decided to get right into the action, reassignment or not. I dropped my belongings off at the "Frat House" at the *Stripes* and decided I would show up at the news desk as soon as the war games operation got going. I didn't have to worry about sewing on new rank chevrons. I was wearing civilian clothes anyway, even in the midst of the military maneuvers.

I was in charge of our own PIO version of *CNN News* long before there was such a thing. It was something we invented as we went along – Odgaard, Maurer, Edwards and I. Odgaard had just gotten out of the Army and was off to civilian life in Nebraska. Edwards got an overseas discharge several months earlier and was hitchhiking around the world. He ended up in Australia. Maurer and I were the old pros by then, and our new helpers simply took orders. For this field exercise I had three support photographers and two writers. No directives, no schedules, no requisitions and no officers or sergeants in charge. That was how it was.

Our "battlefront" covered nearly 80 miles because it was to be a simulated nuclear deployment. Troops had to be spread out to reduce losses. I was soon to get a very big lesson in battlefield logistics.

I was lost by the end of the first afternoon, even with the secret coordinates and battle plan in hand. The last I saw of my colleagues, we were all trying to figure out which of the half dozen *Hausens* on the map might have been the one we were looking for.

Hausen, we learned later, is German for "houses." What we were seeing on the map were simply notations for random clusters or groups of houses. We couldn't find any of the towns we thought we were looking for because they weren't towns at all.

Approaching panic, I gathered as much information as I could. My 7 p.m. story deadline was approaching. I had no photos at all. I couldn't find any of the photographers. I decided to do what I could with what I had. It was a war game, so I would pretend we were really at war. Photos would not be available. My photographers were lost in the action.

I stopped at a gasthaus in the first village I could find. It was a friendly one. I ordered two shots of Schinkenhager schnapps, a couple of large German beers, a fantastic Hasenpfeffer dinner from the menu, and dove into writing the battle story of the day in the style of the *Stars and Stripes*.

My creative mind was going wild. I was lost, out of touch and rapidly getting drunk. I was in the middle of a mock-nuclear confrontation. Forget about the "mock" part. This was serious business.

Checking my secret schedule of messages, I was able to project my story ahead for the morning edition. I wrote one of the most realistic reports of a military maneuver published since World War II, complete with appropriate uncertainty about casualties.

I called the story in over the German phone system with my apologies for not getting to Darmstadt with hard copy and film. The desk editor on the other end of the line wrote down my story exactly as I dictated it and signed off with many thanks. There must have been a shortage of military news that night.

My story the next morning was a sensation. My friends at the *Stripes* said Army lifer wives were calling in to find out if their husbands were safe. (Since I was lost when I wrote the story, I couldn't be certain about anything. For the totally casual reader, my written uncertainty about casualties might have implied there were some.) The editors at the *Stripes* were probably pulling my leg, but I took it as a tribute to my realistic style. My stories were featured for the entire week. Once I located our photographers, I was able to supply the military news pages with photos of the action as well.

The *Stars and Stripes* was now my home base, although I never got a copy of my offficial orders. Who had time for details? I just showed up as a staffer when the big war game ended, and everyone was fine with my being there. By that time I had become a familiar face around the campus.

There I was, at last, sitting at the home of the best in journalism, as far as I was concerned, and perhaps the best in the world. I had my own full-time tutors in writing, editing and producing headlines. I was getting better every day!

Keeping track of time remaining in the military had gone from one of my highest priorities to my lowest. All of a sudden I was down to my last month in the Army. Where did those thousand days go? What was I going do next with my life?

My editing mentor, a civilian from New York and a veteran copy editor, was understandably curious. He wanted his wife to meet me and also to meet Elke, who had just been featured in the special interest section of the paper. They invited us to dinner at a restaurant in Heidelberg.

His wife was an exceptionally striking blond, born and raised in Athens, Greece, and educated in the States. That night she looked even more beautiful than her norm in a black dress and sparkling jewelry. Both were interested in knowing what I would be doing next and what Elke would be doing.

It was a delightful evening for me, with stimulating conversation, a great meal and fine wine. What I didn't know was that during the entire evening Elke was feeling miserably uncomfortable and outclassed, sitting at the same table as "Helen of Troy." Of course she didn't say anything until we went to the car to head for home.

Being as naïve as I always have been, I never caught on to her discomfort at dinner. She was nearly crying.

Outclassed? Uncomfortable? Inferior? I would never have guessed. Of all stupid things.

How could Elke be outclassed by anyone? Or be considered inferior to anyone? Leave it to a German to come up with something as ridiculous as that!

I was pissed. How could she feel that way? Outclassed?

"She was so beautiful," Elke wept, "and I'm so plain."

Shit! I thought without speaking. "Helen" was good looking for sure, but not *that* good looking.

"And she was so intelligent," she wept, "and I felt so ignorant. I hardly know enough to carry on a conversation."

Shit! My thoughts were flaring again. "Helen" was intelligent, but not *that* intelligent.

And besides (my temper was getting the best of me), if there was anything to feel sick about, it would be me feeling sick over having to end our relationship in just a few short weeks! It was our agreement. Elke was to go her way and I would go mine. We didn't talk about it, but I sure thought a lot about it. That might be something worth feeling sick about.

My mind skipped over my imminent loss and turned to anger over her feelings of inadequacy! Ridiculous! Stupid! Maddening! I was boiling over for the first time in nearly a year.

I drove Elke to her apartment, made an abrupt stop at the curb and didn't get out or offer to open the door. I just stopped. She got out, glared at me, then slammed the car door, obviously very angry with me for being so insensitive.

And I was gone.

My VW must have agreed with me in this bit of macho irritation. If a VW could screech its tires, my Buddy would have. I tore off like a racing car driver behind the wheel of a Porsche, accelerator to the floor, gear jammed into first, then a very quick shift into second. Then a scree-e-e-eech for real! This time the tires were clawing against the pavement in a frantic attempt to stop.

A military police car was making a routine turn right into my path. The two MPs jerked out of the way and squealed to a halt. I ran up onto the curb and into an electric pole.

"Shit!" Then silence.

"Maybe this serves her right!" I thought as if I had done something to get even. Elke had no idea that anything was happening. She must have gone off sulking to her tiny apartment. I was in the middle of the street a few blocks away in one heck of a pickle.

The MPs brought me into police headquarters.

There I was, in Heidelberg, only a PFC (I hadn't bothered to upgrade my ID), beyond the 50-mile travel limit, out after the midnight curfew, appearing to be AWOL, lacking appropriate papers, driving recklessly, causing a near collision with a military police car, and I had been drinking besides.

I was assured that the incident would make for a very lengthy delinquency report (DR), and who knew what might come in the form of penalties.

Since I hadn't picked up my formal written orders, I assumed I was being sent to the *Stripes* on verbal command and was still on my old outfit's rosters. I told the MPs I was assigned to the 509th of the 8th Infantry in Gonsenheim. It was well after midnight by then. The night duty officer at Lee Barracks could find no record of my assignment, either there or anywhere else, or any evidence of my existence. I was not on any roster.

The MPs were cordial, but really making a drama out of having a hot violator. I was witnessing a military-style episode of *Dragnet*. One of the MPs was playing Sgt. Friday, complete with the deep monotone voice. The other was the straight man. They offered me coffee and let me hang around the desk. I could sit in the cell if I wanted to, or I could stay with them.

Finally, at about 2:30 a.m., after several unsuccessful attempts to find my assigned post within the 8th Infantry Division, I suggested they contact the *Stars and Stripes* in Darmstadt, which they finally did, but very reluctantly. They got the old *Forest Meister* sergeant out of bed, and he assured them I was under his command. He would send someone down to pick me up.

Two hours later a jeep and driver arrived from Darmstadt to fetch me.

I thanked the MPs for their hospitality and help in finding my home base and managed to make a point of telling them my good spirits were largely due to the fact that I was getting out of the Army in about two weeks.

"Two weeks! Out of the Army in two weeks!" They both laughed.

"That's what you think," Sgt. Friday droned in as friendly way as he could. "With a DR like that, you might be around for quite a while."

I smiled, declined comment, offered a hand in appreciation and left. My car was dented, but drivable, so I followed the jeep up the autobahn to Darmstadt.

The cafeteria at the *Stripes* that morning was alive with chatter. I couldn't sleep anyway, so I went right on in. The buzz was about me.

"That rascal Fred spent the night in the Heidelberg jail."

The talk was all accompanied by grins and smiles, no notions of dire consequences. "About time something interesting happened around this place."

"What was it all about?"

"Oh, not much. He just ran an MP car off the road!"

"And he hit a telephone pole!"

"And he was out after curfew?"

"Beyond the 50-mile restriction after hours? Who ever bothers about that anyway?"

"Reckless driving? Oh, no, not him!"

"No orders? Nobody would claim him!"

"Great job, Caruso! If you are going to do it, do it right! You did it right, Caruso!"

I was a mini-celebrity. My desk editor had no idea that his wife had precipitated the whole affair and I wasn't going to tell.

No matter anyway! It was good for a laugh. And laugh we did, especially me.

Later in the day, just as a precaution, I called Mike Farmer, the fellow who shared our PIO offices and who roomed with us at Lee Barracks. He was in charge of the one-man base communications center. I told him the mess I had gotten into. He, in turn, after a good laugh of his own, assured me there was no problem. He would call his counterparts at the communications centers between Lee Barracks and Heidelberg. The delinquency report would never get through. No way.

I soon got over the stress of spending a night in jail, albeit a very casual, coffee-drinking, nighttime TV show drama. Just another day in the life of the brand new Specialist Fourth Class Fred Caruso, ace paratrooper, ace reporter for the *Stars and Stripes*, ace photographer, and very soon to be an ace civilian.

I had only one weekend left before I had to ship my car to New York. It was my last opportunity to see Elke. It was February and it was snowing that weekend. We took a long drive through the Black Forest south of Baden Baden. The hills were covered white and snow was piling up on the roadway, but I never worried. My

VW could drive through anything.

There was no mention of the incident the weekend before and virtually no mention of the fact that the end was at hand. She had her commitments and I had mine. We had known the situation for more than a year. How could two people be so matter-of-fact about something so final? It was a great play. The snow made for a beautiful final touch. That was just the way it was to be.

My final day of reckoning had come, so to speak. The *Stars and Stripes* experience was fantastic right up to the last moment. I was to go back to Lee Barracks for my actual departure.

I was packed and ready to go before I even got there. All I had left to do was to make it through a short exit interview with my old company commander and, by now, First Sgt. Williams, both of whom had devoted the past two years of their lives trying to ruin my career.

I was feeling a great sense of relief that my super DR from the Heidelberg incident had not passed through our carefully monitored checkpoints. No one along the messaging system reported having seen it. The MPs were not waiting with handcuffs at the exit interview. Everything seemed to be in order, nothing unusual. The time had come, and I was soon to be home free.

Here I was, after all of these months with one foot out the door. A thousand days and more had passed. After all of that counting, how could it be? It seemed like I had just arrived.

I was sad beyond belief, grief-stricken at the thought of losing everything — my friends, my job, the airborne and even my mortal enemies. I was standing in their presence for one final time with only seconds remaining. What would life be without them? Sgt. Williams, that kindly, caring, good-natured, nasty son-of-a-bitch, was standing right there, close to the door, ready to trip me up, no doubt. Did I really have to leave?

Damn, they were great guys!

My mind was running over with euphoric feelings of appreciation — no, much more than that — joyous feelings of love. Was this all for real? It couldn't be happening this way. After waiting a thousand days and a wake up, could this be it?

"Great guys they are," I was thinking and bursting with feelings of goodwill and camaraderie, "every last one of them. I love 'em!"

My emotions were getting the best of me. My mind blazed through a montage of memories, of photos, the maneuvers, the stressful times, but mostly a lot of good times, warm friendship, support and fun.

"Even Sgt. Williams, I'm going to miss him. My God, Sgt. Williams, what a great guy he was! I think he really cared for me. And I always loved that guy, even though he hated me."

The company commander broke the ice.

He stiffened slightly, and, as straight-faced as possible, stuck out his hand to shake.

"It's time to go. Good luck to you Caruso," he said.

I stood at attention as best I could in preparation for a departing salute.

After a slight pause to allow me to get myself together, he continued.

"And by the way, Caruso, that was one hell of a DR you got in Heidelberg."

With a twinkle in his eye, he added, "You had better get on out of here."

"What a guy! One hell of a DR in Heidelberg. How did he find out? How did he get his hands on it? What the hell!"

I was overwhelmed. I thanked them as profusely, but as quickly as possible. I gave a salute as best as I could in my faltering condition, shook hands with Sgt. Williams, and broke into a near run through the halls and down the stairs to the waiting jeep, crying all the way.

I really didn't want to go, but I didn't want to stay either.

The driver left me to my parting thoughts and my unparatrooper-like sadness. He must have seen it before. Tough paratrooper talk right up until the moment of departure. Then the real person comes out.

We headed off to the gathering point in Mainz. From there, I joined a handful of others from units around the area who were to be delivered by truck to Bremerhaffen. From there we were to leave by troopship, even though in my case I had specific orders to go by air. My trusty VW "Buddy," repaired by then, had been sent off a few days earlier by ocean freighter.

As contrary as it might sound, in view of my disastrous trip over to Europe, I requested that I fly back to the States rather than endure a week on a troopship, rolling and pitching over a wild and frigid ocean. I felt my chances of being in another airplane crash were slim to none, but death by ship was another story.

My doctor prescribed a flight home to the States, but, the Army, being what the Army is, managed to confuse the issue. I was going home by troopship, with no time to argue. My consolation was that I was to be left alone, with no special duty on ship. I just had to hang out until we got to New York. I was handed a supply of tranquilizers and seasickness pills and started taking them days before I left Mainz to make sure I wouldn't be troubled by the water.

By sailing time I was so lethargic I could fall asleep in a minute or two, no matter where I was. The seas were rough the instant we left Bremerhaffen and got steadily worse. Most of the others got sick within an hour or so, but I was medicated beyond that possibility. I wasn't going to let on that I might be well enough to take on any work details. There would be no KP or special duty for me. I stayed hidden in my bunk, reading a lot, but mostly napping while under the influence of seasickness medication.

Considering how much I disliked the thoughts of another episode of exposure to seawater, I went up on top once or twice to watch the waves and the ice building on deck. Otherwise I simply hid out except for meal times. I slept until I got hungry, then I ate until I got tired. Even troopship chow served the purposes well under those circumstances.

We entered New York Harbor, passed the Statue of Liberty, passed Ellis Island where my Italian ancestors were processed into America, on to Brooklyn, and were let out.

A gruff, unshaven transportation worker, who looked like he had just gotten out of bed, grabbed the duffle bag I had dragged along for the past 5,000 miles out of my hand and thrust his free hand forward for a tip. Caught somewhat by surprise by the gratuity-seeking welcoming committee, I dug into my pocket for the only coin I had, an American 25-cent piece, a quarter.

He said nothing, showing only a grimace. My tip was indeed ungenerous. You could tell by looking at him. I knew I was on home turf once again.

I took the bus to the Port Authority bus station in Manhattan and from there, on to Nanuet. I got off at the Nanuet Hotel, where my Gumbadi Dominick's younger son, Alex, already in his 40s, worked as chief pizza chef. I popped in to say hello, made a phone call to announce my arrival, and my father came to pick me up.

I was back, at last, at the center of the universe.

Part III

Drawn
Into the Vortex

Chapter 16

Back in the U.S. of A.

*O*nce in the U.S., I was faced with decisions. I had to do something with my life, but had hardly given it a thought. As the saying goes, it was time for me to "fish or cut bait."

My relatives were mostly in the construction trades, as bricklayers and stonemasons, or were factory workers. I loved my job in the Army, but newspaper work never seriously entered my mind. Army people did Army things, and civilians did civilian things. I would wait to see what civilian life would mean for me.

The trauma of the Flying Tiger episode seemed to be under control. With few mood swings or flashbacks, the whole affair was fading into the past. But not completely. The crash was still a popular conversation topic. Talking about it kept bringing Ireland to my mind. I was rescued and taken there by helicopter. I was, after all, born again as an Irishman at Mercy Hospital in Cork.

Unfortunately, I knew no one of Irish descent in my corner of New York. My Jewish friends and Italian relatives shared no interest at all in Ireland. Most had little to no awareness of the very existence of the tiny island, much as was my case before I discovered it by accident. I found myself mentioning the Irish part of my rescue less and less.

There I was, back on the streets of Nanuet, Nyack, Monsey and Spring Valley after three years away, with no savings at all and very little spending money.

Bob Godwin, a renovation contractor and brother to my Army sign-up buddy, helped me out with a job. We were hired to paint the Monsey VFW headquarters, a massive World War II quonset hut, with a new type of high-tech silicon paint. It was a great, minimum-thought job, just exactly what I needed, and Bob paid cash.

In those days, before Bob "took the pledge," the afternoon beer runs were more numerous than the morning coffee runs. This made working on those extra-tall and rubber-like aluminum ladders very precarious and a lot like airborne sport. Work started at 9 in the morning, and our morning ended at 10. From there on it was afternoon beer time. The whole arrangement suited me just fine.

I signed up with an employment counselor who suggested I apply for a job at a newspaper, but that didn't excite me. The only people I knew in the real world who did what I did in the Army were newspaper hacks. They pounded the local city beat, read the police crime blotters and wrote obituaries. Sitting in a cloud of cigarette smoke, they hacked out their stories on a well-used typewriter, pasting together what they had in order to beat each deadline. They were paid very little and had even less respect. In Germany, the term "journalist" had a different meaning. Journalists there had status, a degree of social respect. My being an Army journalist didn't seem to diminish the status. I was a journalist, just as important as the next one. Not so at home.

I followed up on only one reporting lead. It was an opening for a sports reporter for a Tarrytown, New York, newspaper. I gave the editor a call, but wrote it off immediately when I learned of the salary. It began at about half of what I could earn as a common laborer. Besides, I never did find organized sports to be particularly exciting or satisfying. At least with the construction trades, I could look back and say, "See what I did. I built that." I hadn't yet made the same connection with writing when, in fact, that was one of the things I liked best about writing. I could always see the results of my work.

During the day, when not working, I went from old friend to

old friend, just to say hello. At night, I raised hell. I was still a paratrooper, if not on paper, in the corners of my mind.

My Jewish "Godmother," Molly Nordhauser, was working since her husband Frank died and her son Frankie went off to college. She was rarely home. I wanted to see her so I decided to drop in at her work. She was delighted.

Molly was the lone cashier for the book department at Shopper's Paradise, a genuine Yiddish bargain house in Spring Valley. My mother went there regularly to find a sale, knowing that the Jewish patrons would accept nothing less than a genuine bargain.

The book department was a respectable shop with a good supply of best sellers and reference works. It was somewhat separated from the rest of the store, to the right of the entrance. Molly was her delightful, cheerful self. Her department was nearly empty, and I was happy for the quiet time. I thumbed through books close to the cash register so we could talk without having her look like she was slouching on the job.

Molly finally got around to asking me what I was going to do next — the dreaded question of the day — and I had to 'fess up that I didn't really know. I told her I was into journalism and photography in the Army, but that didn't sound like a very good job in civilian life.

"Journalism is a wonderful field," she told me as she smiled with her godmotherly assurance, as if she knew a lot more about it than I did, which was very likely the case.

She then handed me a thick, heavy book from a nearby shelf. It was *Lovejoy's Guide to Colleges*. She told me it was the best reference for all colleges in the United States. I briskly thumbed through the pages, going directly to the subject of journalism. Only 30 colleges or so were listed and one of them caught my eye — the University of Montana School of Journalism.

It literally jumped off the page and called me to attention.

I really hadn't seen the word, journalism, in the context of a discipline, something you might learn and train for at college. Reporters weren't really journalists, were they? Here, this catalog of colleges said the magic word. It wasn't just a job. It was a profession, a career. Journalism was not simply reporting. It had status.

And the school, "Where was that?" I mused, "Montana? Isn't that somewhere out west? The land of the cowboys?"

Molly and I talked a little more, and then it became clear to me. Henry Larom, my creative writing instructor and the first Dean at Rockland Community College, was recruited from the University of Montana to take charge of our brand new school in suburban New York. I was in the first graduating class of only 44 students. I survived the Flying Tiger airplane crash with only two possessions: my Army dog tags and my RCC graduation ring. I used RCC and my associates degree to leverage my way into writing press releases at Lee Barracks.

Montana was where Henry Larom got all of those crazy ideas that made our college events so interesting. He used to dream up reasons for parades around campus, with him leading the festivities in his old jalopy mounted with cow horns on the hood. It was Montana that caused our class to be known as "Pioneers" instead of something more Eastern, like "Pilgrims." Montana had to be very unusual. I had to talk to him right away.

After stretching my welcome as long as possible without putting Molly's job at risk, I gave her a hug and a kiss and headed home. I didn't even feel like hitting the local hangout for a quick beer on the way. I wanted to get up early to go to RCC.

At the campus, Henry Larom appeared to be waiting for me behind his big, dark wooden dean's desk, just as he was the last time I saw him. Grinning behind a dark, bushy mustache, clutching a pipe between his teeth, he made time for me that morning, even though I didn't have an appointment. We had a great reunion. He wanted to hear everything about the airplane crash and listened intently until I got to the business of what to do next. I mentioned the University of Montana and journalism.

He quit listening, put his pipe aside and picked up the phone.

"I've got to talk to someone," he said. He dialed a number and reached someone of obvious authority. It turned out to be Ed Dugan, who was serving as the acting Dean of the UM J-School, as well as holding down his professorship.

Larom told Dugan that he had someone with an unusual background, an older student who just got out of the Army and who had experience writing for the *Stars and Stripes*. He told Dugan I had an interesting story to bring along, about the airplane crash. I was in his first graduating class and he would vouch for me as a good prospect. Dugan told him to send me out.

I had to apply for admission, of course, but I was accepted almost immediately, and that was it. After a summer of working at the Orangeburg Concrete Company, just a few miles from home, I was headed for Missoula, Montana, to become a professional journalist.

Before leaving New York, a friend gave me a book by John Steinbeck to help pump up my enthusiasm for a new adventure. It was *Travels with Charlie.*

Steinbeck toured the United States in his camper pickup truck with his companion dog named Charlie, and he wrote about his adventures as he traveled. He was fascinated by just about everything he saw and everyone he met along the way until he got to Montana, at which point he went into orbit.

"I am in love with Montana," Steinbeck confessed. "For other states I have admiration, respect, recognition, even some affection, but with Montana, it is love."

He went on to say, "If Montana had a seacoast, or if I could live away from the sea, I would instantly move there and petition for admission."

Try to ignore that kind of endorsement while your heart is already beating at a galloping pace. Steinbeck went on to relate the sights and sounds of the old west and the friendliness of the people in the Big Sky Country. His excitement passed right through me, and I could hardly wait to get there.

By early September, I was on my way with everything I owned worth taking, all packed in the tiny front-end trunk and equally tiny back seat of my faithful VW. I was thrilled with my new home base, and I hadn't even arrived.

Very soon I would find myself much closer to Ireland, even though I was moving two thousand miles further away from it.

Chapter 17

Big Sky Montana

Crossing into Montana that September afternoon was a profound experience for me. I could feel an exciting "something" vibrating in the air, the skies and the landscape around me. As I soaked in the panoramic views and the unfolding hills of the wild west, I was indeed moving much closer to my ultimate destination. I was tingling with excitement but unable to pin down a source.

Everything I saw that day seemed to be a part of a grand plan designed to convince me I was heading home.

Even the highway at the state border shouted out to me, "Welcome, Fred Caruso!" The black tarmac roadway was painted red for nearly a quarter mile as I drove in from the Badlands of North Dakota. An oversized billboard with a mounted cowboy waving his western hat drew me in.

I assumed the red carpet entry must have been the State Chamber of Commerce's response to John Steinbeck's book and all the great things he had to say about the state. I learned later that the painting was left over from the Montana Centennial celebration of the previous year when red-carpet welcomes and long bushy pioneer beards were very common sights. In any case, red-painted roadways are a nice touch.

Big things were happening for my benefit, far above those blue skies, and it started some 90 years earlier. It was that "something" behind the tingling and vibrating sensation I was experiencing as I crossed the state border. My stars were coming into alignment.

It began for me in the 1850s. An Irish immigrant, destitute but fired with optimism, arrived in New York to begin his western trek, first to San Francisco, then to Utah, and finally to the wild, empty frontier of Montana. He settled in the town of Anaconda, a short way from the city of Butte, where thousands of other Irishmen were headed to seek their fortune in mining for copper, silver and gold. By 1881, that previously poor, uneducated farmer had struck it rich. He built a smelter in Anaconda and became one of Montana's most famous Copper Kings. His name was Marcus Daly, from the parish of Derrylea, near the village of Ballyjamesduff, in County Cavan, Ireland.

After years of praise for the opportunities in America, he succeeded in luring his childhood neighbor and shirt-tail cousin to Montana Territory, convincing him to take a chance at its ranching fortunes rather than mining. The United States was giving away free land to those willing to nurture it.

Patrick Lynch arrived in 1883 at a site in Eastern Montana along Rosebud Creek. The trip was arranged by Marcus Daly's cattle boss. When he arrived with his wife, the former Margaret Callan, their eight children, one nephew and everything they owned in a rickety horse-drawn wagon, they found a side of beef and a sack of flour waiting for them – a small gift from their former neighbor to help them through the winter.

The journeys of these two men and how they intersected with mine would not be known to me for some time. All I knew at that moment was that I was tingling with excitement. I was in "Big Sky Country, Montana" and heading west to the Rocky Mountains. I was headed for adventure, for the University, and possibly a real working career as a professional journalist.

The city of Missoula is situated in a vast valley, the flat bottom of an ancient glacial lake, surrounded by smooth, grass-covered, rounded mountains, one of the most prominent of which is branded with a giant "M" right above the University campus. The climate in the valley tends to be considerably milder than the rest of the state, with less wind, more moisture and moderate temperatures. Its trees acquire a brilliant golden glow in late September and early October, giving rise to reflections of a New England autumn.

I knew before leaving New York that Missoula was the head-quarters for the U.S. Forest Service Smoke Jumpers. They are dropped by parachute to fight remote forest fires. I briefly considered signing up, but dismissed the idea. Jumping into enemy fire as a soldier was one thing. Jumping voluntarily into a fire with real flames that might cause pain and disfigurement was too much for me.

At that point in time, Missoula had a unique and often unpleasant, semisweet odor, tainted with smoke from burning pine sawdust. The odor was from the paper pulp mills at the far edge of town. Given the right temperature and humidity, the pungent vapors mixed with the burning waste from nearby lumber mills to form a dark grey and choking layer of smog and created an acrid, obnoxious stink. On occasion, the smog was so thick one could barely see across the street.

Fortunately, the clear days far outnumbered the "weather inversions." The paper mills and sawdust burners were on their way out. The valley had become a hotbed for the national environmental movement. Public outrage drove the teepee-shaped sawdust burners into extinction and forced the pulp mills to relocate or contain their emissions. Even though the polluters are long gone, I can still recall the aroma at the mere mention of the name, Missoula.

Aside from the odor, which one soon learned to ignore, the campus and surrounding countryside were beautiful beyond my New York ability to imagine. I was one of the oldest students on campus at the time even though I had only recently turned 24. The student body was young, bright, energetic, somewhat naive and completely welcoming.

The drama of the Flying Tiger continued to fade, but the stories of the crash and my survival preceded me. I found plenty of opportunity to impress just about anyone who would listen. I was from New York, that mysterious Mecca of the East. I was confident, outspoken and very fit, far more so than the typical young man about campus.

Thanks to those long months of coaching by Alberto Maurer, I was comfortable with any social scene. I had traveled far and survived an ordeal most would only read about. I liked being noticed and took a keen liking to being liked by others. To me, I had found a social paradise.

Even my classes were a treat. All were small, rarely more than 20 students, and highly interactive. Many were held around the "rim," a U-shaped table found in most newsrooms. The subject matter was exactly what I was craving, my classmates were pleasantly compatible in thinking, if not as experienced in the trade, and the teachers were exceptional.

One of my favorite professors was an odd looking woman in her late 60s. Dorothy M. Johnson, our magazine journalism instructor, was a world-class celebrity writer.

In many ways, Dorothy Johnson reminded me of Molly Nordhauser. She looked very much like a Jewish grandmother from the big city, with curly gray hair, thick glasses and a stern and serious look on her face when she wasn't intentionally smiling, which, fortunately, was most of the time. She was short and, frankly, as she would say of herself, rather "dumpy," but with a radiance that made her a star. You wouldn't even think of missing one of her classes. She was too much fun and had entirely too much wisdom to share.

She was a former magazine editor from New York City and a prolific writer, most notably of stories about cowboys and Indians. By time I met her, *The Hanging Tree* and *The Man Who Shot Liberty Valance* had already been made into motion pictures starring Gary Cooper and Jimmy Stewart. *A Man Named Horse*, a story about an Englishman who was captured by a savage Indian tribe and eventually becomes one of the braves himself, was on scheduled for filming.

A story that still circulates around the J-School recalls the day Dorothy came to class holding her right hand high into the air. She held it up for the full 50 minutes, never mentioning why she held it up as she proceeded with her lecture. Finally, as the class was about to adjourn, and since no one pointed attention to her gesture, she broke the ice with an explanation.

"You might be wondering about my upraised hand. I'm going to tell you even if you weren't wondering. I just had a meeting with Gary Cooper who is starring in one of my films," she said.

"This, my student friends," she said gesturing at her upraised hand, "is the hand that was kissed by Gary Cooper."

Ed Dugan, Henry Larom's friend, who was serving as acting Dean of the Journalism School when I applied, proved to be a prince of a human being as well as a great teacher. His good humor, strong support for everyone, and his critical eye for good journalism made him one of the most popular of the instructors. Most of my classes were far too short for what we covered, and I don't believe I missed a single one of them.

My intent was to complete the full school year, which consisted of three 10-week quarters, but a lawsuit against the Flying Tiger Air Line was heating up. The attorney wanted to move the case to trial to force a settlement. He didn't ask me to show up, but I was eager to get into the fray. My course work was actually running ahead of schedule, so I decided to return to New York at the end of my second quarter to be on standby.

The Federal Aviation Administration had already issued a skimpy 32-page report on the crash. Most of the blame for the engine failures was laid on the flight engineer, who was said to have been unfamiliar with the aircraft. Before he died in the crash, he was alleged to have accidentally turned off the oil circulation to an engine on the opposite side of the plane from where the fire started. He had mistaken the oil switch for a fire-extinguisher switch. He wasn't there to offer a better explanation. My attorney was concerned with issues beyond who was to blame. He was interested in aircraft safety.

Soon after I got back to Nanuet, a settlement was arranged. No trial. I got a check for $10,000, one-third of which went directly to the attorney. Even after a few additional legal fees, I was left with more than $6,000 to spend, in any way I wanted. Easy money it was. All I had to do was be in an airplane crash.

In addition to the money, which by today's standards of mega-million dollar settlements seems hardly worth the effort, a number of changes were made in aviation safety as a result of Flying Tiger 923's demise.

Life rafts on board at the time of our crash in 1962 had a definite top and bottom. Our raft inflated upside down. No one could see or rectify that error in the dark and chaos of the crash, and survivors began piling in. As a result, no one could access the emergency first aid kit and rescue flares zipped into the floor of the raft, unless everyone was willing to get out long enough to flip the raft over. We had to get by with the only flashlight available, which came from inside the aircraft itself.

Another issue was the emergency lighting that encircled the rim of the raft. When the raft flipped upside down, the emergency lighting was facing downward, into the water. The planes above couldn't see us.

Those defects were changed. Life rafts are now reversible. Safety lights and first aid and rescue kits are available on both sides.

Another point was that the passengers on Flight 923 were boarded by manifest, or roster as was typical of the military, rather than with separate tickets. This happened even though ours was a commercial flight with a schedule number, not a military flight.

At the time of the crash, an airline's total liability in the event of death on an international flight was limited to about $8,300. This was originally established to protect small, struggling national airlines. All tickets for international flights had a separate slip inside explaining the liability limit and suggested passengers purchase additional insurance, should they wish more coverage. We were not notified of this limitation.

The liability limit for international flights was subsequently raised and later dropped altogether. In the meantime, I had been wronged by this oversight, so I received a small award.

Suddenly, I had a windfall of easy money.

And what would I be doing with it?

Well, it didn't take long for me to decide to do the same thing any other red-blooded, ex-paratrooper might do. I bought a motorcycle — a rugged, high-powered, off-the-road mountain scrambler— and set out to become a wild, reckless rider of the west.

I had to practice first — that is riding as wildly and as recklessly as possible. I learned this takes a lot more strength and practice than the more practical, common-sense approach. I was still in good physical condition and, compared to my settled, conservative, civilian friends, I was reckless to the edge of total irresponsibility. The streets of Nanuet, Nyack, Spring Valley and Suffern were my own motorcycle proving grounds.

With the Flying Tiger case behind me, I was in a new holding pattern, not really going anywhere, but feeling like I was on my way. I had to graduate from college first.

The University was never far from my mind during this holding period. I was taking one evening course, two nights a week at Rockland Community College in order to complete my required two years of Spanish. This would allow me to graduate the following June and gave me a fine reason to go to RCC to mix with all of the 18 to 21-year-olds. I wasn't wasting time with boredom. Two midweek classes almost always set me up for the weekend but, with or without a date, there was always a lot to do about town.

"Not to worry and not to hurry," I supposed. I was an "old" single man, just turned 25 and still in school, while most of my friends were at least three years out and married and well into a career and raising a family. What the heck! I was having fun. All of the rest could come later.

Unfortunately, New York, with its mid-'60s obsession with abruptness, rudeness, violence and crime, began wearing me down.

In Germany, I was isolated with the troops. We had very little exposure to the local news media. Our view of the world came at a fairly high level through the eyes of the *Stars and Stripes*. There was very little sensationalism tainting our view of the world around us.

This was not the case in the New York metro area, where the daily tabloids featured a new murder every day in two-inch headlines. The radio blasted the scene a dozen times between songs in 3-D, echo chamber, ultra-loud high-fidelity.

You couldn't get away from it. Stories of murder, rape and the constant threat of the escalating war in Viet Nam were paraded before your eyes and ears on the news pages, on TV and over the radio. You felt lucky to have made it through the day without disaster striking your own home.

Driving the short five or six miles to and from work became an ordeal. I had become a "news addict" and drove my car just so I could tune in to the radio. The motorcycle was strictly for moments of escape after hours. I had to keep up with the news. I kept imagining in the back of my mind, again and again, the sensation that must have been created around the airplane crash: "Local boy missing at sea!" repeated over and over again. How pathetic it must have been.

Murder, rape, sickness and catastrophe. Was it all worth the effort? My feelings of anxiety grew nearly to the level felt after the Flying Tiger — that generalized feeling that all was *not* good and that all might suddenly get a lot worse.

It seemed as if a person (like me) could live through an airplane crash and three years of Army hell and end up the victim of a gruesome murder. It might happen while stepping outside just long enough to pick up the daily newspaper. What were the odds? Judging from the news, the odds seemed pretty good. It hardly seemed fair. While I feared no one — anxiety cast a shadow everywhere. Danger seemed to stalk every corner — hidden, outside danger that is. My own recklessness didn't count, nor did anyone I could see eye-to-eye.

Serial killers created an unusually high level of anxiety in my mind. That kind of killer had to be a sick person. The Richard Speck mass murder in July 1966 was the last straw.

I woke to the news being repeated over and over again. Speck had killed seven nurses in a Chicago apartment, one at a time, with each hiding under a bed, waiting her turn. He killed them mercilessly and pitifully. They were reported to be Filipino, and I assumed they were petite, beautiful and as kind as a young Asian nurse could be. Murder! Murder! Murder! That son-of-a-bitch! He murdered those lovely, helpless nurses.

Why did he do it? There was no reason that I could understand, except maybe for the fun of it. By time I got to Orangeburg Concrete I had heard the headline story at least 30 times. I was devastated by the wretched condition of the world. Going back to the peace and safety of Montana was as close as I could get to escaping.

I didn't report to my work area that morning. I drove right to the main office and told the boss I was leaving in two weeks and I did.

I bought a trailer for my motorcycle and a trailer hitch for my Volkswagen. I packed my belongings, loaded a black and gold shipping trunk on each side of the motorcycle trailer, kissed my mother and sisters good-bye, clasped hands with my father, and barely told anyone I was leaving.

What a relief! For all I cared at that point in time my family could start telling everyone that "Fred is dead."

Good-bye, folks. To hell with the world. I was gone.

I had nearly a month of free time to kill before school started, and I was going to spend it as far out of range of New York as I could.

My first stop after a short nap at a highway truck stop near Chicago was to see Jack Odgaard, the old 8th Infantry Division *Arrow* news hog. He was working as madly as ever at his hometown of Columbus, Nebraska, at the *Columbus Daily News* and apparently enjoying it as much as he did the weekly Army paper.

I left Columbus for Montana charged up with the notion that "This is America! Land of the free!"

Frankly, I had a lot to be charged up about. The Beach Boys were filling the airwaves with the latest pop and the Beatles kept coming out with more interesting and modern tunes. I drove onto a levee along the Missouri River to pretend my little VW was a Chevy long before the famous song was even written. My memory of that event always has me singing the tune, but my levee was running full. There was nothing dry about it!

After Columbus, I had another stop to make. I wanted to see a J-School friend who lived in a remote, offbeat place known as Lodge Grass, in the southeast part of Montana, very close to where destiny would draw me within the next few months.

My friend, Loretta Lynde, was one of the most clever, creative and interesting of all the young women in my classes at UM. She had become by then the resident cartoonist for the *Kaimin* newspaper, which published her "Protester" cartoons nearly every day. When it came to one-liners, many of which showed up in her drawings, no one could match her.

Cartooning ran in the family. Her brother, Stan, was the creator of "Rick O'Shea," a cowboy cartoon that ran in the New York newspapers as I grew up. I had seen Montana portrayed in the cartoon strip, not knowing what it was really about, of course, but enjoying the deep messages about beautiful scenery, wildlife and the love of nature.

Easterners have no idea what "dry" means. Montana gets kindling-wood dry by the end of summer, and you may well be drafted into fighting a wild fire whether you want to or not. That has always left me with a feeling of apprehension because of my loathing of fires. Prairie fires seemed to pop up spontaneously on the Montana dry lands.

By time I got to Lodge Grass, fires were raging everywhere. It was one of the driest seasons on record, and the Lynde ranch was not to escape the scourge.

A grass fire started within a mile or so of the main ranch house and was racing toward two very large and valuable haystacks. It had to be stopped, I was told. All of the workers and men from neighboring ranches dropped their duties for the day and headed for the fire control mission.

I was touring the ranch with Loretta in my trusty, all-terrain beetle. My motorcycle and other possessions were parked safely away from danger near the main house.

When we learned of the fire, Loretta knew what to do and I did not. In fact, I was inclined to head another direction, away from the fire, and let others more qualified worry about it. Loretta needed a vehicle – a truck, a jeep, or anything that could cross the open country – and my poor bug was the closest thing at hand. From the high life of Europe, my poor little car was pressed into fire service in Montana.

The fire was about a quarter of a mile wide. The dry hay fields were ablaze, and the wind was causing the flames to race ever faster toward the haystacks. If those stacks burned, much of the ranch's winter feed would be gone.

Loretta got behind the wheel and jammed my tiny VW into first gear. Off we went, straight ahead, across the fields and directly toward the raging inferno.

Being the "dude" I was from the East, I had no idea how fires worked. I was too deep in shock to do or say anything constructive.

"Holy mackerel!" I gasped, as I clutched the "Oh, Jesus" bar above the passenger side door. What I really meant to say was, "Holy shit, Loretta! What the hell are you doing!"

She drove my car right into the wall of fire as I hung on for dear life.

"My God, Loretta! You're crazy!"

I could imagine the explosion of gasoline. I could feel the flesh searing off my bones. I could see my little car turned into a napalm bomb on wheels! My God, I was a goner!

Well, it turns out that while a grass fire looks like a huge inferno, the fire itself is limited to a narrow ring of flames hardly more than five to ten feet wide. Beyond that, in the center of the ring, it is all burnt out black.

It is a weird feeling to be inside the ring of fire, very much the way Johnny Cash describes it in his song. We were surrounded by flames, but Loretta had no fear even though she could not see beyond the curtain of smoke and flame. We kept on racing through the blackened and smoldering center and then on through to the opposite side and back into the blaze. She acted as if she did it every day.

We got to the other side of the pasture in time, alive, and helped the crew stop the fire from getting to the haystacks. We beat it to death with the flat side of shovels, heavy brooms and sticks with wet rags tied to one end.

What I learned on that leg of the trip was this: "Don't go to Montana at the end of August unless you don't mind fighting fires." I "got out of Dodge" as soon as possible. My hero days were over. Invincible or not, I was beginning to dread pain a lot more than I might relish the thrill of glory. I was headed for the safety of the university campus.

Missoula was as beautiful and serene as it could possibly be. No more New York for me. The center of my universe had shifted 2,300 miles west. I was a senior in college and the world was my oyster.

As soon as I got to town, I went to a rental agency and took the cheapest apartment I could get. It was $55 a month at 555 South Broadway, a one-room efficiency, with a kitchenette. An open sleeping area hung out over an empty space below, providing a handy parking spot for my motorcycle. There was a sofa and table and room for study. What more could I need?

In the apartment below, I soon learned, were three fellows — Dave Sloat, Mark Bunyan and Nick Sokal — who had just arrived from Santa Rosa, California. They were a trio of fun-loving, upbeat bandits who soon became known as "the California Boys."

Our apartments were so dilapidated that you would not dare write home and tell the truth about them. I think they might have been used as movie stage sets for films about derelict drunks and druggies before they burned down some five years later. In the meantime, they served our purpose. They were cheap and stood up to our abuse.

The California Boys were all motorcycle buffs. I had my own

bike when we met, but by that time, I was already trying to sell it. I had lost enough skin off my back and stomach from sliding down hills to cause me to think twice about the whole idea of biking to fame. I'd leave the glory to Montana's own daredevil stunt man, Evel Knievel. The end, I realized, might be horrifically agonizing as I slid one final time along the rough and unforgiving pavement.

My new neighbors came from crowded California to be free. They saw Montana as 'unplugged,' where a guy could spread his wings and do the wildest things, and no one seemed to care.

I did my best to raise their expectations. The first day we met I told them that I would have a party to prove my point. I went to the local grocery store and found enough young women out shopping to populate our party. I had no need to prove my handle on the social scene after that. What I could not pull off, the California Boys were very adept at improvising on their own. I fit right in. We lived like there was no tomorrow until late the day before classes began.

I thought with the beginning of my senior year I should clean up my act a bit and I should start by kicking my smoking addition.

I picked up the nasty habit during my first month in Army basic training, while in the hospital with pneumonia. It was hard to see smoking as a health hazard when everyone around you was physically fit and the picture of health. And besides, if you didn't smoke, you picked up cigarette butts for the others who did during the mandatory, hourly 10-minute smoke breaks.

I was so badly into the habit that I found myself one afternoon attempting to smoke a pipe, as any intellectual university student might, while at the same time attempting to light up another cigarette, while I already had one lit and sitting in the ash try. I ran out of hands. I decided right then and there that I had had enough.

I quit. Done. Period. No more cigarettes. With a little help from a package of over-the-counter Bantron nicotine tablets, my biggest challenge was breaking the automatic motion of reaching to the pocket for another smoke. It was just too bad for Pall Mall non-filtered butts. Sorry, guys.

The next day would be a smoke-free day and the start of a new era for the Italian boy from New York.

Chapter 18

The Green-eyed Irish Cowgirl

*I*t was the first day of my senior year. Everything I owned, including my motorcycle, any insurance I needed, and my tuition
and expenses were paid in advance or held in reserve. No need to
work. Just study and play.

I had just given up smoking the day before. I was getting edgy
by noon, trying to stop those mindless, habitual motions to find
and light a cigarette whether you wanted one or not. I was determined to beat it. I was a man in control of his life.

Classes that day went well, until about 7 p.m. when I was to
start working at a newspaper editing lab. We were required to work
one night a week on the student daily newspaper, the *Kaimin*, until
the pages were closed and turned over to the printers some time
after midnight. All of this was done under the direction of a student night editor. The printers would put the paper on the presses
in the basement of the J-school, and the day's edition would be
distributed throughout the campus by 7 a.m.

I showed up for editing lab in my sharpest outfit: black chino
pants, a white dress shirt with sleeves rolled up, which I wore
regularly to show off my suntan, and my smooth-heeled, brown
suede European motorcycle boots.

The *Kaimin* editor for the night was Ellen Broadus. She was a
girl and her qualifications went downhill from there. She was barely
20 years old, just by a week or so, a junior, and was from a far-off

ranch in Eastern Montana, near a tiny Northern Cheyenne Indian village named Lame Deer. She rode a tractor all summer long, baling hay along Rosebud Creek, and that was the extent of her professional work history. She had no working journalism experience. She was to be the Monday night newspaper boss. She was to be *my* boss!

Where had she been? I had not seen her one single time during my two quarters of class the year before, nor had she seen me. The J-school was simply not that big. How had we avoided crossing paths? She seemed to pop up out of nowhere.

Ellen Broadus! She barely tipped the scales at 100 pounds. She looked younger than a freshman and *she* was the editor-in-charge. I was an "apprentice" copy editor and headline writer. That was way, *way* too much for me.

She had a cute personality, perky, witty and cheerful, and was easy to look at, with dark brown hair and dark green eyes. But petite features, cute personality, intellect and good looks can only go so far.

I lived through my shift, trying to be my very social and well-experienced self. I just had a hard time handling the humiliation of working for a young inexperienced girl. Early the next day I went to the administrative office and switched nights.

I did a second night of editing that week to make sure I'd have a smooth transition. I didn't want to lose any time during my last year. The editor on my second night was a young fellow — a boy in my mind — totally lacking in experience and absent of any of that cuteness the young female brought to the table. By the end of that session, I was ready to switch nights again. Fortunately, the University administration was accommodating. So there I was, reassigned to Ellen's editing desk at my own request and quite relieved. What was I doing to myself?

There was something about Ellen Broadus.

I learned along the way that she had been editor of the college *M-Book*, which was a student guide to campus activities and facilities. It was a publication that I would never read, simply because I never read instructional manuals or guidebooks, but it looked and sounded impressive. The *M-Book* was named for the giant white "M" that stood on the side of the mountain above the University's Main Hall.

I wanted to let everyone on the editing desk know that I had been through all this, but I was being more polite than usual, trying hard to fit in. I was going through what I call "my decent phase."

Among several of my minor reforms, aimed at making me a little more decent by Montana standards, was that I had pretty much written all profanities out of my vocabulary. I made up my mind that profanities should be saved for airborne fighting machines. I decided that profanity was the Army's way of generating a little more hatred in order to make killing easier. I didn't want any part of fighting, or hatred, or killing. No more! I was becoming a man of peace.

What was happening to me? I seemed to be falling to pieces.

I was going to every class and studying long hours between party sessions with my neighbors. I was polite to everyone and rarely raised my voice, even during our rowdy social events. It wasn't as abrupt as my quitting smoking, but I was definitely slowing down on my vices as well as giving up a few.

Even with my reforms, Ellen Broadus was a real stretch. I wanted to ask her for a date, but found myself fearing rejection, a possibility I seldom if ever considered in the past. I finally got up my nerve and asked her out, being careful, of course, to appear as confident as ever. She was agreeable. It was something out of her norm — a motorcycle ride and a few hours at one of the wild California flings — but otherwise quite innocent.

We seemed to be a serious mismatch. She was a Delta Gamma sorority girl and I had a major aversion to sororities and fraternities. The airborne fraternity was enough of that stuff for me. Her sorority kept her fairly regimented in the beginning, but we soon figured our way around the rules.

I was 25, an old man on campus at the time, and even at 20, she appeared to be a mere child, cute, petite and naïve. We were both Roman Catholic, but hers was a family of Irish Catholics.

I was a black sheep in my family when it came to religion. I was anything but a good Italian Catholic, but she didn't seem to object. Her father was Protestant, but not a churchgoer. He not only tolerated the Catholics in the family, but encouraged their faith and made sure they never missed Mass on Sunday.

Although I was becoming a peace-loving man, I was in great physical condition and still acted close to invincible. I feared no one and had little regard for danger, but that attitude was changing rapidly. I suppose I was maturing, but I was resisting as best I could. The *Animal House* life style that came with living in the apartment above the California Boys was fantastic. We were wild-west crazy, but there was no doubt about it, I was weakening. I wanted to tame down, but I didn't want to "melt down" altogether.

The California Boys thought I had lost my mind. Ellen was so straight! She was precise, well dressed, upright, and to my surprise appeared to be accepting and non-judgmental. She seemed to party as hard as everyone else, yet she maintained her bearings while others didn't. When the boys revved up their bikes and drove them in circles through the apartment living room and bedrooms, she simply stood to the side, out of their way, her hands over her ears to quell the noise, and watched the show. When they began their crazy, no-win drinking games, she watched in amazement and discretely avoided joining in. I tried to hang on to the wild side as long as possible, but I was starting to lose interest in the party life unless I could have Ellen along with me.

Wait and see. If Ellen could tolerate me, the real me, and my friends, I guessed, I couldn't ask for much more. I loved journalism, I loved Missoula, I loved working on the *Kaimin*, I loved UM, and I loved the moment. It all seemed like a lot of love to me.

The local Gestapo, whom they called house mother at the Delta Gamma sorority, wasn't as pleased with me as Ellen was. I had to lay low — keep out of sight where possible — just to keep Ellen from getting a reprimand or having a negative report sent to her parents at the ranch. I worked at becoming more acceptable, but I had a very long way to go. I hardly ever went near the sorority house except to escort her home after wrapping up the paper at about 1 a.m. every Monday night. Ellen had applied for a special dispensation to allow her to come home after hours due to her job at the *Kaimin.*

I had sold my motorcycle during the first week of school to a fellow in Helena, some 120 miles over the mountain to the east, in part to reduce my chances of a premature death, but the California Boys — Dave, Nick and Mark — made sure I was never without a bike, should the urge return. They had a milder version of the Honda scrambler I bought after the Flying Tiger settlement. I enjoyed theirs a lot more because it rode lower and my feet could comfortably touch the ground. I could jump off the bike in a tight spot, something I couldn't do as easily before. They also had a British-built Triumph road bike that could handily top 110 miles an hour on the highway. I was welcome to use them any time I wanted.

Ellen was always game for a ride on either one.

We went everywhere together and especially liked Saturday motorcycle outings on the logging trails up Blue Mountain. Our formal début as "a couple" came at Halloween, at a sorority costume party held in a downtown hotel ballroom. We arrived in black leather and denim, complete with chains, dressed as California Hell's Angels, riding in on a motorcycle of course. There was no doubt in my mind she was the cutest Hell's Angels Mama this side of the Mississippi. Our entrance did not go unnoticed.

It wasn't long before we acquired the nickname, "Frelen." The ever-in-a-hurry-to-the-next-party California Boys decided one name for the two of us would be a lot easier than going through the formalities of two separate names. "Hi Fred, Hi Ellen" simply became, "Hi Frelen."

Of course she was interested in my Flying Tiger story. To my surprise, however, she was as much interested in the Irish evacuation part of the story as she was in the crash itself. She seemed to delight in my impressions of the Irish people and the notion that I felt that I had been born again as an Irishman.

Her name is actually Margaret Ellen. Her mother was also a

171

Margaret, and Ellen wanted her own identity. Ellen happened to be the granddaughter of Alice Lynch, whose father was Patrick Lynch from County Cavan. The entire Lynch family emigrated to Rosebud Creek, Montana, to get into cattle ranching.

It was either Irish stubbornness or her Montana frontier lack of sophistication that allowed her to persist in dealing with me. She seemed to look beyond my desperate, reckless side, and it wasn't long before we started talking about the possibility of meeting her family back at the ranch.

Unfortunately, tragedy struck before I got there. Her father, Bill Broadus, died suddenly on Election Day, just before Thanksgiving break. I took her to the Missoula airport for that terribly sad trip to the ranch for the funeral, and I went my own way later for Thanksgiving. By time the break was over, I was desperate to be with her.

Election Day, by the way, became a very significant day for us in Montana. Ellen's uncle Haston Broadus was running for Sheriff of Hill County, which had only one real town, Havre. Her mother and father were visiting that election day to be there during the counting of the ballots. Bill Broadus died of a heart attack, just as the voting polls closed, while striking a match on the bottom of his boot.

I never got to meet him and it was probably just as well that he never got to meet me. From what I have learned about him, I cannot think of a single redeeming characteristic about my New York, Italian, blunt and abrupt airborne self he might have liked.

By Christmas time the family was ready to meet the more polished, but only slightly improved, me. Brother Hugh, who had just turned 28, was taking over the ranch after his father's death at a time when far older men dominated ranching. It was a lot of responsibility for a fellow his age, caring for 20,000 acres of range land, which ran some 15 miles from the front gate to the back.

I was making my debut only 60 miles from General Custer's famous "Last Stand," some 10 miles north of the Indian village of Lame Deer, the headquarters of the Northern Cheyenne Indian Reservation.

Hugh set me up for a horseback ride with Ellen. I was to ride Jack, a tall chestnut quarter horse. Ellen, who was an expert at rounding up cattle, rode a horse that she knew and could easily handle. She had always ridden Jack with little to no effort and figured he would fit me fine.

Jack had his own opinion. He didn't like me at first sight. As a matter of fact, I've not yet found a horse that did like me. Jack, it turns out, was a Sgt. Williams in animal form. He hated me.

That miserable horse bucked me off against a brilliant orange Montana sunset and on top of a huge prickly pear cactus. I went on home to New York for Christmas the next day in total pain and virtually incapable of stepping up or down a street curb. I was the big, ex-airborne, ex-motorcycle maniac, ex-wild-eyed New Yorker, tamed down and put in my place by a wild Montana horse that I learned later hated all men as a matter of routine, and especially me.

It wasn't long before I realized that I could hardly stand the thought of living without Ellen.

Besides all of her assets, her family roots were in Ireland. That very word, "Ireland," had a magic ring to it. I could not get enough information about her origins and how Ireland and Montana shaped her family. I was exhilarated at the very mention of it, Ireland.

Ellen's favorite aunts were from Butte, a two-hour drive from Missoula. There was Aunt Agnes Lynch and Aunt Rosie O'Grady. They soon became my favorite aunts as well. And there were cousins.

Ralph Olsen, was married to her cousin, Monica, a niece of Aunt Agnes. He was "Irish" by marriage. His brother, Arnold, was into politics, a Congressman. The name, Olsen, may have been Norwegian, but not to bother. In those days, in Butte, everyone was Irish, and there was no way around it. Congressman Olsen was Irish by politics.

Irish immigrants dominated Butte and Anaconda. They came to work the copper mines, and they left their mark. There were hundreds of Lynches, and many more O'Sullivans and O'Sheas in the phone book. Many of them emigrated back to West Cork, Ireland, when Butte's copper mines closed down, but they were as evident as ever. Even the local accent sounded more Irish than any other place in the U.S.

I got to know all of the relatives pretty early on and to know about Marcus Daly too. He was the Copper King from County Cavan, the neighbor and distant cousin from across the lane who made it big. You learned about Marcus Daly if you spent any time at all in Montana simply because he played such a big role in the development of the territory.

The more I knew about Ellen and her family, the more I wanted to know. I wasn't even out of college, but I wanted to marry Ellen Broadus — Margaret Ellen Lynch Bailey Broadus to be more precise.

I figured that name, Broadus, could do no harm as it was the name of a town about 100 miles east of the ranch, named after her grandfather and his brothers who served as pioneer postmen, carrying mail by horseback. You couldn't get to be much more of a pioneer than that, having a town named after your family.

Without consulting anyone, we set a date, June 17th. We were going to be married at the tiny Blessed Sacrament Catholic Church in the village of Lame Deer, just 10 miles south of the ranch.

Father Fabian Fehring, a Capuchin monk who ministered to the Indians on the reservation and to nearby ranchers, and a longtime friend of the family, was to perform the service. It was to be one week after my graduation. Since there were no public facilities within 50 miles in any direction, except for the tiny chapel itself, we assumed the reception would be held at the ranch house.

Ellen's mother was thrilled, or at least put on a good act, although she was fretting over the whole affair as any mother would. She pulled it off on one of the most beautiful blue-sky, cloudless days in Eastern Montana history.

As the wedding plans proceeded, we cruised through the remaining months of journalism school. I was a graduating senior, but Ellen was a junior and would be setting her journalism studies

174

aside for a time. Getting married was exciting enough. We weren't worried about what she would be doing next.

My parents came out to my graduation in Missoula while Ellen went home to help with the final wedding plans. I drove my parents to the ranch by way of Yellowstone Park.

Her brother, Cowboy Hugh, initiated my teetotaling father to cowboy whiskey while on an errand to Forsyth, some 60 miles north. They both came back to the ranch quite inebriated, my father with a card in hand, given to him by a religious Good Samaritan. The card said, to his mortification, "We think you have a problem. Please call if we can be of help."

We still laugh about that single day of cowboy recklessness.

All in all, the entire event, which lasted several days, including the final preparation and pre-parties, was as memorable as it was stunning. The ceremony at the Lame Deer chapel was overflowing with guests who followed us 10 miles north to the reception at the ranch. Well over 200 joined in the party. Montana's big skies were more deeply blue than usual that day and provided a most dramatic backdrop to Ellen's beautiful white wedding gown.

I was married to a green-eyed Irish cowgirl.

Chapter 19

Europe on $5 a Day

*O*ur destination as we left our wedding revelers behind was the New York metro area and a great European adventure.

We did a lot of planning for our first trip. We wanted to tour Europe on a motorcycle and photograph and write about our travels. It seemed like a natural, since we started our romance around motorcycles and by then considered ourselves a team of seasoned journalists. Ellen's literary polish went well with my rough-hewn military reporting style.

The plan was to find a motorcycle manufacturer to underwrite our adventures in return for great volumes of publicity. We sent out proposals, but, unfortunately, found no takers. No one from Harley Davidson, BMW, or any other motorcycle manufacturer would even talk to us.

One rejection letter suggested that the company might consider sponsoring us if we took a trip first and then wrote a credible story afterward. That was reasonable for them, but not for us. It was the cash for the motorcycle part that we were most lacking, and, frankly, we didn't have much set aside for travel expenses, either. What little was left from the Flying Tiger settlement was gone by the end of the school year.

"So, to heck with them!" we decided. We were going on our own, even if we couldn't afford it. We would find a way.

A little accident occurred a few weeks before the wedding. It was to be our last Saturday motorcycle outing in Missoula, part of which was to include a run up the side of our favorite mountain. I don't know what I was thinking. Instead of taking the rough-riding mountain scrambler, I chose the smooth and powerful green and gold Triumph road bike. It was a great machine for speed, but it was not fit for hill climbing.

A few hundred feet up the side of the mountain that rose above the campus, the bike tipped backward in a stall, kicking up a cloud of smoke and dust in the performance, falling on top of both of us. I was thrown to the side, but Ellen was pinned beneath as gasoline splashed from the fuel tank over her riding jacket. As dry as it was in the heat of the day, it was pure luck that no fire erupted. I pulled the bike away and did what I could to soothe her shoulder.

With no visible damage to the bike and not nearly the damage to ourselves as we might have had, we gathered up our belongings and "limped" back to campus atop the Triumph. We quietly resolved to never again use a road bike as a mountain climber, and, from that point on, to consider approaching life with a little more caution. We were soon to be married. Ellen's left shoulder was back to full function by wedding day, but was prone to pain for some months to come.

The accident caused us to rethink the whole idea of traveling as a married couple by motorcycle. The good news was it helped ease the disappointment of rejection by the motorcycle companies.

The one guidebook for which I granted an exception to my macho-man "never read manuals" rule was a popular travel book of the day, *Europe on $5 a Day*. It was a persuasive reference that talked the traveler through the steps, from city to city, from breakfast to dinner, with expenses adding up to only $5 a day. I remembered Europe as being very inexpensive. I was a free-wheeling GI at the time, with low expectations when it came to meals and accommodations. Nonetheless, I was certain prices couldn't have gone up very much and that we could do Europe on half as much if we worked at it.

Our big day at the ranch was suddenly happening. It was June 17th. Everyone was there and the wedding party was going strong. We couldn't simply slip away. Ellen changed from her stunning white wedding dress into her pink "going-away" outfit. The teenagers had marked up the Volkswagen with the appropriate "Just Married" slogans and attached strings of tin cans so everyone would know we were trying to disappear. Those capers were all in good humor, and we left feeling as if we were sailing away on a boatload of good wishes.

Within a few miles of the ranch, a hubcap full of gravel spun off. We hunted through the sagebrush, but we soon abandoned the search, eager to get on with our journey.

We were married. What was to unfold for us was a total adventure, a complete unknown. We were open to all options. We would make only one side stop on our way to New York, and that was for a job interview.

It was at the marketing department of Caterpillar Tractor Company in Peoria, Illinois which gave us the opportunity for a detour. That part of the trip, from Missoula to Peoria and back, was to be at their expense under a generous interview package. This actually paid for our entire trip to New York. In addition, we would have a night in a fancy hotel and a grand dinner with one of the public relations section bosses and his wife.

If I were to work for Caterpillar, I would start out as a technical writer in the marketing department in Peoria, but was assured that I could soon work my way up to the regional manager of marketing at some nifty place like Atlanta, Georgia.

Coming fresh from Big Sky Montana, the prospects of living in Atlanta left me feeling queasy. Visions of a relapse of Army-style prickly heat in the Georgia boondocks gave me serious cause to consider where I should start my career. In any event, the interview was an interesting and uplifting experience for both of us, a great boost to the morale. I had one offer in hand.

From Peoria, we headed to Nanuet to introduce Ellen to the East Coast family. Within a few days of our arrival, I got an official letter from Judge Advertising and Public Relations in Helena. I had interviewed with the owner of the small company shortly before graduation.

My emphasis in journalism school was advertising and public relations. The owner, Tom Judge, was impressed with my maturity and Army work experience but couldn't offer much in the way of salary. The letter offered me $25 a month less than we had discussed during the interview. I felt we needed that extra few dollars to pay for health insurance. As a married couple, we had to think of those things.

The offer was discouraging. Twenty-five dollars was quite a bit at that time and especially in view of the embarrassingly paltry starting salary. I would be earning less with a bachelor's degree than I was earning two years earlier without a degree as a soldier at the *Stars and Stripes*, where I got medical coverage, free housing and lots of military privileges besides my pay. Nonetheless, it was a starting point in Big Sky Country, so I decided to take it without protest. We were happy about the decision, simply knowing we would be returning to Montana.

So there I was, a married man, calm and collected, and professionally employed. Let the chips fall where they may. Frelen was open to anything that came our way.

My parents held a backyard family reunion so the new bride could meet the family. At least 50 of the relatives were there, including my Great Aunt Elizabeth and all of my other great and lesser aunts and uncles.

What a party it was! The entire family seemed to be in good spirits and not one person had a premonition to foretell our future, or at least no one reported any. There was plenty of God bless this and God bless that, but, otherwise, everyone seemed to be acting perfectly normal — nearly Montana-like. Either time was mellowing everyone, or I was becoming less cynical of their old-world traditions.

After experiencing an eastern celebration of the Fourth of July, Ireland was to be our next stop, and $5 a day was our limit, just as the book said. Fueled with the optimism and high spirits of youth, we were off to Shannon, on a Boeing 707 jetliner leaving from New York Kennedy Airport.

Excitement built as we made our way across the dark ocean. I had no fear. My chances of being in an airplane crash twice, at least over the same route, were close to nil. Excitement leaped during those last minutes of approach to Shannon and soon we were standing on Irish soil. We caught a bus to the Limerick train station. From there, we headed to Cork, the site of my second birth, and our bed and breakfast, which was recommended by the guide book.

Our B&B in Cork City had a fluffy feather bed, which, being as jet-lagged as we were, and being newly married besides, was more inviting than the local countryside. It was chilly and raining.

We took a nap and got up only long enough to find a restaurant just before closing time. Our first dinner in Ireland was, of all things, spaghetti bolognese, anything but a traditional local dish, but it tasted great. We weren't into the pub scene at that point and weren't even aware of its significance to Irish culture.

The very next day, we digressed from the guidebook and rented a car so we could explore the city and surrounding countryside. It was our first experience driving on the left-hand side of the road.

Our first challenge was to find Mercy Hospital, the scene of my joyous rebirth. It was nowhere to be found. Nor was the beautiful lake with all of those big white swans I had seen on the way to the hospital. Of course, if you have ever been to Cork City and tried to find anything for the first time while driving, you would appreciate how those landmarks proved to be so elusive.

The real reason I couldn't find them was my stubborn, New York male notion of refusing to ask directions. I was certain I could find the hospital and the swans by instinct, if not by memory, and I lost out on both accounts. They would have to wait for another trip.

We headed a few miles out of town to Blarney Castle to kiss the famous stone. Ellen had never been to a castle before, while I had been to dozens of them in Germany. We then headed west toward Bantry Bay and Glengarriff, where we took photos at the village grotto, and then on north over a very tiny, rugged mountain road to Killarney.

It was all new to us, especially coming from the wide open arid Montana west. Many of the rural lanes were like tunnels making their way through forests of trees and vines, a sight you would never see at home. Tall stone walls, covered with grass and flowers, lined the roadway with openings every so often to allow farmers access to their fields. At nearly every entryway stood a "leprechaun" — an older man dressed in a dark jacket, woolen work pants, green boots and a cap — keenly watching us as we drove by. And there was also one on every doorstep.

Prosperity was still a long way off for Ireland. Very few houses were painted at all, and those were painted a traditional common white. Miles of homes that butted against the roadway throughout Cork City, one adjacent to the other, were unpainted, dirty gray. Rural homes were tiny and not well kept. We learned that it was partly tradition. Spiffy homes garnered higher taxes during the time of British rule, so people avoided anything that might appear extravagant. Of course, the main reason was money. Ireland had been very poor for centuries and was only beginning to see a little economic hope for the future. Irish youth were still the nation's largest export.

Killarney was a beautiful sight. Horse-drawn carriages were everywhere, leading us to believe that horses were still the main mode of transportation. That was at least the case for tourists.

And everywhere we looked were those "leprechauns" standing in the openings of the walls along the roadway, watching us drive by. Actually they were local farmers, taking a break along the roadway. Their dress and intense curiosity made them appear as real leprechauns to us.

We experienced one of those damp spells the Irish dread and tourists often talk about. It was wet and chilly during our entire stay in Ireland, but we ignored the weather as best we could. We kept the car and drove on to Dublin for one night in the country's largest city, where we met two young fellows in a pub. It was on

O'Connell Street. The young lads seemed quite excited about local politics and eager to show us a new alteration to the landscape. Only a few weeks before, rebels had blown up a monument in the center of the roadway, just a few yards from our pub. They walked us to the site to show us what had been done. We were getting a taste of politics in Ireland, not knowing that politics would soon become a major part of our life back in the States.

We dropped the car in Dublin and took a train to Limerick, staying our last night at the Railroad Hotel.

After dinner, we sat in the pub to reflect on our travels of the past two days and plan our next steps. The pub had a television set. The riots and burning of Newark, New Jersey, was the featured news of the day. The Irish were keenly interested in American events. One family, consisting of a father and four children ranging from three years to thirteen, all sat at the bar, arranged as if according to plan by size, with father at the left, moving down to the smallest, watching the news.

The Railroad Hotel was not fancy, but it was affordable. We already knew we had to watch our expenses as $5 a day seemed to be lasting only until noon.

The next day we were off to Amsterdam and then to Mainz to see the PIO legacy my buddies and I had left behind.

Security at Lee Barracks at the time was at a low ebb, and we were welcomed to look in at whatever we wished. To my astonishment, there was not a single trace of me or the existence of our PIO team from just a little more than two years earlier. It was as if we were never there. There were no photo labs, no writing offices, and no one doing what we had done. How sad. How could they get along without us?

Life goes on, and we had to move on, too. Our next stop was one of my favorite spots from my Army travels, Lucerne, Switzerland, an exceptionally picturesque, medieval village on a lake surrounded by mountains. By that point we were really sensing a need to start trimming expenses. We decided to take to the roads for a hitchhiking adventure across the Alps to the city of Lugano, near the Italian border. We were running out of cash.

Somehow in planning for our trip, we missed the all-important part of the *Europe on $5 a Day* formula. It was $5 per person per day, and not $5 per couple. Even though we counted ourselves as one Frelen, economic realities dictated otherwise. We were two by the book, not one.

Fortunately, no one checked our math before we left; otherwise, we might have considered an alternate plan that would have skipped Europe. Hard facts have a way of throwing rain on a parade. We were spared the rainfall.

There was no turning back now. Hitchhiking at the time was popular and safe. It was worth a try.

Off we went, two innocent-looking tourists with thumbs outcast and luggage at our feet. We struck luck on the first leg of trip, catching a ride with an older German woman who was happy to have me do the driving. She had a VW Bug just like mine and I felt right at home crossing the Alps with Ellen at my side and the German woman in the back seat. She managed to go through a complete change of clothing as I drove, without distracting me in the least. Such is the power of being a newlywed.

Tracing our steps back a few days later was another matter entirely. Two young and obviously well-to-do Egyptian fellows in a red sports car picked us up. They took off over the winding alpine passes with Arabian "snake-dancing" music blasting full tilt and driving as if they were practicing for the next Grand Prix event. Ellen and I looked at each other in disbelief and horror, wondering if we would make it around the next turn. The fellows up front didn't seem the least bit concerned.

We got out at the first town we could find with a railroad stop, thanking our foreign hosts for their generosity and the ride, and took the train the rest of the way to Zurich where we caught a plane to Rome. Our flights had been prepaid, thank goodness.

While we loved the Coliseum and the Vatican and all of the Roman monuments, the congestion of the city was entirely too much for us. The heat, the noise, the wild, arm-waving, hyper-dramatic

Italian taxicab drivers were enough to get us thinking about going back to Montana. This was not to mention the costs that were quickly depleting the budget. But good fortune saved the day.

Before our wedding, I had gotten my godfather's address in Italy in order to send him an invitation. He had retired, after spending 40 years or more in the States. His wife had died. He was back to his roots in his remote home village of Casamassima, just a few miles south of Bari, on the Adriatic Sea.

We didn't expect him to come to the ceremony in Montana, but I did want him to know the news. We were hoping to see him at his home on our honeymoon and hoped the invitation would open his doors to us.

Once we got to Europe, we sent Dominick a postcard and a letter saying we wanted to visit him, but we had no way of knowing if he ever got our messages or our earlier invitation. We wanted to see his village in any case and proceeded on blind faith by train from Rome after sending one last message by telegraph, telling him when we would arrive.

It was a long, slow and crowded train ride. We were hopeful, but prepared for the worse. But to our delight, there to greet us at the train station in Casamassima was a cheerful, short and heavy-set man who kept calling out, "Caruso, Caruso, Fred and Ellen Caruso." It was my Gumbadi Dominick Fasano's son, himself already a senior citizen. My God! What a welcome.

Dominick's apartment had a room set aside for us newlyweds. He had a full-time housekeeper and cook and a steady stream of visitors, all of whom he wanted us to meet. It was an easy decision. We would spend the rest of our honeymoon with my godfather, who was small in stature, but clearly a very big man in his village.

His kindness and generosity swept our lack of resources under the carpet. The possibility of touring Europe on $5 a day had become pretty much of a myth by then for an individual, we had to concede, and certainly didn't work for a couple. We decided to skip our visit to Spain.

And what a wonderful time we had with my very own Gumbadi.

Everyone in town knew him and acknowledged him as we walked by. His wife had been memorialized with a bronze plaque on a stone monument, as tall and as wide as a person, in the village square. She was acknowledged as a midwife who helped hundreds of women give birth, many of whom were important citizens of the community. We saw the sights, enjoyed a family picnic overlooking the Adriatic Sea, and generally prepared ourselves for our trip home and the start of a life together.

Chapter 20

Fresh Out of the Box

With Europe behind us, Ellen and I were ready to start on our Montana adventure. We had so little money left after the honeymoon that we couldn't afford to eat out or stay in a motel on our cross-country drive. We were too proud to mention our economic straits to anyone in New York.

We slept in our trusty VW Buddy, my old Army friend, at a truck stop along the toll road around Chicago between two very noisy but familiar-smelling cattle trucks. Then we drove nonstop to the Big Sky Country.

After a brief stop at the ranch to pick up what wedding gifts would fit in the Bug, we headed for Helena. We found a small and inexpensive furnished apartment right across the street from the copper-domed State Capitol. The landlady knew my new boss, Tom Judge and his family, all longtime residents. She agreed to let us move in without paying a deposit. She also agreed to wait for the first month's rent until after I got my first paycheck as a married man.

We felt like Montana pioneers all over again. We were "fresh out of the box" and ready to roll.

It turned out that Judge Advertising and Public Relations was far more interesting and diverse than the run-of-the-mill ad agency. The firm did very little commercial advertising as you might expect from the company name. Instead, it specialized in advertising campaigns for political candidates during the active political seasons and public relations and publicity campaigns for a few corporations during the off-season. But the firm's bread-and-butter commitment was to "association management."

The company owner was an up-and-coming politician. State Senator Tom Judge was weaving his way through the political ranks to becoming governor. He was in his early thirties at the time, very affable and distinguished looking and well-known around the state. Somehow he managed to juggle a hectic political career, an even more hectic business venture, an active social life and some semblance of family life.

While I spent nearly five hours being interviewed for the job just a few weeks before graduation, I was so green to the real business world that I didn't even take note of his political party. Not that it would have mattered. Having not yet voted in an election of any kind anywhere, I was not the least bit in tune to the political world. I soon found out that Judge was a Democrat and was preparing for his next race, for Lieutenant Governor. I was soon to learn a lot about the world of politics, and I would learn it very quickly.

Even now, after decades of doing it, I still have a hard time explaining it. It was the association management side of the business that fascinated me and changed my life. It was that – the management of nonprofit organizations – that led me to what I came to believe was my purpose in life, the reason God saved me from death the night of the Flying Tiger crash. I became convinced I might be destined to make a major contribution to the field of association management.

Our office served as the headquarters for a variety of statewide, nonprofit trade associations and professional societies. Our clients included the associations for architects, lawyers, radio and TV broadcasters, savings and loan institutions, mobile home dealers, public health officials, optometrists, veterinarians and a half a dozen others. Each organization paid a monthly retainer fee that

188

covered all staff services.

Our staff of three arranged conventions and education programs for all of the organizations, handled all of the finances and dues billings, designed and carried out membership campaigns, wrote and edited the newsletters and publications, and issued press releases. Each association benefited from the lower cost of shared offices, equipment and staff and from the use of systems developed by others.

I soon learned that associations are communications systems and we were in charge of managing those systems. Journalism was a natural part of the job.

Associations are also very political and can be extremely influential. Judge parlayed his business into a political power base. He could go to any town in the state, open a phone book and find a dozen people he had never met, but yet could call them and say he was calling as the executive director of their professional or trade association. He had an instant and solid contact, even if they weren't active members of the organization. Certainly they had a vested interest in their profession or their business, members or not, and that was good enough.

Political advertising dominated our activity during campaign years, and a big year was coming up. As a totally green recruit, with no experience, I was assigned three campaigns: a small one for the state treasurer candidate, a larger one for state attorney general, and a very big campaign for a U.S. Congressman.

The congressman happened to be Ellen's shirt-tail cousin, incumbent Arnold Olsen of Butte. I couldn't afford to damage his campaign just because I didn't know what I was doing. I had to learn the tricks very quickly or perish. But to fail was not an option. To do so would mean the end of my client's career as well as my own.

Work at Judge Advertising made my Army PIO job seem like a long and extravagant vacation. No one noticed if our stories or photos didn't get published in the Army papers. If we did get published, we were instant heroes.

With political advertising, you walked a tightrope every inch of the way. Your job was to get the right ads out, in the right media and at the right time You were always noticed, especially if you fell short. Late breaking news made advertisements placed yesterday obsolete. Advertising deadlines were firm. Making the placement of ads all the more difficult was the fact that all media purchases had to be paid in advance and in full. There was no credit and no IOUs for political ads. (Evidently, there are few things more difficult than collecting debts from a defeated candidate.)

It happened that my congressional candidate was a key figure in the city of Butte and its strongly Democratic and solidly Irish community. While filming a series of TV commercials in the mining center of the state, I was swept up by the Irishness of the people whom he called his own. It was almost like being in Ireland, except for the landscape that was dominated by a huge open pit copper mine that nearly gobbled up the old downtown. Many of the people we filmed spoke with a heavy Irish brogue.

Congressman Olsen and I spent an entire week together, filming everything from fly-fishing, to touring gigantic mining equipment in the open pit mines, to interviewing school superintendents and city officials. I used my own 35-mm camera equipment to get all of the black-and-white still shots we needed, while a professional cameraman handled the filming. We won the campaign by a fairly large margin, but not without a lot of pressure along the way.

Between campaigns I made up lost time with the association clients. This work steadily and increasingly captured my interest. Unfortunately, my association high was being interrupted regularly by political campaigns. It took less than two years to figure out that political campaigning was not my thing. Judge Advertising was a great stepping-stone for Tom Judge in his career, but not necessarily for me.

I wanted to develop my own business with my own focus. I would become a free-lance publicity agent. I would develop public relations programs, write reports, build audiovisual presentations and provide association management services for anyone or any organization needing them.

There seemed to be no shortage of small nonprofit organizations needing help, but there was a very large shortage of groups with money and a willingness to spend it on management. Regardless, Ellen and I were able to put together a decent living and an impressive client list relatively quickly, and did so without competing head to head with my previous employer. I focused on the business, and Ellen worked at various journalistic endeavors.

Two years had passed since our wedding and my graduation from UM. We were living in Helena. Ellen was working at Carroll College as student activities coordinator and taking classes part-time. Soon after our first child, Andrea, was born, we decided it was time to go back to Missoula so Ellen could finish her bachelor's degree. She still had one year to go when she left the J-School to marry me.

Congress had recently reinstated the GI education bill, largely in response to the Viet Nam conflict. The benefits and the payments were very generous and I qualified as a veteran, provided I enrolled in a graduate program. The GI bill, combined with our business income, would allow us to live fairly well.

So back to Missoula we headed at the end of summer in a rented U-Haul truck, 120 miles over the mountain with everything we owned, including our new business. We had outgrown our Volkswagen Beetle as our moving van.

No one seemed to catch on that we had moved to another city, not even our business clients, and we enjoyed the anonymity. We had all of our mail forwarded and I showed up at all necessary meetings at the State Capitol, just 90 minutes away. Montana still had no daytime speed limit and we drove very fast. There was very little traffic to slow you down.

Ellen enrolled for her final year in journalism, and I became a graduate student in sociology. I would study the workings of nonprofit organizations, trade associations and professional societies from the inside, using my business as my research laboratory. It was a very handy arrangement.

Our return to Missoula was an exceptionally happy and peaceful time for both of us. We enjoyed a new dimension of status and a surprisingly high level of financial security. We were not the typical starving students about campus.

Our second daughter, Tanya, was born right in the middle of winter semester, but that didn't slow Ellen down for a minute. She went to class looking as if she would soon give birth to a watermelon, riding her bicycle across campus on Monday. By Thursday she was back in class again looking just like everyone else, no less for the strain.

The wild paratrooper, the crazy motorcycle madman of a few years earlier, had settled down and was achieving a degree of respectability. Ellen graduated with two baby girls in tow, and I was accumulating hours toward my Master's degree and was well into gathering information and interviews for my thesis. We were enjoying the good life.

And then the telephone rang!

I should have stayed in the library that day or never answered the phone. The phone call was from the chairman of the Montana Republican State Central Committee.

The Republicans were reorganizing and preparing for the next campaign. He had heard that I was an expert in political advertising. He had heard about my slide show from the last campaign. I photographed every political advertisement in the Helena *Daily Independent* newspaper, every day of the campaign. Simply by showing the daily progression of advertising, a candidate could catch on to the very basic principles of political advertising. I had already presented my program to a number of clubs, including the Young Republican Club, just for the fun of it.

The party chairman also knew I was very familiar with the Republicans' chief rival of the next campaign, my former boss, Tom Judge.

I agreed to meet him for dinner in Great Falls, some 165 miles away. That was a big mistake, simply because when you go that far, you become invested in the opportunity. The offer was enticing. I would start with a very good salary, would be in a prestigious position, and could do as much independent work with Republican candidates as I wished.

After a few days of debate, we decided to give up my university studies and go back to Helena to take on the GOP. I decided I would manage the Republicans as if they were an "association." We'd keep the business and Ellen would continue to work with our association clients out of a home office.

It was an exciting job. I loved the contact with high officials and I loved the political game. But, as many who have been in politics can attest, the whole business can become a "love-hate" affair. It is great when it is great, but it can be horrible. Common sense and civility often vanish under the strain.

I focused as much as I could on the parts of the job that I liked. And what I especially liked was the chance to do extra assignments for nothing more than the challenge and goodwill it generated. I loved helping candidates with their campaign publicity and advertising.

Candidates for the state House or Senate might come to Helena for a meeting. I would run them up to the Capitol, take five or six stock photos with them standing on the Capitol steps with hand outreached as if greeting an old friend, or at the speaker's podium inside the legislative chambers. I would then get a little biographical information and mock up a photo brochure and advertising campaign for distribution back at home. Montana was so big in size, and districts so isolated, that there was never a fear of overlapping or duplicating campaign designs. Every one I helped turned out to be a winner.

My favorite candidate, and soon to be my closest friend in Montana, was Glen Drake, a Helena attorney. He was a leader in urban planning circles, a family man with six kids, and a friend to everyone. Without discussing the matter with anyone outside of his immediate family, he decided on the last day for candidate registration to run for State Senate. His opponent was one of the wealthiest men in the state. Glen was virtually dirt-poor at the time, but his heart was clearly in his commitment to do a good job. I agreed to handle his campaign even though the odds were stacked against him.

We created a campaign theme, "Glen Drake is a common man," a man with common values and simple interests. Everyone knew his opponent and his wealth, which was often mentioned in the newspapers.

Drawing from my Army photo experience, we created a world-class portfolio. Although shy and modest, Glen Drake was indeed photogenic and willing to pose in any situation I suggested. The photos told his story in our brochures, our newspaper ads and our TV commercials. He was a common man and a family man, just like the average Joe. His opponent's campaign did very little to hide a rich man's life-style, and we won handily.

Politics being what it is, our man Drake found himself in a re-districting fight, so he had to run again halfway through his original four-year term. He wasn't feeling well at the time and had serious second thoughts about another campaign. I convinced him to turn his campaign fund over to me and I would take care of his marketing just as I had before. We won again by a wide margin.

I still liked pressure and I still liked to work. I got a lot of satisfaction out of accomplishment, but I wasn't sure I was going in the right direction. I found myself asking, "Is this my mission in life? Is this why I was saved from the clutches of the Flying Tiger that dreadful night at sea?"

It was a successful time, politically and economically, but anxiety was returning. I was beginning to suffer from a new attack of wanderlust. I resigned my job as Central Committee executive soon after the elections of 1972, and, after cleaning up the aftermath, stayed on as a half-time fundraiser for another six months. Ellen kept our association management business going the entire time I was involved in the GOP. New business was plentiful and we had acquired new value as legislative lobbyists.

It was the first day of the legislative session, a very exciting day in

Montana since the legislature only met every other year. It was January 1973. Newly re-elected Senator Glen Drake was the keynote speaker at the Helena Kiwanis Club luncheon, and I was there to cheer him on.

After his exceptionally rousing speech about the pros and cons of the National Women's Rights Amendment, I walked boldly up to the podium to congratulate him.

He was still up front, organizing himself to leave. Most of the Kiwanians were rushing out the door to get on with their day. He was looking slightly dazed when he saw me, clasped his chest, and fell over in pain. He was suffering from a massive heart attack.

There was a doctor among those who remained, and he jumped in to help. My man Glen was moved to a sofa and given air. The next two months were a nightmare.

Glen Drake had become a lot more than a friend. He and his wife were nearly 15 years our senior, and Ellen and I had become part of their family. The closest medical center for heart surgery at that time was in Salt Lake City, nearly 800 miles away. We took in the youngest of his six children while he and his wife, Jo Mae, were away for the then new form of heart bypass surgery.

Soon after returning from the hospital, Drake began an exercise regimen that included walking a mile twice a day. Our house was exactly at the half-mile point. We got to check on him twice a day at his turning point, and he could stop by for a respite if he felt inclined.

We looked forward to seeing him and started celebrating his success at his turning point with a glass of wine, and then several glasses of wine. The walking seemed to work well in spite of our added therapy. He went back to his official duties on the very last day of the legislative session to a resounding standing ovation. He had missed the entire session between the first and last day, but no one seemed to mind.

As a result of his experience, we were shocked into the reality of our own vulnerability. That caused us to look more closely toward the things we really cared about, like Ireland. It was becoming our "special place, someday." It sometimes takes a long time for the important things in life to percolate to the top.

Chapter 21

D.C. Detour

*I*n the world of associations and politics, Washington, D.C., is the Holy City, and I knew I was missing something by not being there. After an especially long, cold Montana winter, when the temperature never rose above zero (minus 18°C) for 25 consecutive days and the temperature on the mountain pass plunged to 45 below (minus 43°C). Ellen and I found ourselves coming down with what Montanans call a serious case of "cabin fever."

Adding to our restlessness and our curiosity about what we might be missing in the world beyond Montana was the arrival of a young high school exchange student from Rio de Janeiro. She came to Helena by random assignment and was soon bored and uncomfortable in the icy cold winter surroundings, having grown up along the beach. She was looking for an after-school job doing anything at all that might broaden her American experience. Ellen hired her to take care of our daughters every afternoon so she could keep up with our association management business.

Sandra's accent, her exotic look, her curiosity and her worldly perspective at the age of 17 caused me to think more and more of the good times I had with my Peruvian friend, Alberto Maurer, in Germany.

And, wouldn't you know, at about that same time, we began getting phone calls from Alberto himself, who was making regular trips to the States as an importer and exporter of chemicals and

raw materials. With Sandra caring for the girls, and Alberto calling, we had a steady series of reminders that there was more to the
world than Helena.

I began exploring career options and locations, and we decided
Washington, D.C., had the most to offer. I soon found a job as
director of state legislative affairs for the Mobile Home
Manufacturer's Association. I knew the industry from my two years
of prior part-time experience as executive director of the Montana
Mobile Home Association, which had been one of Judge
Advertising's clients.

By the time of our move, Jack Odgaard had become a press secre-
tary and legislative aide to a Nebraska congressman and was well-
established in D.C. He was as much the hyper-enthusiastic PR
man in civilian life as he was in the Army and his enthusiasm
fueled my fever for D.C. My new employer was headquartered
out of the city, in its own modern building in the fields and forests
of northern Virginia near the new Dulles Airport. The country was
green, lush and hardly congested.

The transition from Helena to D.C. was surprisingly easy.

We soon found a home not far from my headquarters, some 15
miles out of the city in a romantic-sounding community called
Sugarland Run. Small creeks and rivers in northern Virginia were
called "runs," and we were close to some of the most historic runs
of the Civil War. Sugarland Run itself was the site of a minor civil
war battle and a tributary to the famous Bull Run.

A brand new campus of the newly created Northern Virginia
Community College was being built at the entrance to our community, and Ellen was hired as its first communications director.
She couldn't have found a more interesting or convenient arrangement than that.

Alberto Maurer dropped into our lives soon after we arrived,
while we were still in temporary quarters waiting for our new home
to be completed. Eight years had already passed since we left the
Army.

Alberto was a man of the world, flitting here and there, making huge deals, brokering chemicals and raw materials by the ship-load. Nonetheless, he maintained that suave, easygoing, carefree South American manner.

My job as state legislative affairs director meant I worked with people all across the country in state capitols who were doing what I had done locally in Montana. It required a lot of travel, but that seldom took me away for more than two nights in a row. Because of D.C.'s location in the center of the populated East Coast, it was not uncommon to attend a business lunch in Boston, Chicago or Atlanta and be back the same evening.

As a one-person department within the larger public affairs division of the association, I soon learned that most of the field work was to be accomplished with independent contractors and outside attorneys. Our most effective agent was a distinguished-looking older gentleman, Harold Gray, who became a very close friend and mentor.

Harold was 64 years old and starting a second career as a consultant for state and local affairs after his retirement from the National Highway Users Federation. His job of the previous 35 years had been developing and executing grass-roots political campaigns to gain support for the expansion of the U.S. highway system, as well as managing the activity of a dozen field agents working under his direction. No transportation system was ever built without strong opposition from one sector or another. Diplomatic Harold was an expert in overcoming the opposition.

Harold was my man for getting a state to change its regulations. He would go to a state and meet with transportation officials at every level, including county commissioners and legislators, over a period of three or four weeks on their home turf. He would explain the need for regulatory adjustments and, before long, a major change in our favor would be announced. It seemed like magic to me, but it was routine for him.

If Harold was in the field when I had occasion to be nearby, he always made it a point to meet me to show me around as if Any Town, U.S.A., was his own hometown. He had been everywhere in his first career and had taken the time to learn about each locale and its uniqueness, no matter where it was. He was always eager to share his local knowledge as if he had lived there all his life.

Being closer to the center of association activity and working with an organization with substantial financial resources made it possible for me to bring Ellen to national meetings and trade shows that we wouldn't have attended if we were living in Montana.

We nearly always found the Irish Tourist Board to be a prominent exhibitor at these events, promoting travel to the Emerald Isle, along with a host of prominent Irish hotels, and the national airline, Aer Lingus. We started looking forward to those conferences just to feel the thrill of being so close to Irish names and Irish faces and people with endless enthusiasm for the homeland.

The "D.C. Detour" became a time of study and speculation. I was on that never-ending quest for purpose, the contribution to the world that was to be my legacy from the Flying Tiger incident. It had to have something to do with my work.

I thought my obsession with nonprofit associations was my calling, but I wasn't sure. I knew that associations were influential in the fields they served. I knew, for instance, that Ireland's bed and breakfast associations were helping the country's growing tourism industry.

The B & B associations established standards, while helping thousands create instant guest accommodations throughout the country before the existence of a low-cost hotel network. The millions of tourist dollars spent at these mini-lodges, many of which were little more than private homes with an extra bedroom for rent, eventually made their way into the Irish economy. I had been studying how this entire process worked. The people who worked for the Irish Tourist Board always seemed to be interested in what I was doing.

I dusted off my graduate school research in associations, eventually developing it into a book, and took advantage of the proximity of the American Society of Association Executives by attending as many of its education sessions as I could. After completing the arduous application requirements and passing the eight-hour exam, I reached my dream goal of becoming a Certified Association Executive, a CAE.

So I was learning and becoming known as an expert in my field. But was that my purpose?

My mother continued to remind me that I had one, whatever it was. She was still making novenas for me. The airplane crash was years in the past, but it kept popping up as a conversation topic.

It was the crash that allowed me to be born again Irish, you know. Or was it that the crash *caused* me to be born again Irish? In either case, was I any closer to Ireland?

Was I any closer to knowing and reaching my purpose now than I was a few years earlier?

Was my family any better off on the East Coast than it was in the West?

Was my career path the right path?

How could a person reach a goal without knowing what it was? I simply didn't know.

Our neighborhood was full of young people from all corners of the world, all of whom seemed to have interesting careers. They were well-read and interested in an endlessly diverse number of global topics. Our home was brand new, of California contemporary design with high vaulted ceilings and sweeping roof lines, and in a beautiful setting above a tiny creek. The children loved their preschool. Yet, after nearly two years, it felt that Washington, D.C., was not taking me to where I hoped to be and, in all likelihood, it never would.

Most of the professionals we knew in the D.C. area certainly appeared to speak and think on a higher intellectual level than our colleagues in the West. Eventually, however, we realized that their actions tended to lag far behind their conversation. They were not especially adventurous or bold, and certainly were not as daring as most of those we knew in Montana. They were just like everyone else, no matter what they did or said. I expected more.

In Montana, for example, politics and political office was a way of life. A person might be 10 to 20 times more likely to be a state legislator in Montana than in New York or California simply because of the ratio of legislators to citizens. Serving in political office was conceivably within reach of anyone with determination and persistence. The rest of the world, we learned, didn't see it that way at all.

One evening at dinner with friends who had also migrated to the D.C. area, I mentioned that more than likely both Ellen and I would be serving in the state legislature, either in the house or senate or both, had we stayed in Montana. With our positions and experience it would have been expected of us.

I went on to speculate that I had no doubt that Ellen could have launched a campaign for the U.S. Congress, had we stayed, and would have had a very good chance of winning, partly on the basis of her family name, Broadus. Montana had a long history of women in politics, including the first female member of the U.S. House of Representatives, Congresswoman Jeannette Rankin. She was elected in 1914, six years before the rest of the nation had universal voting rights for women. We were not talking new ideas for women in the 1970s, at least as far as Montana was concerned. We had actually discussed the possibility of Ellen running for office on several occasions in private.

The response I got shocked me.

The other two couples burst into guffaws. The whole idea was absurdly ridiculous to them, but the possibility was perfectly sound and realistic to us. Ellen took the conversation personally and was disheartened, even though we both knew better.

While D.C. offered many new opportunities, it lacked others. That little social incident confirmed our suspicions.

Another motive for moving to D.C. was to be closer to New York. Our kids would have an opportunity to get to know the grandparents and relatives on the East Coast.

Much to our surprise, within a year of our moving east, my parents took early retirement and moved to Lakeland, Florida. We had one opportunity for Thanksgiving and Christmas in New York as a family, and that was it.

Then the economy tanked and a middle-east oil crisis threw

life into turmoil. It was 1975, and the Richard Nixon/Watergate affair had dropped a depressing pall across the political scene. The Viet Nam War was very ugly.

So, after two interesting and mind-expanding years in the lush Virginia countryside, we decided it was a good time to take stock of options one more time. We were suffering from another outbreak of cabin fever, and we weren't anywhere close to a cabin.

One night, after the girls went to sleep, we took a map of the United States and started crossing off states in which we had no interest. We wanted to avoid areas with a strong regional accent. We would avoid states that were too remote, or too limited in opportunities for young people or for women. The flat-land states of the American bread basket were ruled out as well. Too much farming.

Eventually all we had left on the map were Colorado and Montana, and as a distant third, California. The lure of John Denver's folk music and the lyrics of his song, "Rocky Mountain High," made Colorado seem just like Montana.

Next came finding something worth pursuing.

I started spending more time in downtown D.C., between my field trips, visiting other associations to learn how the rest of the world was getting along. Today we call it networking. One long-standing contact was the executive director of the National Reclamation Association, who was reading a newsletter from one of the state affiliates as I walked into his office.

What a coincidence. The Colorado Water Congress was looking for an executive director. It was an organization that had money and needed management. Might I know someone who would be interested in a job in Colorado?

Well, I did know someone.

In fact, the person I knew had two years of experience with an affiliated organization, the Montana Water Development Association. He had all kinds of good qualifications and experience. As a matter of fact, he happened to be looking right now.

"How do I apply for the job?"

Chapter 22

Approaching the Center of the Vortex

*I*t is characteristic of whirlpools and spirals, no matter how large and powerful, to tug ever so lightly as an unsuspecting visitor approaches. The earliest tugging is so slight, so tentative in fact, that it might not be noticed. As the visitor draws closer, the force increases. If the visitor moves away soon enough, and fast enough, the force can be broken. If the visitor hesitates, however, and looks inward, unaware of the tugging, the spiral tightens its grip, pulling ever stronger in wide, circular sweeps. The intruder finally vanishes into the center of the vortex.

In the spectrum of the universe, it may take a tiny star a hundred million years or more to make its first revolution around the edge of a mysterious black hole. Little by little, the star nudges closer as its rotation accelerates. Round and round it goes, faster and faster, until eventually it is swallowed by the center.

The vortex of fate that began tugging at me as I crossed the Montana border years earlier had been slowly pulling at the two of us as if we were a pair of slow-moving, wandering stars, Fred and Ellen, approaching the unseen force. We hardly noticed.

We were intrigued by Ireland but maintained our foothold in Colorado as we worked on our careers and raised our family. All things "Irish-like" attracted our attention: the accents, faces, names, books, songs, holidays and even the daily news, but we had our duties. We had to paddle the outer fringes of the spiral in order to take care of our priorities.

The D.C. Detour hadn't taken us to a dead end when it came to our long journey to Ireland. On the contrary, the D.C. experience fueled our interest in Ireland and gave us even more opportunities for accumulating Irish points.

We started a tradition of celebrating St. Patrick's Day in Montana and continued it in D.C. We listened to Irish music whenever possible. We spoke of Ireland at every opportunity with friends who shared the interest, or who were polite enough to tolerate our conversation. We spent hours at the Irish Tourist Board exhibits talking about Irish economic development and tourism with real live Irish people.

All of these "things Irish" seemed to be adding up. One interest led to another of even greater interest. Keeping Ireland in mind, by whatever means, fueled our passion and longing and affection for Ireland itself.

Colorado proved to be a treasure chest of opportunity for accumulating Irish points. Unfortunately, the move to Denver turned out to be more painful than we expected.

Colorado was known at the time as a cowboy state and Denver itself as a cow town, perhaps even more so than any place in Montana. We realized very quickly that Colorado, and especially the Denver metro area, was hardly another Montana. In fact, it suffered from urban sprawl.

More than four times the population of Montana lives in about half the land area, and nearly half of Colorado's population resides in metropolitan Denver. For me, that meant in one 16-mile commute I would drive past more people and more houses than were in the entire state of Montana. I could see each and every house because of the lack of trees and hills.

On the positive side, Denver's population makes it a regional center for transportation, communications and education, all of which translates into many more opportunities for jobs, culture and entertainment.

As the brand new executive director of the Colorado Water Congress, I arrived to find that there was very little water over which to preside, much less over which to hold a congress. Colorado's shortage of water, of course, was exactly the reason the organization even existed. The Water Congress helped referee disputes over what precious little water there was and mediated in controversial plans to store and distribute it.

I eventually settled into what was the most interesting job I've ever had. Water was an economic and political medium and the center of endless debate.

Our conferences always featured the top leaders of both political parties. One luncheon program featured our Governor and both U.S. Senators, with yours truly serving as master of ceremonies. It happened to be Valentine's Day.

I arranged to have Ellen and our daughters at the luncheon. The Governor agreed to take charge of a "Heartfelt Thanks" awards ceremony, which involved distributing boxes of candy to our female supporters. Each in turn was called forward by the Governor and given a heart-shaped box of candy, including at last, Ellen, Andrea, then age 9, and Tanya, age 8.

Our Governor had hardly begun to speak when our two girls proceeded with one mind to tear open the crinkly, cellophane wrappers that covered their heart-shaped candy boxes. There was no stopping them. Governor Lamm graciously ignored the sounds coming from the table closest to the microphone and even cast an approving smile. The audience loved it.

We gave a lot of thought to moving back to Montana and starting over again with our association management business. That was, until quite innocently, we fell upon the attraction that lures so many to Colorado and its mountains, and the glue that holds so many there — the sport of downhill skiing.

Finally, we were connected. Colorado is not about cows and cowboys, or farming or mining, but about skiing and snowboarding. It is a commitment and a way of life.

Skiing rarely takes less than a full day, from dawn to dark, and it seems like everyone does it. Skiing was exactly what we needed to maintain our balance on the outer edges of the vortex of fate that was drawing us to Ireland. Skiing infused a lot of energy into what was otherwise the mundane passing of time. It was the energy required to fight the force. We were experiencing the "Colorado Rocky Mountain High."

With that issue out of the way — to stay in Colorado or to move north to Montana — we were able to focus on work, family, and developing a network of friends, many of whom had a high level of interest and some with deep ties to Ireland.

Two of my work colleagues were married to Irish-born women. Tom Pitts, a water engineer, was married to Enid, and they had a daughter, Erin. Jack Ross, a water lawyer, was married to Una, and they had a daughter named Fiona.

Jack and his wife took a trip to Ireland and returned with fascinating tales of security challenges resulting from the "troubles" in the north. It was hard to imagine but was very exciting to hear. They had little trouble finding accommodations as they traveled and were amazed at the economic progress they had seen since their last trip.

Tom and Enid took two weeks to visit her family's farm. It had been in the family for 400 years, having known little more than extreme hardship and poverty during that time. Recently, however, conditions were improving. There was money to be had, at least enough for painting and fixing up the house and for the luxury of a color TV.

We learned from the travels of our friends that Ireland was on the rise. More than a decade had passed since our honeymoon visit. The possibility of another visit to Ireland some day, a longer one than our honeymoon allowed, was not as remote or unrealistic as it seemed before.

After four years on the job with the Colorado Water Congress, I decided there had to be opportunities for higher income, even though I knew I would miss the excitement and controversy that surrounded water. Skiing was an expensive sport, and a fatter paycheck would help.

I hardly started to think about a new job, when I got a phone call from my former boss in Washington, D.C. John Martin had since become the president of the National Lumber Dealers Association. He called to tell me that a five-state, regional lumber dealers association headquartered in Denver was looking for a new chief executive. He wanted to know if I might be interested.

It was an easy shift for me. It was a different type of association with a much larger territory, but the work involved most of the same activity: newsletters, conventions, education programs and some governmental lobbying. The best news was that the association had a much larger budget and had money in the bank.

Ellen was working at the University of Colorado at Denver as director of alumni and government relations, a job she found shortly after we arrived in the metro area. After five successful years on her job, and soon after I made my change, UCD campus administrators changed, and, as is often the case, staff was ripe for change, too. Ellen decided take the plunge as an entrepreneur to launch an association management business similar to what we had going in Montana. Within weeks, she was set up with client organizations representing physical therapy, home care and a local building materials supply group. The Carusos were back in the association management business.

Family ski trips gave us long days together for sharing stories of terrifyingly steep ski runs, of driving through blinding blizzards to and from the mountains, and of interesting people we met on the ski lifts. We found out why so many of our neighborhood acquaintances appeared to be too busy to be sociable. We skied 28 days one season. That was the same as giving up the entire month of February to a hobby, leaving only 11 months to fit in everything else. With that short of a year, time passes very quickly.

Another way we satisfied our need for adventure during this period was travel. My job with the lumber dealers provided plenty of opportunities to travel with the family as a business expense.

Visits from Alberto Maurer and stories of Sandra, our exchange student from Brazil, who had become an airline hostess and contacted us frequently by phone, exposed the kids to people from faraway places.

With a widening sphere of friends who shared the Irish interest, it wasn't difficult to find ways of adding to our Irish points. Denver became a major center for an annual St. Patrick's Day parade and festivities. We did our part by hosting an annual neighborhood party at our home. We began to get into the spirit by playing Irish music for two weeks steady before the official date and for many days afterward. We served kegs of beer that had been dyed green at the brewery. Irish party hats, paper plates and napkins with an Irish theme, and green tee-shirts embossed with "Thank God I'm Irish" became standard.

It seemed like no time at all before the girls were starting to plan their futures. Of course there would be college, but before that would come a high school foreign exchange experience.

We decided that Andrea and Tanya should spend one semester, or just half of a school year abroad, to avoid any delay in their stateside graduations. We decided to arrange a direct exchange, without the aid of an established exchange organization. That way we could control their destination and their length of stay. We had hosted a German student for a year directly through parents and friends, so we knew it could be done.

The question was where the girls would be going. It was to be somewhere in Europe. Ireland was Mom and Dad's first choice, but the girls wanted to see their options first, and it would be their own decision. We started planning a three-week family trip — a familiarization tour — to see what was out there.

Finally, after months of preparation, with Andrea and Tanya each saving their own cash for the trip, we were ready to start our big European Family Adventure. Our first stop was Ireland.

All hearts were beating fast as the pilot announced our approach to Shannon, and especially mine. I was getting a funny feeling. I was coming home.

Our first night in Ireland was in the village of Dingle, some three hours southwest of Shannon airport. And why were we going to Dingle first, instead of say, Cork? That was simple.

Dingle was the home of the University of Dingle, the well-respected alma mater of the famous Beatles drummer, Ringo Starr. Tanya heard all about it from Ringo himself in an interview reported on the cover of a record album. Any town with a college good enough for Ringo Starr had to be good enough for our family.

Exhausted from the overnight journey, we couldn't make it all the way to Dingle without a nap. We found a small church parking lot along the side of the road and slept in our car. No one protested.

Refreshed by our roadside respite, we proceeded to Dingle. As we got closer to the very rural and isolated village, Tanya's confidence began slipping. It was possible, maybe, that it was simply a hoax. Ringo Star had a reputation for telling tall tales. We didn't want to hear about it. We were committed and by that time we were almost there.

And so it turned out there was no University of Dingle and there never was, but not to bother! There should have been one. Dingle is a wonderful, quaint little village, a great place for a university.

Our dinner that night was at the Armada Restaurant, where we learned of the influence of the Spanish Armada nearly four centuries earlier. Dozens of the Armada's ships were battered to pieces by a violent storm right off the western coast on approximately the same day and nearly the same place as the wreck of the Flying Tiger. Hundreds of seamen were washed to shore. Of those who lived, many stayed in Ireland.

Ellen told the owner of the Armada that her roots were in County Cavan. He immediately treated her to a song which has been one of our favorites ever since, *Come Back Paddy Reilly to Ballyjamesduff.*

In less time than it takes to pay a restaurant bill, Andrea and Tanya, who were by then 14 and 15 years old, found the gathering point for local teenagers. These were mostly boys, of course, allowing the fashionable Americans to hold center stage. This gave us a chance to see what was happening at the local pub, just a few yards away, with the girls checking in periodically to report on progress.

Before long it was closing time for the pub, and the girls were gone. Oh, yes. They mentioned something about a dance.

The locals all knew about it. The Bishop himself was in town to cut the ribbon. Everyone would be there. So, after midnight in a soft rain in a foreign land we set out to find our daughters.

"Not to worry," we were told. The pubs were all closed. "Everyone will be there."

And it seemed as if everyone was there, hundreds of them of all ages. "When do the Irish sleep?" I wondered.

We followed the crowd to the hot spot disco. It was 12:30 by then, and revelers were into the music. After paying our entry fee, we elbowed our way into the hall and found ourselves joining in a festive rendition of Bruce Springsteen's *Born in the U.S.A.*

Right in the middle of the shouting and cheering crowd were none other than Andrea and Tanya Caruso. The Irish had taken them in.

Before leaving Dingle the next day we had to stop at McKenna's sweater shop where several of the teenage boys worked. The girls forgot to swap addresses the night before. That was a good excuse to shop for Irish woolen ski wear. Nothing was intended for skiers, but we would start something new.

And something else caught my eye. I loved those plush, soft Irish sheep skins and had to have one.

I asked the salesman, "Where do you get those beautiful sheep skins? They are fantastic."

He smiled at me as if I was expecting him to say something like they were imported from China or Japan, but he didn't.

"We get our skins," he said, "from the little fellers up there on the hill," pointing toward the window.

"The what?" I asked as if I didn't hear correctly.

"The little fellers," he said again. "The ones up there on the hill." He smiled as he pointed to the grazing sheep.

"I need four of them, the best ones you have," I said, smiling by then as well. "We will keep them right along side the bed and think of Ireland first thing every morning."

From the Dingle Peninsula, we headed south to Cork to kiss the Blarney Stone. Along the way the girls told us of a conversation they had with the Irish boys. Somehow the subject of heritage came up. The boys were pure Irish, of course. Andrea and Tanya told them they were part Italian and Sicilian, part Irish, some Welsh and a bit of German.

"We're just mutts," they said. "We're a little bit of everything." The boys nearly recoiled in horror.

"Oh, no," they said, "You're not mutts. You're beautiful." Naturally the girls enjoyed the compliment. The notion of cultural diversity was pretty new to Ireland.

After Cork, we shot back north to Galway City, then north to Yeats country, Sligo, and east to County Cavan, which we knew by then was the origin of both Marcus Daly, the Montana Copper King, and Ellen's great grandfather, Patrick Lynch.

Ellen brought along a letter written in 1919 by one of the Irish cousins. Jack Callan told of his journey home after World War I. It was one of the few pieces of real evidence we had of the connection to County Cavan. Jack named the towns and significant landmarks, and you could feel his enthusiasm grow the closer he got to home. We zeroed in on a few of those names on a map and found the center of family activity, just out of Ballyjamesduff, in an area called Darrylea, near the village of Kilnaleck.

Kilnaleck, with a population of barely 200, had 11 pubs, or about one for every 18 of its residents. One of the most brightly painted of them all was Patrick Lynch's Pub and Feed and Grain.

What better place might there be for starting the search for our roots than at Patrick Lynch's place?

Ellen marched right up to the door, intent on finding a blood relative. The proprietor was an elderly, frail, but jovial fellow, well into his late 80s and appreciative of the attention.

"No," he assured us. While his name was Patrick Lynch, he was not related. There were several unrelated Lynch families in the area. It was possible that a bloodline was out there. He suspected that the fellow at the pub on the corner was married to someone who would know. All we had to do was walk a few doors down and ask.

Paddy Smith, proprietor of the Central Bar, was married to one of the sisters of the O'Reilly family line, cousins of the Lynches. He made a phone call and by evening, we were having an official family reunion with Paddy's wife, Kathleen, and her children. We found home. We knew we would return.

Schedule-bound, we headed off to London, and then onto Germany. Andrea and Tanya had to see Lee Barracks, of course, and I was eager to show them. The Gonsenheim Village Firemen were having their annual festival that weekend, and we just happened to be there to help them celebrate. And thus began the family quest for festivals all along the way, on into Austria, Switzerland, northern Italy, southern France and back into the Black Forest of southern Germany. Teenagers seem to have a sixth sense for parties and can read a festival poster in any language, we discovered, even from the back seat of a fast moving automobile.

Our final evening in Europe was in the village of Weinheim, just a little north of Heidelberg and south of Darmstadt. We had time on our last morning, a very quiet Sunday, to make a stop for old time's sake at the *Stars and Stripes*.

I was sure I could find my way, even though it had been a very long time since my adventure as the Army airborne, photojournalist, the indestructible "Mr. Invincible Man."

My God! The Flying Tiger crash was nearly a quarter century into the past.

The autobahn exit looked the same, but Darmstadt had grown up. The old landmarks were missing and the entrance to the *Stripes* was nowhere to be found. I stopped at a nearby gas station and learned the entry had been moved. We were very close and in a minute we were there.

Just as I remembered it, we were on the doorsteps of the *Stars and Stripes*. It looked incredibly similar to the Journalism Building in Missoula. The *Stripes* always had the feel of a college campus in my view. It was silent and beautiful and there seemed to be not a soul around.

Tanya, the younger and more impetuous, punched at a button in a moment of mindless fidgeting, and to our surprise a voice called out of the intercom, "Can we help you?"

There were people inside. The voice was that of a young military reporter, an Air Force man. I told them who I was and that I had worked there 20 years ago while in the Army. He invited us in.

There were only four people in the newsroom, which was all centralized by then and totally electronic. I introduced my family and then myself, noting my experience there. One of the four was an old timer, a civilian. To our astonishment, he said, "Yes, Fred Caruso, I do remember you."

He smiled and shook hands. My daughters were impressed.

After a brief update on what had happened at the *Stripes* in my absence, my family reminded me of our flight home. The plane would leave without us if we didn't show on time. So we left, all pretty much in awe that I had found someone there who remembered me. And that was it.

Both daughters decided to study German and settled on Southern Germany for their student exchange program. Andrea chose Wasserburg on the Inn River east of Munich, and Tanya selected the city of Lörrach, just a few miles north of Basel, Switzerland, at the base of the Black Forest. With relatively little help from us, aside from our writing a few letters and making a few phone calls on their behalf, both were able to arrange host families, and each had a great student experience.

From that point on, Europe was in our blood and Ireland became number-one destination for mom and dad. We had become loyal subscribers to *Ireland of the Welcomes* magazine and daily users of Irish Spring soap. The Dingle sheep skins at the side of our beds were our first sensation of the day.

We realized by then that we had been accumulating Irish points by doing things Irish all along. It was becoming a game, even though we never assigned a value to any aspect of the process. The points began to add up quickly.

With the girls advancing through school, we had more free time and found ourselves drifting closer to the center of the vortex.

Part IV

The
Road Home
to Ireland

Chapter 23

The Cavan Connection

*J*ack Callan's letter of 1919 led us through the green rolling hills of County Cavan to the right village and even to the right neighborhood, but it took Ellen's persistence with the elderly Patrick Lynch to get us to the right pub just two doors away. From there, at the Central Bar, through Kathleen and Paddy Smith, we established the long-missing and vital Cavan connection.

The curious names of Kilnaleck, Ballyjamesduff, Darrylea, Lough Sheelin, Crosserlough, Mount Nugent, and Coot Hill all became household words. Percy French's ballad, *Come Back, Paddy Reilly to Ballyjamesduff* became a family anthem.

The Montana relatives were delighted and astonished with the news of living blood cousins. Aunt Agnes Lynch's son had gone to County Cavan a few years earlier to trace his grandfather's steps but wasn't able to make contact. He must have thought that Patrick Lynch's Pub and Feed and Grain was entirely too coincidental to be the real thing, or else he popped in when the senior Patrick Lynch was on an errand. In any case, he never learned that the key to the family code was just a few yards away.

Our discoveries sparked a new interest in the family's Irish roots.

How was it that Patrick Lynch found his way to Rosebud Creek? We knew a little of that story, but very little. And why had the Montana relatives never heard a word from Ireland, except through that lone letter of 1919? And how was it that those in Ireland seemed to know nothing of what happened to the Lynch family after they left Ireland so many years ago?

Through an exchange of letters after our trip, we connected with the family of Fergus and Nuala Lynch. They owned a bed and breakfast fishing lodge known as Holywell on Lough Sheelin, a beautiful lake near the village of Kilnaleck.

I realized I had probably spoken to Nuala's daughter the year before when I tried to book a room in their B&B. We came across the Holywell B&B listed in the Irish tourist guidebook. The book named the proprietress as Mrs. Lynch. Of course, we wanted to stay there since Lynch was the family name. Who knows, we thought, maybe they were relatives.

I rang by phone from Denver in hopes of a room but learned to our disappointment that the B&B was closed for the season. I was speaking to Nuala's daughter, Deirdre, but neither of us had a clue that there might be a connection. I never will forget the sound of that young Irish voice with the cheerful Irish brogue, even though I was sorry there was no room for us at Mrs. Lynch's lodge.

That was history. Now we knew we would be visiting the next time as guests of the family, only a few miles from the original Patrick Lynch farm. In our minds at least, we would be visiting as a genuine part of the clan.

Nuala and Fergus Lynch spent half their lives in the States, in New York City and New Jersey, and returned to Ireland when Fergus learned of the opportunity to buy the rundown Holywell estate. He landed a job as a civil engineer for the county, supervising water and sewer projects. Four of their eight children stayed in the States and the others chose to relocate to Ireland.

We didn't want our excitement in discovering our roots to become a burden to our newfound relatives, so we planned sightseeing visits to different parts of Ireland, either before or after stopping at Cavan. Two or three days of visiting, we reasoned, was probably more than enough during any given trip. As a consequence, we got to see a lot of the country.

Ellen's mother, Margaret, had recently turned 80. We decided we should take her to see her roots while she was able to travel. So, with grandmother and daughters, we toured the English and Welsh countryside by van, and took a ferry from Fishguard, the port in Wales, to Rosslare, Ireland. We then drove to Cork City and Blarney Castle, where Gram earned a certificate for having climbed the hundreds of stairs up the castle towers in order to kiss the magic stone.

From there we headed north to County Cavan, where we stayed at Nuala's Holywell Fishing Lodge on Lough Sheelin. From that as our base, we explored the hills and lanes with the next-door neighbor and cousin, Maureen Gill.

Maureen was the family chronicler. She knew all the lines from one family to the next and knew all of the old home sites and country lanes as well.

Our first stop that brilliant, sunny morning was to visit Maureen's mother and her bachelor brother, Phillip "the Farmer." Their bright, lemon-colored cottage in the center of a lush green cattle farm had been Maureen's home as a child. In the sunlight, the cottage glowed like a precious gem.

The young and spirited 94-year-old Margaret O'Reilly was well dressed for our visit and assisted by her granddaughter, Olivia. Farmer Phillip stood close, but it was clear that the ladies were in charge of the household social arrangements.

"Would ye have a wee drink?" Margaret O'Reilly asked in a very high-pitched voice with the volume of someone very hard of hearing.

I could see Ellen and her mother checking their mental clocks, noting that it was only 11 a.m. I was game for an 11 a.m. tip of Irish whisky, but I could see they were taken aback by the thought of a drink so early in the day. Ellen and her mother politely declined the offer.

The Grand Lady Margaret O'Reilly ignored their retreat and asked again in an even louder, high-pitched voice, "Would ye have a wee drink to warm the house?"

Daughter Maureen leaned forward and whispered to us, nodding her head, as she spoke, "Mom would really like you to have a drink. It's a tradition. It's a way of blessing the house."

Ellen and her Mother hesitated still, but Maureen cast a commanding glance as she told them, "She really would be hurt if you didn't."

"By all means have a *wee drink,*" I thought to myself from my quiet corner of the room.

Still somewhat astonished, Ellen announced for the three of us, "That would be wonderful."

I stood by quietly, nearly overjoyed.

We gathered around the table in the tidy kitchen and within minutes, Farmer Phillip came out with tall drinking glasses filled nearly to the brim with Irish whiskey.

Cousin Maureen beamed. Ellen and her mom looked at their nearly overflowing glasses with a degree of hesitation. I was having a hard time containing my enthusiasm for the Irish sense of priorities. I was afraid we might have had to settle for tea and scones. Surely we were home.

With Maureen in the lead, we all gave the traditional toast, "*Sláinte!*" and proceeded to have a delightful conversation and a lovely day. No one died from the effects of tippling so early in the day. No one fainted and no one tripped over anything, although it took an hour or so to get through the toast. It simply was the tradition.

From the brilliant cottage in the center of a lush green farm, we proceeded to the neighborhood of the old Patrick Lynch family farmstead. I could tell the day was having a powerful effect on everyone. Ellen and her mother were nearly speechless in anticipation. Maureen was pausing frequently with the profoundness of the occasion. I was getting choked up myself, and it felt good knowing that I had something to do with organizing it.

Maureen took Ellen's mother by the arm and walked her down the very lane where Margaret's mother, Alice Lynch, walked as a child, and where Patrick Lynch and Margaret Callan courted so many years ago.

They might as well have been my parents and grandparents for what I was feeling. My "born again Irishness" was coming to the surface. I could hardly hold back the tears. I walked a few feet away to look at the blackberry bushes loaded down with fruit to hide my own flushed face.

Cousin Sean O'Reilly was farming the land and led us into the original family farmyard. At one end of the cow shed was the old hearth that would have been the gathering point for the family for warmth and food so many years earlier. Maureen told us that she always heard "it was a sad day when Patrick Lynch turned the key of the cottage for the last time and headed off to America." That was more than 100 years earlier, in 1881. It took nearly two years for the family to make their way to their final stopping place in Montana.

As we toured with Maureen, some of the mysteries of the family history and the legacy of Ireland came to light.

Owing to the English Penal Laws of the time, the Irish were not allowed to attend school. Illiteracy for the Irish had been written into law. Patrick Lynch and his family were unable to read and write, as were their neighbors and friends. That explained the lack of correspondence once they left.

The poverty and forced illiteracy generated a malaise that dulled enthusiasm and pride. Many emigrants of the era simply could not bear to reestablish contact with the past. Those who stayed behind experienced the same limits. Many others would have packed up, except for the need to care for their aging parents. The sadness and despondency caused many to retreat within themselves. No news was often viewed as good news.

Cousin Maureen pointed out plenty of examples of the impacts of the poor conditions of the time, but one situation especially stood out.

As we walked the lanes, it was obvious that some of the farms were absolutely beautiful, while large stretches of land seemed to be little more than marshy bogs. We learned from Maureen that

223

when the British lords moved in, they claimed all of the high, dry and fertile lands for their own. The Irish peasants got what was left over, mainly the low boggy wetlands.

Irish farmers could work as hard as they might and still end up with a very poor crop because they were farming a very poor plot of land. Within a generation or so the conditions were accepted as normal and, owing in part to the lack of education, many Irish grew to believe that they themselves were the reason for poor crops. They believed they were poor farmers and ignorant of what it took to succeed, when, in fact, it was the condition of the land that had been discarded by the British lords.

The history of Ireland is indeed one of sadness, tragedy and starvation. It took on a new level of intrigue, a mystery to which I wished to be a part. Despite the misery of the past, there seemed to be virtually no expression of bitterness or martyrdom, similar to what I saw among Italian immigrants. I wondered how this could be. I began taking mental notes on everything I saw and read.

Maureen's husband, Paddy, was a schoolteacher. By the time we met him he was having difficulty with the changing attitudes of Irish youth. They had no respect, he lamented, no discipline. He sounded just like the teachers we knew in the States. Both Gills had their hands full with eight children in a tiny house. Together they were managing to shepherd them through school, several of whom landed engineering degrees.

Paddy Gill's family, we learned, lived on the larger of the Aran Islands, that remote and barren set of islands off the coast of Galway Bay. Grandmother Margaret Gill was well into her 90s by the time we met. She made frequent trips to Cavan to see the grandchildren. Always in good spirits when we saw her, after a week or so with a house full of so many grandchildren, she was always pleased to retreat home to the total silence of the islands.

Another cousin, Phillip "the Horseman" O'Reilly, lived nearby in great, great grandfather Lynch's house and farmstead. He raised and bred Irish racing horses, one of which he had recently sold to the stables of the Queen of England. By that time British money was being happily accepted. Business in Ireland was moving into the modern world.

We got to know and love all of the Irish cousins and virtually all of Ireland, as well, through our many side trips before and after Cavan. There was always something new to discover and always another beautiful spot we had not yet seen.

Donegal and its barren seacoast, its peculiar Errigal Mountain and the fairyland forests, although often chilly, became one of our favorite stops. Leo Brennan's pub in Bunbeg near the sea, we learned, was home base of the popular New Age singers Enya, Máire and Clannad. Leo himself performed frequently and introduced many new artists to the stage. Dozens of gold and platinum records earned by family members lined the pub walls.

What fun it was to visit Leo's pub for the first time. Ellen talked to the barman, as he poured us a Guinness.

"I'm looking for Leo Brennan," she said. "Do you know where I might find him?"

"You're looking at him, young lady!" the barman answered with a wry smile as he poured the foaming brew. We stayed the day, making friends with locals, and joined in the singing that night. Leo himself sang his own version of *Come Back Paddy Reilly to Ballyjamesduff.*

And how beautiful it is in County Mayo in May when the purple rhododendrons are in bloom!

When stopping at a remote but grand fishing lodge in Leenane for a bit of a snack, we learned that the dramatic fight scene from the movie, *The Field*, was filmed at the base of the waterfall at the head of the pond right across the roadway. Richard Harris and Tom Berringer spent weeks in the area creating an Irish classic.

Leenane is very near the famed mountain of Crough Patrick, where St. Patrick himself retreated for 40 days and 40 nights some 1,500 years earlier. He was not there to avoid a flood, but to find his place with God. While he was there, legend has it, he chased the snakes out of Ireland once and for all. There are a number of myths surrounding this event, but the truth is Ireland never had any snakes to chase away. The island was cut off from the mainland by open seas during the Ice Ages, before snakes could migrate across the land.

We always stayed at home-style bed and breakfast accommodations and used those occasions to get to know what was going on locally and to make new friendships. Each trip, each personal contact and friendship, each stay at a B&B and each bit of Irish knowledge drove our interest even higher. The Irish points were adding up at an astonishing rate, although we had yet to assign any numbers to our game.

We even began looking at property in County Cavan, around the many lakes in the area. At one point we composed a letter to cousin Sean O'Reilly asking if he might sell the site of the old Lynch family cottage, but we never mailed it. The kids still had a way to go to finish college, and we had other matters to attend. We decided it was too soon for us to make a commitment.

Chapter 24

The Good,
the Bad and Superman

*T*he years that followed our first visit to County Cavan were mixed
with the normal challenges of raising a family with two teenage
daughters, meeting the scheduling demands of a lot of skiing and
frequent family trips to Montana, growing responsibilities at our
work, and in my case, somewhat faltering health.

As we found ourselves moving closer to the vortex, we also
found ourselves working hard to stay along the edges. It felt at
times as if we were engaged in a tug of war, mentally ready to
pack up and leave for Ireland, but inescapably tied to a life in
Colorado.

The Cavan connection sparked a major wave of interest in family
history on the Montana front.

Ellen's mother, who already had the reputation as the family
storyteller, took my challenge on one of our visits to write her
memoir before it was forgotten. A few months later she surprised
us with nearly 200 pages of rough-typed manuscript. For the next
two years I found myself editing, revising and probing more deeply
into the family history based at the ranch on Rosebud Creek.

The end product was a lovely book entitled *Through the Rosebuds: Tales of Rosebud Creek, Montana.* We sold out the entire

printing within six months, mostly to Montana libraries, schools, history buffs, friends and relatives.

The book project spurned even more interest in the family roots, and that gave us still another excuse for shoring up connections in Ireland. We gave a copy of the *Rosebuds* book to each family in Cavan so they would know of their ties to Montana, and we donated a copy to the Cavan town library as well.

The chief librarian at the Cavan library was delighted and staged a photo shoot of the "handing over" ceremony for the Cavan newspaper. He then offered to help us find the family birth records.

Most vital records for the county were stored in that very same library building. Within an hour we found ourselves viewing the original birth registration for Alice Lynch, Ellen's grandmother, who was born on March 29, 1876.

Every entry on the ledger page was preceded with an "x" and a signature, which, upon close examination, was by the same hand. The librarian reminded us that none of the local Irish could read or write. The local notary signed for them.

We were looking at her grandmother's official birth record — a key document in the process of establishing citizenship for Ellen, should we ever want to do so. With only a few more documents such as marriage certificates, she would have everything she needed. Ellen decided to apply. The process of gathering the remaining papers took at least a year, but we were in no rush.

Even while immersed in producing *Through the Rosebuds*, I was often distracted and distressed over the notion that my real purpose in life might be to make some kind of earth-shaking contribution to the world of trade associations. I gave dozens of presentations on the subject and wrote numerous articles for association publications.

Feeling very intellectual at one point and much like a crusader, I signed up for a People-to-People Economic Study Tour to Eastern Europe, soon after the fall of the Berlin Wall. It was that wall, which brought me over to Europe so long ago when it went up, that brought me back yet again, but for another reason.

The days of our study tour were filled with a series of meetings and lectures in Berlin, Budapest, Prague, and Warsaw. The nights were filled with social functions involving business leaders and government officials. A former U.S. Ambassador to Czechoslovakia was our tour guide. I kept pace with the tour, but I knew I was not functioning very well. My health was slipping, causing me to sleep on the bus rides between sessions and location. I couldn't put a finger on what was wearing me down.

Then, after almost a decade of nearly continuous success as head of the retail lumber association, my job started falling to pieces. The association side of the office was doing exceptionally well. From all outward appearances, everything was rosy and an example to many of my colleagues throughout the country.

Unfortunately, the health insurance program, which occupied the other side of the office and was a primary benefit for about a third of our members, was on a fast track to disaster. We couldn't raise the rates fast enough to pay for the group's rising medical costs, and the Association was accumulating an enormous debt. I began to fear that the retail lumber dealers had the least healthy group of employees in the entire world.

Once the insurance committee accepted the fact that the future was hopeless, I was asked to make a commitment for the next two years to serve as "captain of the sinking ship."

Our objective was to reduce debt as much as possible through a rapid succession of rate increases and then liquidate at a point where the financial damage would be minimal. The association side of the office remained very strong and active throughout the drama, while the health insurance side of the office continued to crumble away, destroying my future along with it.

A most critical part of my job as "captain" was to keep all of this a secret and to keep on smiling, no matter how bad the future appeared. We couldn't afford a panic that would cause a complete financial collapse.

It shouldn't have come as a surprise, but I had a hard time dealing with the situation. If I were to consult with a trauma specialist today, I would know that an episode such as the Flying Tiger crash so many years ago does not strengthen the spirit. In fact, major trauma tends to undermine a person's ability to deal with prolonged stress in the future.

I wasn't the steel-willed and invincible storm trooper I used to be. The only remnants of my "blood and guts" era were the frequent bursts of pent-up anger I had worked so hard to bring under control. I found myself fantasizing ingenious methods and means of merciless revenge for those responsible for my pain.

Sick thoughts, I've heard, can lead one to real sickness. Far too often I found my face smiling while my brain proceeded to process an entirely different script. Some of those guys — businessmen they like to call themselves — became in my mind little more than sniveling cheaters, whining and crying over the relatively small financial assessment needed to cover their prior underpayments and dismal hiring practices.

It was during this period that the long-suppressed thought with its roots in that horrid night of the Flying Tiger — the thought I could never divulge in conversation and that I had virtually forced out of my mind after my session with the shrink in Bad Kreuznach more than two decades earlier — rose again to the surface.

How I wished some of those complainers had been floating with me in the freezing ocean among the debris of the Flying Tiger. I wanted to show them what a real disaster was like. I even fantasized with sadistic pleasure, refusing to help them into the life raft, or maybe pulling them part way in, then letting my hands slip away. In fits of rage — even the most professionally suppressed fits of rage — thoughts like that can bring a person close to nausea.

I was paid well to stay to the bitter end and I did so, even though it was not a good decision on my part. By liquidation day, the $4 million mountain of debt was cut by nearly 90 percent to less than four hundred thousand dollars.

Unfortunately, even that level of success was little cause for joy. To many people, any level of loss in business is totally unacceptable. I was a hero to no one and a sleazeball to many.

Once the dust settled, I was free to leave.

But not to worry! Ellen's association management business had grown beyond her capacity to handle it alone, so I didn't have to look for another job. We were working again as "Frelen," pretty much as we had nearly three decades earlier in Montana. I was soon doing exactly the same type of work I had been doing with the lumber association, but I was doing it for several more interesting organizations, without any involvement in health insurance programs.

Even with a safety chute close at hand, losing a job for any reason is a blow to the ego. I was feeling very badly beaten.

It was worse than one might expect under similar conditions. I assumed I was down in the dumps about business. It might have been stress and depression, repressed anger and frustration, but the condition slowly worsened even when life was good. I was always tired, increasingly irritable and sometimes light headed and dizzy. I could hardly stay awake at meetings. I was going to bed early and getting up late and still felt as if I hadn't even gone to bed.

My prolonged ailment, which grew over a period of several years, was becoming chronic.

Our family physician couldn't find any physical deficiencies. Tests showed no obvious medical issues. In view of my history with the Flying Tiger and the past several years of stress on the job, my doctor suggested I make an appointment with a medical psychiatrist for an introductory consultation. Under normal circumstances I would have objected at even the suggestion I might need a headshrinker, but by that time I was in no condition to argue.

To ensure that I wouldn't fall in the hands of a shrink who might be experiencing a slow time at the office or in need of new business, I made appointments with two different doctors in the same week. I wanted an immediate second opinion.

Both psychiatrists drew the same conclusion within the first ten minutes of my visit. I was a walking zombie due to lack of sleep. I wasn't going nuts after all.

Even though I appeared to be sleeping longer and longer all of the time, they both suspected I was suffering from an advanced case of sleep apnea due to obstructed breathing. I was hardly sleeping. The minute I fell asleep, my throat tissues relaxed, breathing stopped, and I abruptly awoke, only to repeat the process hundreds of times a night. The condition could not be detected while awake.

My long months of sleep deprivation, compounded by a prolonged bout of depression, caused a series of damaging side effects. Most challenging for me was the destruction of several basic and important emotional mood-states.

I lost the ability to experience exhilaration, elation and delight, all of which are associated with the joy of skiing — such as when you break air on a jump on a steep slope covered with fresh powder. It should be a thrill to race down the hill, but I had lost the feeling. You could have thrown me out of an airplane, without a parachute, and I would have quietly and unemotionally waited for the sudden stop. It was surprising to me to experience how important those feelings are to one's everyday motivation. Yes, it was depression, but chronic fatigue compounded the damage.

Throat surgery cleared the breathing obstructions, and reasonably normal sleep was restored. But that was only a start. I had to try to get my psyche back to normal. My medical and psychiatric advisors had very few suggestions, so I began my own therapy. My objective was to restore joy and exhilaration.

How did I do it? I committed myself to a regimen of all things uplifting, joyful *and* Irish.

Every possible moment was spent listening to audiotapes of Irish jokes — silly, rib-tickling nonsense — starting with my favorite, Hal Roach, who was then considered the King of Irish Comedy. Owing to my extremely short memory for jokes, each time I heard the same silly story, I found myself laughing harder than the previous time. I began laughing my way back to enthusiasm.

The joke tapes were eventually supplemented with lively Irish music — hours and hours of Irish jigs and reels and beautiful Irish airs that elevate the heart. And then there were as many Irish-theme movies as I could find, such as *Ryan's Daughter*, *The Playboys*, *The Quiet Man*, *The Field*, and my favorite, *The Secret of Roan Inish*, about a remote cluster of islands off the coast of Ireland where "seal people," *selkies*, become real people.

Ireland became my therapy.

Ireland was making me human again, and I began to make up for the many Irish points I passed up during my period of low energy.

Ireland lifted my spirits. I wanted to be more Irish.

But wasn't I meant for something special? Certainly whatever it was had to be more important than chasing leprechauns and fairies and much more important than listening to harps and jigs.

The notion continued to nag at me — that God saved me to do something special, whatever that something was — and I was disliking the idea just a little more each time it came to mind. It simply didn't seem fair that I should have to be the one to figure out why I was saved.

It was that damned plane crash!

Fate put me in the wrong airplane at the wrong time only to find salvation in the perfectly right rubber life raft floating at the perfectly right point in the ocean during just the right windstorm. Frankly, I thought that Lady Luck could have done better than that.

Couldn't I have won the lottery instead?

I could hardly enjoy doing what I liked to do while burdened with the need to find that other elusive, but more worthy purpose.

That was until one Saturday morning when my clock radio turned on to a program commemorating the 50th anniversary of the comic superhero, the caped man of steel, Superman.

I was ready for a kick in the butt, and Superman was about to do just that. His own identity crisis put my lifelong drama into a different perspective.

It was *Weekend Edition* on National Public Radio. Scott Simon was interviewing the owner of the Superman comic franchise. It was a lively, upbeat segment where both marveled at the super hero's accomplishments and his endless string of good deeds over the past 50 years.

The interview was coming to a close.

"One last question," Simon said, adding the words, "and this is a serious question."

He paused for an instant – a pause intended to command attention — and continued:

"A lot of people wonder," he said, hesitating again with a purposeful pause.

"Was Superman Jewish, by chance? Or, was Superman Irish Catholic?"

Both broke into laughter. Simon interrupted, still chuckling, with a clarification, apologizing to listeners who might not understand the inside joke.

Superman, he explained, was never depicted as smiling in the comic books. It was not until the motion picture screen that Superman was ever seen smiling. He was frequently seen in the early comics sitting at Lois Lane's kitchen table, with his Superman cape draped across his hunched shoulders, showing a dour, joyless face as if he was downright depressed.

Superman might have just come in from having rescued a school bus from falling off a cliff, an airplane falling out of the sky or performing any number of superhuman deeds. No matter what the heroics, Superman appeared as if he had gotten very little satisfaction from his accomplishments. Many readers were left wondering about the source of Superman's distress.

Simon played the question a little further.

"While most mortal men would be pounding their chest with joy," he said, "Superman seemed to be trapped in a state of inner conflict."

He said, "People wonder, was Superman suffering from the Jewish sense of inadequacy or guilt because there was so much more to be done?" After all, Simon mused, Superman was sitting there at Lois Lane's table doing nothing. He might have felt he should be flying about doing more good deeds.

"Or," he asked, "was Superman experiencing the Irish sense of humility or embarrassment that one should not be gloating over one's accomplishments? One should be humble, you know."

They both had another chuckle. In either case, they agreed, Superman came across in the comics as a depressed and unhappy super hero, perhaps because of those conflicting emotions.

I wasn't sure. Should I call in to comment? But if I did call in, what would I say? Was it a Jewish influence, or Irish Catholic? In either case, it was pretty silly. I knew that a person's social world shapes the individual's experience of the world, but I hadn't thought about it that way.

That radio interview started of a new line of thinking for me.

Why should accomplishment and success cause apprehension and discomfort? I called the conflict "the Superman Paradox."

I decided that if anyone, Superman included, could feel a certain way because he had unconsciously adopted a way of thinking from his cultural environment — and that another person from another culture experiencing the same situation could experience a different set of feelings for different, but seemingly logical reasons — then, why couldn't I create my own cultural environment? I could pick and choose the parts I liked best and adopt my favorite points of view.

I had come a long way since Father Kennedy gave me his bit of advice some 30 years earlier at Lee Barracks. He made me keenly aware of a bad habit I had acquired from my childhood surroundings. He told me, "Being bitter won't make you better." I really didn't feel bitter but acted that way simply out of habit. It was the way the people I knew acted, but it was not necessarily how they felt. I still had a lot of bad habits holding me back.

Learning about Ireland, its past and its present, and the Irish people, took on a new meaning as I proceeded to discover more about myself. I wanted to adopt what I liked best. I wanted to identify and avoid all bad habits that might diminish my experience. I wanted the best of Ireland and the best of the Irish people. I was on a quest to create my own world of Irishness.

In the meantime, while I spent my days and weeks wandering off on my mental, philosophical journey, listening to Irish jokes and songs and entertaining images of leprechauns and fairies, Ellen kept busy with day-to-day activities.

She set her mind to getting her Irish citizenship as a foreign-born national the moment she learned that she was entitled to it. Her grandmother was born in Derrylea, County Cavan. She had the birth record. She located her grandmother's marriage certificate proving the lineage, and then was able to do the same for her mother, although that proved to be more difficult. Margaret had been delivered by a Cheyenne Indian midwife at the ranch home without a doctor's presence. Her "official" birth record was hard to locate.

It was a long process, but she got it done. I would become eligible for Irish citizenship as the spouse of a foreign-born national three years later.

Months after the Superman interview, during a June visit with Fergus and Nuala Lynch at their Holywell Lodge on the shores of Lough Sheelen, I borrowed a motorboat and made my way across the water to the solitude of Church Island. I wanted to get away, to be alone with my thoughts. I wanted to write a few notes on whatever might come to mind.

As I approached the island, something abruptly happened to the engine. The motor raced wildly, but I stopped moving forward. The propeller seemed to quit turning. I had to row the rest of the way to shore, but I didn't mind. It was so much more peaceful without the sound of an engine.

Once beached on the tiny island, I found a quiet clearing and began thinking about how I wanted to write about my love of Ireland. I felt like I was following in the footsteps of Butler and Yeats. As so many other writers before me, I was overflowing with something to say, but didn't know where to start.

With pen in hand, I opened to a blank page in my notebook. What to say? In the silence of the forest on Church Island, the first word to come out was "Superman," which, by then, I was beginning to suspect I was not. The second word was "Ireland," a place where I wanted to be.

I began writing all that came to mind, making note of the quiet, the water, the solitude and my love affair with Ireland. I was alone and at home. I was at peace at that moment on a secluded island, lost to all humanity.

But not for long!

Within minutes of starting my life story, two burly fishermen walked up to me from along the shore. They could tell I was having trouble with my boat engine and wanted to help. I didn't realize it, but the propeller struck a rock and the sheer pin broke off. That was why I had to row the boat to shore.

I knew I'd have to get back eventually, so I was appreciative of their help. The fishermen fixed my sheer pin and floated off in their boat to let me return to my thoughts. (Damn! It is a wonder any of the world's problems ever get solved with all of those nice people interrupting important thoughts while insisting on doing nice things for people like me.)

I understood at that moment why the Celts and the Vikings and the Christian monks of ancient Ireland always sought out the most remote and rugged islands for their contemplation. At that point I gave up trying to find a destination other than Ireland itself. I decided to quit thinking about what I *should* be doing and focus on what I *was* doing at the moment. I was finally free to experience the magic of Ireland, its history, its drama and its love.

BORN AGAIN IRISH - *O'Caruso*

Chapter 25

Peadar's Wedding and On to Galley Head

*I*t was great news. Cousin Peadar was to be married in Cork City, the home of his bride-to-be, Linda.

Peadar was the first of the Cavan clan to take us up on our invitation to visit Colorado. He was the eldest of Paddy and Maureen Gill's eight children and the only one of the family we had not yet met. He always seemed to be off to school somewhere when we visited his family, so he had to come to see us in order to meet for the first time.

Peadar had just finished his education in what we understood to be electronics, as in perhaps TV repair. We learned that electronics was a more humble way of saying electrical engineering. Peadar decided to take his first few months as a new graduate to work in New York City for an Irish construction contractor. He wanted to see what he might be missing in the States before starting a professional career in Ireland.

I was to meet him at the old Denver Stapleton Airport. All I knew was that he would be wearing a "Prince" T-shirt, whatever that was. I was told you couldn't miss him. He was a very slim and lanky young fellow.

Yes, he was easy to spot. He was the one who looked very lost, very thin and very foreign, carrying only an old gym bag.

And, yes, he was wearing a tattered T-shirt that said, "Prince," something which had no meaning to me but must have been important to him.

It happens that he arrived the same day as our Washington, D.C., friends, Harold and Lyda Gray, who were in Colorado to attend the Central City Jazz Festival. Both were fanatical Dixie Land Jazz buffs. Harold, who by then was in his mid-80s and not looking or acting a day older than 50, was well on his way through the leadership chairs of the National Jazz Federation. Central City was an old mining town about 40 miles west of Denver, recently renovated and converted to a city-wide gambling center.

The Dixie Land Jazz groups moved from one venue to the next, playing about 45 minutes at each, according to an intricate printed schedule. This allowed fans to hear their favorite bands under different conditions in different locations, or to hear different groups playing in one spot. Gambling was available everywhere, of course, but optional.

Everything in Central City had been completely restored to its 1880s splendor. The casino and restaurant workers were required to wear authentic costumes of the period. Barmaids were fitted in the extremely revealing, low-cut dresses of the frontier days, which purposely and effectively emphasized their feminine assets.

One especially well-endowed waitress placed a drink before us — Harold, Peadar and me — pausing in her forward position for a deliberate degree of emphasis as if holding a pose for a photo. I resisted the urge to take a picture. Peadar nearly gasped.

As she turned away, finally, he whispered in his sheepish Cavan accent, "Did you get a good look at that?"

Well, how could I avoid getting a look?

His voice raised to slightly more than a whisper.

"Her frock was putting up a fierce fight just to hold her in." He took a quick breath. "And it looked for a minute as if the frock was going to lose."

The consummate gentleman Harold pretended to pay no attention, although I detected a very serious well-hidden grin. I tried to be indifferent, but Peadar's quip caught me by surprise. I burst into a riot of laughter.

It turned out that the shy and modest Peadar was a "closet comedian" along the lines of W.C. Fields and Woody Allen, as well as being an intellectual and a visionary. He not only tickled my funny bone, but he kept me posted on the progress of the Irish economy. By that point Ireland was beginning to be recognized throughout Europe as the restless and roaring Celtic Tiger.

By the way, Peadar was an Irishman who had taken "the pledge" as a young man, which meant he had taken a religious vow not to ever take a drink, even though others in his family would have a "wee tip" now and again. It was part of the Catholic Church's plan to stamp out the evils of whiskey. The pledge was fairly common during that era.

I arranged a field trip through the Rocky Mountains the day following our visit to Central City to show him around Colorado and to make a few business-related social calls. In three short days, we drove nearly 750 miles, or about three times the length of Ireland, and we did most of it traversing a dozen or more 10,000-foot-high mountain passes and through 14,000-foot snow covered peaks. It gave us plenty of time to get acquainted, to share ideas on the economics and future of Ireland, and share droll Irish jokes.

Peadar could certainly put on a show, acting as I have heard it said of some storytellers, "as bent as a leprechaun's slipper." He filled me in on all of the "Cavan man" jokes and how the Cavan man was known throughout Ireland as being "mean" because of his compulsive frugality.

Everyone knew the jokes so I needed to know them, too. For instance, everyone in Ireland knows that copper wire was invented in Cavan when two men discovered it by accident while fighting over a copper penny.

And everyone knew that the Cavan man learned how to peel an orange in his pocket so he wouldn't have to share it with anyone.

And you know, of course, that all kitchen tables in Cavan came equipped with drawers. That was because the Cavan man ate his dinner in the drawer in case he was surprised by unexpected company. All he had to do was close the drawer to hide his meal. Yes, I learned, everyone in Ireland knew about the mean, stingy and compulsively frugal Cavan man.

It seemed like no time had passed at all when we learned of Cousin Peadar's wedding.

Peadar knew that both Ellen and I were handy with camera equipment and asked if we could consider taking photos of the event. Of course we would. We assumed that maybe there was a shortage of photographers in Cork City as there was in eastern Montana when we were married. We were flattered with the request. Wedding invitations had been extended to Ellen's mother and brother as well.

Although it was an especially busy year for us, we decided nothing was going to stop our being part of the wedding. We would be leading a party that included Cowboy Hugh and his wife, Evelyn, and Grandma Marg. We were veterans at planning Irish travel by then and loved showing others around.

The trip went well from Denver to Newark and onto London-Gatwick Airport, with one exception. The travel bag that had all of my clothing for the trip, including my dress clothes for the wedding, didn't make it as far as we had. Fortunately I carried my camera equipment with me aboard the plane. The airline promised to send the missing bag on to Cork the moment it arrived. We proceeded to Ireland from London.

We stayed at a familiar B&B very near the Blarney Castle, just a few miles north of Cork City. The B&B was owned by Brandon and Maria Dooley, who had become our friends by then through previous trips. In spite of grand promises by the airline and good intentions of the staff, my luggage never showed up. The evening before the wedding, Brandon, who was good at pouring a tall glass of Irish whiskey and offering a strong measure of Irish humor, gave me a semi-dress shirt and a not-so-attractive tie to wear at the event.

By the next morning I had accepted the fact that I would be wearing my weathered Levi western jeans, white athletic sneakers and a shirt that was way too tight for me. I couldn't come close to buttoning the collar, but, what the heck, the garish green tie looked at least a little bit Irish. I couldn't turn down Brandon's offering.

After two frantic hours of preparation at the B&B, which included organizing Ellen's aging mother and her brother and her sister-in-law, as well as piecing together a uniform for myself, we found the church at the edge of Cork City's very confusing downtown. We had a map, but it seemed to be of little help. We were hoping for more time to prepare for our photo shoots, but were happy to have found the church at all.

We were actually a half hour ahead of schedule, even after missing a few turns along the way. That gave us enough time to study the church building, its entrances and exits and the best places for photos with the least disruption. It would be an exquisite affair.

The church was filling up with families, friends and well-wishers, all dressed in their finest. Although I didn't fit very well with the wedding party, all decked out in fine tuxedos and wedding gowns, no one seemed concerned or even acted as if they noticed or even knew who we were.

Ellen loves special events. It's the nature of her business. She enjoyed taking command of the photography and reminded me that I had one particularly important "must do" job before the ceremony really got under way.

My mission was to get photos of the bride and her father at the front of the church as they exited the limousine. They would be organizing for the grand entrance march. Of course, I had never met the bride nor her father before the wedding.

Peadar and his entourage of attending men were in the parking area behind the church organizing for their part of the ceremony. Ellen reminded me of my mission, which was to intercept the bride and her father before they stepped out of the limo. Before, not after!

"Yes, indeed," I assured her. I would fill that request with some of the best photos they had ever seen. Not to worry in the least.

I may not have looked the part, but I certainly knew what I

was doing when it came to taking wedding pictures.

I found the other half of the wedding party out front. The father and bride had just arrived in their limo and I darned near missed it. I began snapping photos the moment the limousine came to a stop to make sure I didn't miss a thing.

It didn't bother me at all that Linda and her father watched me with some degree of skepticism. Admittedly I wasn't dressed for the occasion as I had hoped to be. My shirt was a terrible fit, the green tie bordered on atrocious, but my faded blue jeans and white athletic shoes were fairly decent by Colorado standards. I did wear a belt, but wore no jacket of course - not that it would have added anything.

Not to worry! Photographers tend to be a little eccentric. I wasn't there to look good. I was there to get great photos.

Linda and her father adjusted quickly and were accommodating, perhaps a bit amused. Maybe I helped them relax. I was good at getting people to settle down enough to strike the perfect pose.

After doing a spectacular job of posing and snapping scene one, I reported back to Ellen and Peadar and the gathering groomsmen. They informed me that things were running a wee bit late.

"Way behind schedule," they repeated after I indicated that I hadn't caught a word of what they said. I might as well take a break, they told me. It would be at least another 45 minutes before the other wedding finished. Linda and her father wouldn't be arriving for some time.

"You must be joking," I thought, in total astonishment after what I had just done.

I didn't have to say it. They could see it on my face. I just shot some of the best photos I had taken in years of the wrong father and the wrong bride as they organized for their grand entrance on the other side of the church.

Again, nothing to worry about. We had plenty of film. Ellen took the exposed rolls of film to the right person in the other wedding party to save me the embarrassment of doing so. They were very happy and loved the photos, we learned later, and hardly anyone else was the wiser.

The wedding was a grand affair. The reception was held in a hall in the seaside village of Kinsale, some 15 miles west of Cork City, and our mission was accomplished. Many of the Cavan relatives came south for the event.

There was dancing and drinking and celebrating until the cows came home.

A few more years passed. Ireland grew ever more important in our lives. We tried to keep our minds open to other countries and traveled to other places including England, Scotland, Germany, Ecuador and Peru, but Ireland was always at the top of our list. We could hardly bear to stay away.

Peadar and Linda gave us a good reason to pay close attention to County Cork. They visited us in Colorado with their first child, knowing that a growing family would eventually make stateside travel difficult. At the top of Linda's wish list was to find fresh snow in the mountains. She wanted to make a snow angel, take a photo of it, and bring it home. Southwest Ireland rarely sees snowfall and never enough for making snow angels. The region is noted for its mild climate.

Peadar took an interest in the Flying Tiger crash and did some research at the local library on the Irish newspaper coverage of the event, sending me a thick folder of news stories copied from microfilm archives. One of the stories traced the rescue flight from the *Celerina*, across the Galley Head peninsula and on into Cork. I hadn't seen that amount of detail in the few articles my parents had saved for me. I made a mental note that some day I would like to take a look at that flight path.

It was through Peadar that I became very much aware of Ireland's economic revival and the rise of the Celtic Tiger. I started following news reports. Times were changing and we were witnessing many of the changes during our frequent travels.

Finally, a few years later, it was time for us to make a pilgrimage to that point a little west of Cork City where my eyes first caught sight of Irish soil. It would be in recognition of the 35th anniversary of the Flying Tiger crash.

We spent the evening before at Peadar and Linda's home near Cork Airport. By this time they had two children and were quite involved in the economic future of the Republic. Peadar was at the high-tech center of activity, working as much in Paris and Singapore as he did in Cork. It was obvious that the youth of Ireland were moving into the mainstream of global economics.

A few weeks before our trip, the *Wall Street Journal* ran an article about Kinsale being the hottest recreational area in all of Europe. Peadar and Linda added more information to what we knew and expanded our awareness of Ireland's growing potential.

We proceeded on our pilgrimage after our evening in Cork and drove about 15 miles to the west.

We located the beach on the point known as Galley Head. The fog and mist were lifting over the waters in the bay. Ellen wandered off on the beach far ahead to leave me in my thoughts. I was gripped with emotion.

How long ago? Thirty-five years. Unbelievable. All of those good things that happened since that dreadful night at sea!

The sadness and tears were getting the upper hand. It was not sadness for me or the Flying Tiger, or any of my memories of woe. I was being swept up in a desperate state of grieving for others — the millions and millions of despair-ridden Irish who left the sod against their will. Ireland, the land of their love, the nation of their hearts, the country of their heritage and the soil of their passions. Ireland is so easy to love and so desperately hard to leave.

There I was with barely a hardship in the world except for the troubles we tend to invent and dramatize as a way to rationalize our good fortune. I was not especially wealthy, but certainly better off than many others. Certainly my family and I were rich in freedom of choice — a freedom which so few Irish of years past enjoyed. Starvation and desperation have a way of robbing humanity of options.

The unusually quiet ocean lapped ashore, by now soaking my shoes above the ankles. I was there, exactly where they wanted to be — they being the millions of Irish-born who were forced to

246

leave their love behind, their beloved country, their friends and family, their history and their heritage. I could feel it. Their love for that land right beneath my feet.

They had to accept sorrow and leave, or die of starvation. If only I could have some of this turf. Just a little bit of this Emerald Island that allowed me to start all over, to be literally born again Irish.

My God, I had the freedom those millions did not have. I could stay if I wanted to stay. I couldn't hold back.

Ellen was further along on the beach, thankfully. She shouted something from a distance. The fog was lifting. The landscape was coming clear. I had to see what I hadn't seen before.

I cleared my eyes and was glad for the sunglasses. They hid the tears I couldn't hold inside.

The newspaper story reported that this was where we crossed. Our ship, the *Celerina* was right off shore and the helicopter shuttled us across the terrain to the landing field at the Cork airport.

I couldn't immediately connect the misty land and sea before me with what I had observed from five hundred feet above on a brilliant, sunny day, coming from a completely different direction, but I tried. How I wished I could pinpoint the cottage where that beautiful Irish farm woman abandoned the view of us above to chase the sheep through the back door of her home. What an impression of Ireland. Was she beautiful? Of course she was. Everything was beautiful that day.

No matter, recognize the landscape or not, I was home with a treasure beyond the reach of so many, that freedom to come or go. I wanted to take more steps toward staying.

My purpose was becoming clear.

I was to be more than just "born again Irish." My purpose was to be Irish for real, to be Irish in heart and soul.

Chapter 26

The Jewel
of Glengarriff

*B*antry town and the Beara Peninsula to the west were our destination after reconnecting with Galley Head. We were committed to exploring real estate in West County Cork.

By then we had decided against settling in the rolling hills of County Cavan, right against the southern border of Northern Ireland. Although the borders were open by that time, attitudes and tensions remained relatively high over the "troubles." West Cork was far to the south. Conversations in that corner of the nation reflected the distance. All was calm, friendly and quiet.

Our kids were finished with college and getting on with their lives. Our business was humming along in Colorado, and the Celtic Tiger was beginning to roar throughout Europe.

We had a little money to invest. It wasn't much, but we wanted to see what we could do with what we had. We would look at property for the fun of it, with no pressure to buy.

Bantry is a small, colorful village at the far eastern end of Bantry Bay. It is the point at which you begin to see significant mountains up to 3,000 feet high. It is where the rolling farmland changes to craggy, mountainous grazing fields. Bantry was a good place to begin gathering real estate information.

Real estate sellers like appointments, but we as prospective buyers preferred to take a look from the road to see if the location warranted a stop. We looked at a few properties from the road, but kept on driving, not liking what we saw. We went further west to where the land becomes even more rugged, changing into glacial mountains. We began to feel more at home.

The village of Glengarriff, which sits at the eastern edge of the Beara Peninsula, had an unusually comfortable feel about it, a strong sense of familiarity. Maybe it was the climate that allows palm trees and tropical plants to grow in profusion. Maybe it was the large number of seals sunning in the bay that caught our imagination. It might have been the number of interesting and friendly pubs, or the beautiful religious grotto of the Virgin Mary at the edge of town, or the surrounding mountains and native oak forests. Whatever it was, Glengarriff felt right.

A tiny cottage on an acre of land was available just two miles out of town. It was in need of repair but was in our price range.

I was tired of looking after a long day of seeing mostly undesirable wrecks and after getting stuck in a ditch on the way to the worst of them, but Ellen insisted we stop. It was along our way, on the road toward Kenmare. She was driving and found the obscure, hairpin turn by sheer chance. The entry drive was very steep and rutted and the property was a quarter mile up the hill. I wanted to head back.

We knew we were there when we found, standing in the overgrown walkway, farmer Noel O'Mahoney, a tall, thin, late middle-aged bachelor, in his rubber boots, patched work pants and tattered sweater. Just exactly as we might have expected him to be. It was as if he had been waiting for us at that exact moment, although we hadn't phoned ahead.

Not to bother. He put out his hand in welcome, and, with a friendly smile, invited us to come in. The sun was brilliant and the newly painted cottage was dazzling yellow gold. In that incredible Irish way, Noel led us inside and offered us a wee touch of whiskey. It was well before noon.

Noel's cottage had only the barest of furnishings and a very low ceiling, which we learned was to help keep the heat within. We sat in small metal and plastic armchairs. He sat across from us on a plastic covered couch. He was framed on either side by large portraits of Jesus and the Blessed Virgin. Two built-in, flickering electric candles were on the wall near the portraits, showing his continuous reverence. No doubt about it, we were in Ireland.

The price Noel was seeking for his homestead and the fact that he planned to build very nearby and would keep an eye on things while we were gone seemed to us to be a dream come true. We couldn't stay too long that morning as, in our American way of being, we had a schedule to keep. We would discuss the proposition along the way to our next destination and phone back. We would be returning in a few days on our way back to the airport.

After soaking in as much of the view and the sight of the property as we could, we left with our minds full of ideas.

Before we got to Kenmare, only 20 miles away, we had pages of notes, comparisons and rationale. We wanted to be away from traffic, but fairly close to town. We wanted to be near the sea, but we loved the mountains and forests. The house was affordable and livable. We worked through our wish lists and found every desire met, with a lot more thrown in. Noel's farmstead looked like it was meant to be our Irish home. We rang that evening to assure him of our interest.

After a few evenings of traditional pub music in Galway, we headed back south to Glengarriff. The closer we got, the more our anticipation grew.

We drove past Noel's turn off and went first to our B&B on the other side of town to arrange our room for the night. We then popped in at the old Eccles Hotel Pub for a pint as we us gathered our thoughts.

It was there, at the Eccles, where we learned from a local real estate agent that Noel's property had been on the market for some time. A number of buyers were turned away by one of the aspects that attracted us the most. Others didn't like the idea that the house was in the center of a working livestock farm. Most of the farm buildings were located within sight of the house. Ellen grew up in the center of a working ranch in Montana. Knowing that someone would always be nearby, working with the livestock or the farm equipment, was comforting to her.

We worked out a deal. We would buy the boggy field east of the house and all of the nearest farm buildings, including the big hay shed. Noel would keep the cow barn in his property. It was to the rear of the house and out of sight. We were happy to have Noel use the buildings for a period of years without charge simply for the knowledge that someone was close by, watching the property. He would have to walk by at least twice a day caring for his cows.

Noel had been born in that little cottage and was very protective of the property. Our enthusiasm grew by the minute. We made our verbal commitment and went back to town and our B&B.

As the dark of night advanced, however, an extreme case of buyer's remorse set in. It was the worst case that either of us had experienced in our lives. It is one thing to dream about an ideal, but it is another to be confronted with it as a reality. As we tried to reconstruct our picture of the future, we started asking ourselves, "What if our daughters need our help? Could we afford to help them and buy the cottage, too?"

Our joy turned into despair as we spent an agonizing night thinking about the prospects and knew we had to call the next day to rescind our offer. Maybe it was all too good to be true. Maybe we were being way too hasty. Maybe it was a silly idea.

That morning, from an extremely lonely and depressing phone booth at the edge of the parking area at the Eccles Hotel, I made the phone call to Noel to say we simply couldn't go through with the purchase. I would have preferred being burned at the stake over a slow fire than to make that call, but I did so with a downcast heart. Noel was disappointed, but seemed to be understanding. It was done.

We left Glengarriff in a state of mourning. Two very distraught Americans, driving directly to the Cork airport and barely uttering a word along the way. We turned in our rental car and boarded a plane to London Heathrow. From there we had planned an additional three days of visiting in England with British friends but we were too depressed to stay. Frankly, we were miserable. We paid a very substantial penalty to change our airline tickets to go home on the next available flight, never stepping out of the airport.

Within hours of arriving back in Colorado, both daughters assured us they wouldn't be needing our help. They couldn't believe we would chicken out of such a deal. In fact, they were disappointed. We should have gone ahead with the buy.

It took very little convincing at that point in time. We knew we had made a dreadful mistake. The opportunity of a lifetime had been thrown away to an irrational wave of fear.

Well, maybe not yet. We wanted that little cottage, our farmhouse, our jewel. We wanted it very badly. There might still be a glimmer of hope. Maybe there was a chance.

We scrambled through our notes and papers and crafted a script. We were ready to beg an apology of Noel and ask that we be reconsidered for the purchase. We rang Noel the very next morning, and he answered as if he had been waiting for our call.

Another couple from England had stopped by soon after we left and expressed an interest, but Noel conceded he would rather do business with a couple as committed to Ireland as we appeared to be. The sale was on again.

Thanks be to God! Yahoo! We were overjoyed. The bright yellow farmhouse at the head of the Counrooska River became our very own "Jewel" and our Jewel became our obsession. We were in the process of becoming very long-distance property owners. We were buying our piece of the Emerald Isle.

The first necessity in the complicated legal process was to complete the official land survey. That warranted a return trip that November to assure there was agreement on the boundaries. That trip changed the nature of European travel for us. Vacation journeys gave way to work-filled missions where tasks had to be completed.

I went over for only three working days with one specific objective. Noel was gracious and enthusiastic and helped the surveyor with the placement of the markers. It was a fantastic experience to so carefully walk the property boundaries, cutting through trees and heavy brush and boggy marsh. Nothing stopped our surveyor.

I took careful measurements of the house and detailed photos and videotaped every nook and cranny. We watched the video over and over and got the lay of the land and the house solidly in mind.

I made arrangements with a local solicitor to handle the paperwork, and he outlined what would be required over the next several months. An engineer's structural assessment was one of those formalities.

The engineer's report, which took more than a month to complete, detailed nearly 15 pages of shortcomings. By that time our eyes and ears were closed to all defects we hadn't noticed earlier. We were too excited to care. From the photos and measurements I had taken, I built a scale model of the building from foam board, even replicating the thickness of the walls. My model, as amateurish as it was, fueled our excitement. I painted it a bright yellow, similar to the way the cottage appeared in the bright sunlight the first time we saw it. My model had a black, removable roof, which allowed us to look inside and visualize our plans.

The purchase that began in September finally closed the following May. We were ready to move in. We felt like pioneers in reverse, moving from the western frontier that had been the haven for so many distraught Irish emigrants, back to the heart of the old country they were forced to leave behind.

Our Jewel at the head of the marsh was in worse shape than we had envisioned, but we paid little mind to its shortcomings. We didn't expect that everything would be perfect.

Noel appeared to be happy we were taking over the home of his birth and the place of the hopes and dreams of his parents, Florence and Anna O'Mahoney. We could take their legacy and make it work for us.

Noel wasn't moving very far away. He built a new home down

the lane, considerably beyond our view, but still an easy walk to his livestock. He would be available to keep an eye on things.

Within a week or so of possession, we were back in Glengarriff on holidays to do what painting and fixing up we could. We slept on the floor, using our electrically inflated beds, even though we could hear mice running about the house. They weren't eating much, and, after all, it was their home first. We would tend to them later.

We brought a makeshift shower attachment for the old-time bathtub so we could attempt to shower. The house was a bit rustic and perhaps a bit damp, but it was livable as long as we stayed on the ground floor. The upstairs floor rafters were clearly weak and getting weaker. The engineer warned us about woodworm and the inevitable fact that the wooden rafters and beams would have to be replaced.

None of that slowed us down. The minute we had acquired enough basic chairs and tables, we purchased a small refrigerator and a few kitchen necessities and started entertaining friends. We were getting to know quite a few of the locals and already felt we were part of the community.

Two weeks in June barely got us started in our fix-up campaign, although our painting had made a vast improvement. So we booked another trip to Ireland for September, when we could spend more time on the renovation of the Jewel.

By September, to our dismay, our beautiful new painted walls in the kitchen and bath were nearly black with mold. That was when we learned about Irish dampness.

The walls of the old cottage were nearly two feet thick and built right on the ground with no foundation. The thin cement floors were poured over the dirt. There were no rain gutters or concrete skirting around the building. While we were taught in school that water seeps downward into the earth due to the forces of gravity, dampness — Irish dampness — rises upward by way of capillary action or some magical fairy force. It rises up into the walls and up through the floors.

The thickness of the walls had little effect in keeping out moisture driven by rain showers. The rain water could find its way into the outside walls from a corner high against the northwest wall and find its own path through the wall and out somewhere on the opposite side, most often inside the building.

A major source of dampness was from water seeping up through the ground. New buildings are constructed with damp guards, but the old buildings had no such thing.

Without some form of heating, at least a few hours a day, summer and winter, the humidity created condensation on the walls, providing a breeding ground for mold even where there was no obvious moisture seeping in. While quaint little fireplaces can be fun and romantic, they quickly become a burden. Keeping fires going in three fireplaces to fight off dampness can be a full-time job.

We had a lot to learn and had to do a lot of serious thinking as we planned for the future of the Jewel. It was in need of a major face lift, from top to bottom and everything in between.

Our good fortune took a giant leap on one of the last days of that September trip when Ellen decided she needed to purchase a kitchen table. We were using an old metal and plastic table borrowed from Noel, and she wanted something a little nicer, mold or not. She found a local antique collector who had a table that we had to see that same night since we would be leaving the next day. Besides looking at the table, she wanted me to meet her new friend.

Carey Conrad was no ordinary antique collector. In fact, there was nothing ordinary about her. She was a jewelry designer and sales person by trade, a Wisconsin ex-patriot who fell in love with Ireland some seven years earlier and had gotten into building and renovating houses to be used as rental properties. She marketed over the internet and had good repeat business owing to her flair at decorating even the simplest of cottages. Her business was, at the time, one of the first to use the worldwide web for Irish home rentals.

Before the night was over, we had her up to our Jewel where she bubbled over with ideas and dreams for bringing the Jewel to

256

life. We told her we wanted the Jewel's soul to shine. She agreed to take charge of supervising our first renovation project, the old bathroom. We wanted new fixtures, ceramic tiles and a modern shower. We had no need for a bathtub.

That little demonstration of her expertise was all it took. After seeing the dramatic change in the bathroom, we knew everything had to be upgraded and were certain that Carey could orchestrate it for us.

Everything had to go, from floors and doors to windows, from the staircase and landing to the entire second floor. We wanted to raise the ceiling on the main floor, create one large living area, build a new fireplace, use in-floor heating and remove the exterior stucco, at least on the front of the house, to expose the stone beneath.

Every step was an education in the oddities of Ireland, and those oddities simply cemented our totally out-of-control love for the house, the village and all of the people of West Cork. We were on our way.

Two-foot thick walls alone could not keep the indoors dry, but a lot could be done to reduce the dampness. Workers broke out the thin concrete floors and dug down 18 inches. To make the new floor watertight, they added a thick plastic sheet as a seal, then laid insulating foam board, sand and gravel and in-floor, hot water heating coils. Concrete was poured over it all. A low voltage electric wire was connected to a small transformer to generate a damp-repelling electric field that further retards the invasion of moisture. The house became damp-proof and dry for the first time in 70 years.

Carey and her team of local builders added many touches without even asking — simple things that added great value, such as rounded window wells and doorways and raised window peaks filled in with glass to let in more light. They exposed natural stone walls and the original hearth stone above the fireplace. They completely eliminated the fireplace in the kitchen and installed sky lights to maximize the brightness of daylight.

One interior stone wall was left exposed. The other walls were plastered with cement to give a rough texture that blends with the ceramic tile flooring and exposed wooden ceiling beams. The staircase that split the house down the middle was moved against the back wall of the great room. Made of pinewood, the staircase is now a part of the furnishing.

Enough electrical wiring was installed to ensure that we would never be far from an electrical outlet or a phone jack for computers and the internet. Our intent was to plug our computers in on arrival and to stay connected with our clients in the States. We knew by then that Ireland was one of the most technologically advanced countries in all of Europe, if not the world, and we used that to our advantage.

The Jewel's soul indeed began to shine through.

The outside was not to be ignored. Our skilled workers created an artistic concrete and flagstone walkway completely around the cottage so we could walk around the building in bare feet without stepping in a puddle of mud. This drains water away from the building to minimize dampness even further.

We added a driveway and a cattle guard and plenty of parking space. The old, original entry way was kept as it was, with 12 feet tall fuchsia bushes forming a tunnel through which visitors might arrive.

To help celebrate the completion of our project, after nearly two years of hard work, we staged a gala open house, which just happened to coincide with a string of very mild, sunny days. Ellen insisted on having an American-style kegger party, featuring Irish Harp lager, not knowing about local limitations. There was not a single American-style keg tap available. Our pub contacts scoured the country and finally located an electric system that saved the day. A local musician provided traditional Irish music.

It was a great party, attended by all of the craftsmen, neighbors and relatives of our benefactor, Noel. By then we had more friends in the Glengarriff area than we had in Colorado.

Glengarriff continued to hold a magical attraction as if it were more than just a recently discovered hometown. We dug through our old photos and slides, going way back to our *Europe on $5 a Day* trip. It happens we had stopped in Glengarriff for lunch, and I took a photo of Ellen at the grotto of the Virgin Mary at the edge of town some three decades earlier. The photo was an old-time 35-mm slide we never had printed so it was nearly lost to us. We made a photo print of the slide and now can prove we are "old-timers" to the area after all.

In the midst of this activity, my green-eyed Irish cowgirl and bride became an official "Irish citizen of foreign birth." After three additional years of being married to a citizen (the previous 25 plus years didn't count), I would be eligible to apply for Irish citizenship myself as the spouse of an Irish citizen.

The time passed quickly. I got all of my documentation together. I needed three forms of official photo identification in addition to my passport. Those included my driver's license, my South Suburban Recreation District photo ID (for which I have yet to find a use) and, of all things, my Costco membership card with my photo on the back.

Sending off those documents by U.S. mail to San Francisco sent shivers up my spine. What if they were lost? But I had no choice. Happily, within a week or so, I had my official blessing in the form of an Irish Passport.

Obviously, I had earned enough Irish points to qualify. I had watched enough Irish movies, read enough Irish books, celebrated enough St. Patrick's Day events with appropriate enthusiasm, bathed often enough with Irish Spring, stepped on a sufficient number of genuine Irish sheep skins, and had taken enough trips to Ireland. My Irish points topped the magic number and the Italian New Yorker named Caruso became the official O'Caruso. I was Irish!

Was it spiritual destiny? Was it the vortex of fate? Or was it simply a series of disconnected coincidences? At the very least, it was a lifelong journey that began with an airplane crash. No steps at all. Was I the first to be born again Irish? Will others follow?

Chapter 27

The Fate of the Armada

A Postscript

*H*owling winds pushed the wooden ships up the slopes of monstrous swells. Slowly, grudgingly, they plowed on, no faster than a man can walk, creaking and groaning and thumping against every wave on their way to the ridge. Then a nerve-shattering moment of hesitation as the ships balanced at the ledge. The weakened vessels tipped forward, each in its own turn, plummeting downward in an uncontrollable slide, fighting the angry resistance of choppy white caps all the way to the canyon-sized trench that marked the beginning of the next upward struggle. The sounds of raging water and the vibrations of the shaking hulls drove anxiety through the minds and bodies of even the strongest and most experienced of men.

It was the third week of September in the year of 1588, just a day or two after the autumn equinox. The Armada had been disgraced some seven weeks earlier and was still in its slow and agonizing retreat. The British blocked their southern escape route. It was a long and dangerous way north through the Irish Sea, but it was the only way. At the top of the sea, they sailed west, around the mysterious Island known by the Romans as Hibernia and to mariners as Ireland.

Primo del Bravo's family had a history on the sea, spanning four generations, although this was his first voyage on open waters. He grew up listening to tales of the exploits of the family hero, Cristoforo Colombo, repeated by his father and grandfather as if they had sailed on his ships to discover the New World. You would think Columbus still walked the streets of their home city of Genova, the way they told their stories. You would think he was their commander.

Primo wanted to taste the mariner's life for himself. He wasn't Spanish, but neither was Columbus. He didn't care about the Spanish crown or the purpose of the Armada. He signed on for adventure and the pitifully small purse that went directly to the family to help support his brothers and sisters who stayed behind. Anything, he felt, was better than languishing that summer along the docks and in the squalor at home. That is what he thought at the time, but he knew better now. He had made a very big mistake.

The Spanish Armada arrived at the coast of England near Cornwall in late July with a fleet of 130 ships, including 22 fighting galleons and more than 20,000 fighting men. Within a few short weeks, the entire fleet had been routed from the English Channel by a naval force led by the British Admiral Sir Francis Drake. Few ships were lost and very few men died in the battle, but disease was ravaging the ranks on both sides, especially among those of the Armada.

Thousands died from dysentery and fever before they even began their retreat. The agony of disease that tormented the living was worsened by the relentless movement and dampening chill of the surrounding waters.

Escape was blocked. They were trapped. Commander Medina Sidonia ordered the fleet to retreat north, around the rugged and stormy Irish coast, to the safety of the open western seas. They would escape destruction by the English, but the wrath of nature was threatening to be an even more fearsome enemy.

Winds screamed and howled and tossed buckets of seawater as rain lashed from every direction. Sails had been pulled in days earlier to save the masts. The ships were drifting, fighting the wind and trying to avoid colliding with each other.

"Thank God," Primo thought. He made it this far. Scurvy hadn't shown its symptoms yet, but he was weakening. The motion of swirling seas was tearing at his balance. Would he ever be able to stand upright again? He struggled to hold onto the beams in the dark, damp hull, waiting for the next jolt, trying to guess the next shift in direction. Up or down? Right or left? Fore or aft?

He could tell they were inching up another swell by the sensation in his legs. Slowly, slowly, slowly they moved, pounding water every bit of the way, winds pushing hard from behind. The swells had to be enormous, but he couldn't see. The winds were tossing foaming water against the hull.

Inside, darkness was in command. He could barely see the outline of his shipmate, Rodriego, lying in a sickened heap in a cranny nearby, his arms held tightly to his shoulders and knees pulled into his ribs. He was dying from the fever. He had been drifting in and out of awareness for the past two days. It wouldn't be long before the end.

Their ship, the *Delfin*, was one of the smallest and least stable of the fleet. That was his luck, to be assigned to the smallest.

The *Delfin* reached the crest at the top of another swell. He could feel it. First came that moment of hesitation, an agonizing teetering of the ship as if straining in indecision. How long will it be?

Damn, it was cold. Salt water seeped through cracks in the hull. What was not soaked by seawater was drenched with condensation, forming rivulets of moisture on the interior walls.

Motion, motion. There was no end to the motion.

Here it comes.

The ship lurched forward and downward to begin its slide to the far side of the swell. The bumping and thumping was from the punching and slapping of rogue waves as the defenseless *Delfin* fought its way down, only to crash again.

A common name in Genova, Primo was his father's first born. He was proud to be an Italian mariner and proud to be carrying on the tradition of the seas. But this was not his battle nor Italy's war. The Spanish King sent ships, as he swore he would, but most of the ships he sent were old scows, wrecks that were hardly worthy of sea voyage, much less of battle. His father and his grandfather sailed much more glorious ships, three and four-masted galleons, masters of the seas. It looked as if his end would now arrive in the dank wet hold of a junk ship. He would be the first in his lineage to die in disgrace.

He was praying now, out loud and with passion. Why would God want to listen to him, a wretched sinner. He was praying anyway. He was praying that someone on his ship and on the others nearby would be healthy enough to keep watch. Ships had to keep their distance to avoid collision, but had to avoid getting lost. Sickness decimated watch crews and those able to stand watch were not that well. The danger of a damaging collision was serious indeed.

They had made it past the Port of Galway. They were safer now. The waters were warming.

True mariners knew of Ireland and many had been to Galway. Even Columbus stopped there on his way to Iceland in his early days, not just once, but twice. But Galway was not a welcoming place in these times, something political. The Spanish were bad guys at the moment, and anyone sailing under the Spanish flag was suspect. That danger was now behind them.

They were somewhere off that peninsula with a queer-sounding name. What did they say? Dingle? Dangle? Something like that. He was too sick to care.

What kind of boatman was he? Days and days of motion. Hour after hour, up and down and round and around. It was enough to make anyone toss their guts inside out.

The ship plowed into the bottom of the trough, causing him to sink to his knees. The icy water cascaded over the bow and into every possible opening, even the tiniest seams between the planking.

"My God, help me," Primo shouted in his head. "Help me!"

The boat was bobbing like a bottle cork. With a damaged rudder and no sails, how could they survive?

"Thanks be to God," he thought, the waters were getting warmer. Warm? Shit. Compared to what? Compared to the really cold waters north of Galway, the waters here were warm. But that was very little consolation. No one could last long in that maelstrom, no matter what.

The *Delfin* was climbing again, ever so slowly, up a watery hillside. It was fighting to hold back, but the winds were pushing it upward even with its sails unfurled.

"Again, not again," he thought.

Primo couldn't see outside and didn't dare go topside to look. If he could see outside he might have worried about their sister ship drawing too close for safety. Who was left to watch? How could they navigate anyway? He didn't even want to ask. But who would he ask?

Up, and up, and up they climbed, shaking, vibrating and thumping until they reached the crest, then the slow arch forward amidst the cracking sounds and protests of beams and planking, then the drop forward and down toward the trough below.

"My God, no! Please God." he cried.

He could hear the scraping and cracking sounds — the dreaded agony of two ships leaning and rubbing against the other. Then only the raging sounds of the sea remained.

Where did the other ship go? Or did it go at all? Were the ships still together? Would they scrape again? He couldn't tell what was happening.

They were still in descent.

Then the noise again, a louder scraping and a more violent thump, a crashing sound, a crack like splitting timbers. The ships were touching again, pressing harder this time. Two hulls were stuck and squeezing tighter and tighter. Then there was a horrid, violent snapping sound. The hull was flooding with frothing, frigid water.

Primo grabbed at everything in reach to make it to the deck. He was out of the damp dark hull and facing the fury of the raging sea. He hesitated in dread before the scene of horror.

"My God," he flashed. It was worse than he could have possibly imagined. Mountains and mountains of water were crashing in on them. He couldn't breath amid the fury of the seas outside. The two ships were still wedged together, side by side, two nuts in a tightening vice.

Then a horrifying pop, a splintering crack!

He screamed and grasped and thrashed. A pole, a beam, a barrel, a box. Was there nothing to hold? Was there nothing?

Nowhere to turn. The water was splashing in his face, no way to catch a breath. Splashing from everywhere and every direction. He screamed, "Help me God! Please help me!"

The mast was broken and bent down to within inches of his grasp. It jerked away. The ropes threatened to snatch him under. The ship listed away and began sliding down into the raging depths.

Bags of cargo, bodies, boxes and flotsam were all around. He was gasping for air! He screamed to God for help.

"Please, God! Help me please!"

A monster! No, an evil monster!

The ship had turned on its back. He had never seen the bottom of a ship sticking upright. It was huge, monstrous and menacing, crusted with barnacles and sea life that had slowed its way.

He pushed himself further away. It was evil. The sinking ship was deadly, hoping to snatch him on her way down.

The waves were tearing at him. Icy fingers were grasping at his throat. The water was foaming in his face, never a break between breaths. He was drowning with his head above water as he grasped for a hand hold, anything at all to hold.

He was frantic, panicked, drowning. Something or someone grabbed at him, pulling him down.

Away! Away! He pushed the horror away and screamed a begging and horrifying scream, "My God, please help me!"

He was alone, horribly alone. He was desperate.

It was pitch black, yet the seas glowed with a green florescence. The foam was glowing.

My God! The foam was choking and killing and glowing too.

266

He jerked to his senses.

"Was is that? Something to swim to?"

Something was floating nearby. The waves pulled from behind as he struggled to reach the floating pile. He grabbed at the black mass. It was coarse, covered with netting. It was floating. It was an island of boxes and bags trapped in a netting. It must have escaped from the hold. It was bobbing about. He grabbled the netting and climbed in as far as he could until it rolled on him. He was getting cold, and fatigue was setting in. He nearly drowned before he could push away. The horror!

"My God," he screamed, "I'm drowning! Please help me God. Someone help me"

He could see someone grasping for a hold on the floating debris nearby, and then another. Other crew members were holding on to the netting all around its edges, enough to stabilize the mass.

"My God, help me!" he screamed and clawed his way back to the top of the pile of cartons trapped in the netting. It was flattening on top. He crawled to the center and, holding on as tightly as he could with his back against his floating island, he stared upward to the sky.

Up and down, around and around. The stars were twirling above. He was on his back, looking at the heavens swirling above him. He was oblivious to any sounds of life around him.

The skies were lighter now, and stormy. He could see nothing but waves, mountains and mountains of wildly thrashing waves.

The winds were driving him into shore. He could see no one else in the water now. He was alone in the center of his island, bobbing about wildly, spinning and twisting. Would he get to shore? Might there be a chance? Would there be hostile people? He was Italian, not Spanish.

"My God," he pleaded, "don't let me die!"

He clutched the netting, numb with cold, breathing between breaks in the sea.

Hours passed. He faded in and out of consciousness.

The sun was rising, just a slight glow on the horizon. He could see what looked like land. The seas were calming. The land was becoming visible, so green and so bright, not like the dry dusty hills near Genova.

Primo could see people along the shore, dozens of people! He could hardly raise his head. He could see old people and young people. There were women and children. Were they coming to harm him? Were they scavenging for the spoils of a shipwreck?

Someone caught sight of him as he moved his head upward to catch a glance. The wind and waves were pushing him into shore. People were waving at him. He could hear their voices, their shouts. They were friendly sounds, not hostile cries. They were shouting to him. Did they know his name? No. They couldn't possibly know his name. This was Ireland. The last stop on the voyage west for Italian mariners. To hell with the Spanish! He wasn't Spanish.

Now there were more people rushing toward him. The women were beautiful. Even the men looked kindly. They were shouting to him. He waved and they waved. They were welcoming him.

What was all of this? Was it a dream? His mind was raging. His strength was returning. He was alone. What happened to the others? He didn't know. He was drifting to shore on an island of boxes, and a whole village was out to greet him. What was he anyway? A hero?

No, no, he was no hero! He was only Primo, the firstborn, the unfortunate one. He was the one to do all the work and have none of the luck.

His father reminded him many times. His father was his own father's seventh son. Primo missed out. He would never have the good fortune of being the seventh son of a seventh son. He was first and would settle for less.

Good luck or not, his spirit was soaring. A miracle was happening, and it was happening to him.

His island of cartons trapped in the cargo netting slid onto the rocks. There they were, dozens of them! Beautiful faces, beautiful people, red hair, blue eyes, smiles and smiles, and the cheering crowds! How many were there? Hundreds of them! No, thousands of them. They were cheering for him! Smiling at him! And they were laughing with him! They stepped into the water to reach him and him alone.

What beautiful people! They were saving him.

Joyful young women, caregivers all, were pulling at him. They were soothing him, comforting him.

His mind was raging wild. "My God, my God! What beautiful people!"

He thought he might have died and gone to heaven. It couldn't be real. The people were taking him in! He was home. Another chance. Another life. He might never have all of the luck there was, but he had all the luck he needed.

What luck indeed to be born again Irish.

BORN AGAIN IRISH - *O'Caruso*